Play in Child Development and Psychotherapy

Toward Empirically Supported Practice

Irving B. Weiner, Advisory Editor

Play in Child Development and Psychotherapy

Toward Empirically Supported Practice

Sandra W. Russ
Case Western Reserve University

LEA

LAWRENCE ERLBAUM ASSOCIATES, PUBLISHERS
2004   Mahwah, New Jersey   London

Lawrence Erlbaum Associates, Inc., Publishers
10 Industrial Avenue
Mahwah, New Jersey 07430

Cover design by Kathryn Houghtaling Lacey

Library of Congress Cataloging-in-Publication Data

Russ, Sandra Walker.
Play in child development and psychotherapy : toward empirically supported practice / Sandra W. Russ.
    p. cm.
Includes bibliographical references and index.
ISBN 0-8058-3065-0 (cloth : alk. paper)
1. Play therapy.   2. Play—Psychological aspects.   I. Title.
RC505.P6 R876 2003
618.92′891653—dc21   2002035397
                                                             CIP

Printed in the United States of America
10   9   8   7   6   5   4   3   2

In memory of my parents,
Edith and Wilson Walker,
who provided me the opportunity to play

Contents

Preface

Children's pretend play is a complex phenomenon. Pretend play involves a myriad of processes and behaviors that change from moment to moment. Does pretend play have important functions in child development, or is it simply something children engage in to pass the time—albeit while having fun? This is a central question in the field of child psychology today. It is an especially important question for child therapists. Practitioners of a variety of theoretical persuasions use play in working with children. As of 1992, play in some form was used in child therapy by a majority of clinicians, according to Koocher and D'Angelo (1992), who stated that "play-oriented therapy remains the dominant and most enduring approach to child treatment ... practiced by clinicians (p. 458). Many therapists use play because it is a natural activity and form of communication of young children. Also, different theoretical schools stress the importance of pretend play in the therapy process. Psychoanalytic, psychodynamic, client-centered (nondirective) approaches, and cognitive-behavioral approaches as well, have proposed that change occurs in the child through the process of play.

What is the evidence for this proposition? The movement toward empirically supported treatments is gaining increasing momentum. It is crucial for the development of scientific principles of behavior change. Also, the managed care system will be looking to research for guidance about its policies. If play is to continue to be used as a major treatment modality, its effectiveness must be empirically demonstrated.

The main thesis of this book is that play has an important role in child development and is a major vehicle for change in child psychotherapy. Two extensive bodies of research literature address the functions of play, one focusing on pretend play and child development, one on the use of play in psychotherapy. These two literatures need to be integrated. Play is involved in the development of many cognitive, affective, and personality processes that are important for adaptive functioning in children. Often, those who discuss the effectiveness of play in therapy ignore the accumulating knowledge base in developmental psychology. We have not drawn on this knowledge base in developing play intervention and play prevention programs that can be evaluated empirically.

On the other hand, insights from the theory and research of child therapists are not usually reflected in laboratory research on the role of play in child development. Only more effective two-way communication between clinicians and developmental researchers can enable the evolution of more refined developmentally based play interventions and the formulation of clear guidelines about the next logical steps for play research programs. Finally, the implications for the practice of play therapy of the research that *has* been done thus far need to be spelled out.

This book will attempt to accomplish these three goals: (a) to review and integrate what we have learned from research in the child development and play therapy areas, (b) to suggest directions for future studies, and (c) to present guidelines for practitioners based on current research findings. If we can construct a coherent picture of the current knowledge base, then we can understand more clearly what we should be doing as both researchers and practitioners. This book also identifies play processes and proposes that play interventions should target specific play processes relevant to the goals of the intervention program. Play is especially important in the processing of emotions. This specific approach to the use of play in psychotherapy and prevention programs is a new one.

The book begins with an overview, "Fundamental Play Processes." The processes that occur in play are presented, identified, and classified. Play and emotion are discussed, and a new paradigm for play intervention that targets specific play processes is suggested. Chapter 2, "The Role of Play in the Development of Adaptive Abilities," reviews the research on child development in play and the areas of adaptive functioning of creativity, coping, adjustment, and social behavior. Chapter 3, "The Role of Play in Therapy: The Theories," reviews the major theories of the role of play in child psychotherapy and how change occurs. There is a focus on how the play processes with which therapists work "match up" with the play processes that emerge in the child development research. A model that bridges the two literatures is proposed. Several clinical cases are also presented. Chapter 4, "The Role of Play in Therapy: The Research," reviews studies of child psychotherapy and focused play intervention. One section discusses possible models for understanding the effectiveness of play interventions in reducing anxiety. Consistencies between the child development research and psychotherapy and play intervention research are highlighted.

The next chapter, "The Affect in Play Scale," presents the revised version of this standardized measure. There is a detailed review of the validity studies that I and my students have carried out. The revised version of the scale can be found in the Appendix. The clinical and scientific implications of its further development and use are discussed. Some other measures of play are also discussed. Chapter 6 reviews "Current Trends in the Therapeutic Uses of Play." In chapter 7, "Teaching Children to Play," studies that focus on facilitating play skills in children are presented, together with a pilot program that has developed play intervention scripts. The final chapter, "Future Directions in Research and Practice," offers conclusions and suggestions for research and practice. I hope that the book will inspire clinicians and researchers to play with ideas and build the empirical foundation for play intervention programs.

ACKNOWLEDGMENTS

Special thanks go to Susan Milmoe, Senior Consulting Editor at Lawrence Erlbaum Associates, for her invaluable guidance in this process, and to Lawrence Erlbaum for his encouragement. I also want to thank Gail Gangidine for her word processing expertise. And, as always, a deep thank you to my husband, Tom Brugger, for his constant support of my work over the years.

—Sandra W. Russ

1

Fundamental Play Processes

I was sitting in the cafeteria at the San Diego airport, amidst the usual cha-otic airport scene, when I noticed a little boy, about 6 or 7 years old, sitting at the table next to mine. He was with an older brother or very young fa-ther, who was reading. The boy had laid out in front of him four figures: a cowboy, an Indian, a large monster, and a larger rubber dinosaur. He was totally engrossed in fantasy play with these creatures and was making up dialogue and action. I could not hear all of it, but I could hear, "Do this," "No you won't," "Here's this." Some of the play was with an angry tone, some with a cooperative tone. There was a definite story line. His play went on for about 30 minutes. He was totally engaged and comfortable and was clearly having a good time. Finally, his older companion indicated it was time to leave. He helped the child carefully pack all of the creatures into his knapsack. The boy told one of them to "Have a good day." He kept the dinosaur out and put it under his arm. The older companion was han-dling the situation very well: he was gentle, didn't rush the boy, respected his little creatures, and did not intrude in the play. The boy was totally com-fortable playing in front of him. I don't know what kind of family situation this boy comes from or what kind of stress he's going on to, but I do know that he has a terrific resource—he can use play and he likes to play. He is a good player, and that will help him in a variety of ways (Russ, 1995, p. 365).

While observing that child, I felt that he was fortunate because he could use play as a resource. He had the ability to use play as a vehicle for ex-pressing emotion, channeling aggression, expressing and increasing posi-tive affect, learning to modulate affect, playing with ideas and fantasy, practicing story-telling, and resolving problems and conflicts.

What are the processes expressed in play? By observing children at play, we can identify the cognitive and affective processes that are expressed in play behavior. Before reviewing processes in play, let us begin by defining pretend play.

1

PRETEND PLAY

Pretend play is important both in child development and in child psycho-therapy. When the word *play* is used throughout this book, the specific type of play referred to is pretend play. Pretend play involves pretending, the use of fantasy and make-believe, and the use of symbolism. Fein (1987) stated that pretend play is a symbolic behavior in which "one thing is playfully treated as if it were something else" (p. 282). Fein also stated that pretense is charged with feelings and emotional intensity, so that af-fect is intertwined with pretend play. Fein viewed play as a natural form of creativity.

Fantasy is involved in pretend play. Klinger (1971) concluded that play and fantasy have a common origin. Piaget (1945/1967) conceptualized fantasy as "interiorized play." J. Singer (1981) conceptualized play as the externalization of fantasy, so that play would be an expression of internal fantasy. Vygotsky (1930/1967) stated that creative imagination originated in children's play (Smolucha, 1992). Sherrod and Singer (1979) identified processes involved in both fantasy and pretend play activities: the ability to form images; skill in storing and retrieving formed images; possessing a store of images; skill in recombining and integrating these images as a source of internal stimulation and divorcing them from reality; and rein-forcement for skillful recombining of images. They believed that it is the last two processes that are unique to fantasy and play activities. Young children can differentiate between make-believe play and reality (Golomb & Galasso, 1995; Golomb & Kuersten, 1996).

Krasnor and Pepler (1980) developed a model of play that involves four components: nonliterality, positive affect, intrinsic motivation, and flexi-bility. They believed that "pure play" involves all four components, to varying degrees. They also presented three basic views of the relationship between play and developmental skills. First, play reflects the develop-mental level of the child and, therefore, can be used as a diagnostic tool. Second, play provides an opportunity to practice skills. Third, play is a causal agent in developmental change.

The study of children's play can tell us about cognitive–affective interac-tion (Russ, 1987; J. Singer, 1973; D. Singer & J. Singer, 1990). Because play is an arena in which both cognitive and affective processes are reflected, we can learn about the development of these processes and how they interact. Slade and Wolf (1994) stressed the importance of studying the role of play in both the development of cognitive structure and in the mastering of emo-tions. Historically, these two domains have been studied separately, usually from different theoretical and research traditions (Feist, in press). As Morri-son (1988) has noted, Piaget did not consider affect to be important in cogni-tive development, whereas Freud did. Measures of play processes have reflected this split in research traditions. Rubin, Fein, and Vandenberg (1983) pointed out that most of the measures of children's play have measured cognitive processes, not affective processes. Thus, they referred to the "cognification" of play. Increasingly, there has been a focus on both cognition and affect in play. Investigating both types of processes is important, because cognition and affect often occur simultaneously in play, and they interact. Slade and Wolf (1994) stated that the cognitive and affective functions of play are intertwined: "Just as the development of cognitive structures may play an important role in the resolution of emotional conflict, so emotional consolidation may provide an impetus to cognitive advances and integration" (p. xv). They implied that there is a working together of emotional functioning and cognitive structure.

PROCESSES EXPRESSED IN PLAY

What are the processes that are expressed in play? By observing the behavior of pretend play, we can see the expression of a number of cognitive processes, affective processes, and interpersonal processes. I thought it would be helpful to present a framework for categorizing these expressions early in this book. The following is a framework for thinking about the verbal and behavioral expressions that emerge in pretend play. It is based on theory and research in child development and child psychotherapy. I used this conceptual framework to guide the development of the Affect in Play Scale (Russ, 1987, 1993). The Affect in Play Scale (APS) measures some, but not all, of these processes. The APS is discussed in detail in chapter 4.

What follows is a very brief introduction to these play processes. They are discussed in more detail throughout this book. (See Table 1.1 for a summary.)

Cognitive Processes

- *Organization.* The ability to tell a story, with a logical time sequence and indications of cause and effect. Narratives can vary in elaboration of detail and complexity.
- *Divergent thinking.* The ability to generate a number of different ideas, story themes, and symbols.
- *Symbolism.* The ability to transform ordinary objects (blocks, Legos) into representations of other objects (e.g., a block becomes a telephone).
- *Fantasy/Make-believe.* The ability to engage in the "as if" play behavior—to pretend to be in a different time and space.

Affective Processes

- *Expression of emotion.* The ability to express affect states in a pretend play situation. Both positive and negative affect are expressed. For example, the child expresses happiness by having a doll clap her hands and jump up and down with joy.
- *Expression of affect themes.* The ability to express affect-laden images and content themes in play. The child builds a fortress with guns to prepare for a battle. This is aggressive ideation, even though no actual fight is occurring. Children differ in the range of emotion and affect content themes they express in play.
- *Comfort and enjoyment in the play.* The ability to enjoy and "get lost" in the play experience. The ability to experience pleasure and joy in the play situation.
- *Emotion regulation and modulation of affect.* The ability to contain and modulate both positive and negative emotion. Both cognitive and affective processes are involved.
- *Cognitive integration of affect.* The ability to integrate affect into a cognitive context. Affect is expressed within a narrative and cognitive context. For example, aggression is expressed within a story about a boxing match.

Interpersonal Processes

- *Empathy.* The expression of concern for and caring about others.
- *Interpersonal schema/Self–other representation.* The level of development of self–other differentiation and capacity for trusting others.
- *Communication.* The ability to communicate with others, to express ideas and emotions to others.

Problem Solving/Conflict Resolution Processes

- *Approach to problems and conflicts.* The tendency to try to find solutions to problems that arise.
- *Problem solving/conflict resolution.* The ability to work things out and resolve problems. The effectiveness of the problem-solving attempt.

These are some of the major processes that can be observed and assessed in play. There may be other processes, and some of these categories could be broken into more specific processes. These cognitive, affective, and interpersonal processes are important in many areas of child development.

TABLE 1.1
Processes in Play

Cognitive Processes
> Organization
>
> Divergent thinking
>
> Symbolism
>
> Fantasy/Make-believe

Affective Processes
> Expression of emotion
>
> Expression of affect themes
>
> Comfort/Enjoyment of play
>
> Emotion regulation/modulation
>
> Cognitive integration of affect

Interpersonal Processes
> Empathy
>
> Interpersonal schema
>
> Communication

Problem Solving Processes
> Approach to problems
>
> Problem solving/Conflict resolution ability

PLAY AND EMOTION

One of the most important areas in psychology today is emotion, the processing of emotion, and the implications of these emotional processes for adaptive and maladaptive behaviors. Play is a major arena in which children learn to express emotion, process emotion, modulate and regulate emotion, and use emotion in adaptive ways. This view of play and emotion is consistent with a number of recent conceptualizations of emotion and mental health.

The construct of emotion regulation is especially important in the area of child development. Emotion regulation has been defined by a number of researchers. Mennin, Heimberg, Turk, and Fresco (2002) have an excellent review of the emotion regulation area. They quoted Gross's (1998) definition of emotion regulation as "the process by which individuals influence which emotions they have, when they have them, and how they experience and express these emotions" (p. 275). Sheilds and Ciccheti (1998) defined emotion regulation as the ability to modulate emotions and engage in an adaptive way with environment. Mennin et al. (2002) concluded that an emotion regulation perspective would have as goals of treatment to help individuals (a) become more comfortable with arousing emotional experience, (b) be more able to access and utilize emotional information in adaptive problem solving, and (c) be better able to modulate emotional experience and expression.

What is not yet widely recognized nor empirically tested is the idea that play is one activity through which children learn these various aspects of emotion regulation. The affective processes identified in Table 1.1 (affective expression of emotion and affective ideation, enjoyment of play, emotion regulation, and cognitive integration of affect) are consistent with current definitions of emotion regulation. The role of play in modulating and integrating emotions in psychotherapy is discussed in detail later.

PLAY PROCESSES AND INTERVENTION: A NEW PARADIGM

Ideally, play intervention approaches would evolve from the research on play and child development. We should build our play interventions around the play processes that have been found to be related to important areas in child development. Play intervention should have a developmental foundation. Clinical theory and case studies should inform the research as to which processes can be changed in psychotherapy and are important in areas of adaptive functioning. Many of these play processes have been used by play therapists to effect change, although usually in an unsystematic fashion.

Cognitive, affective, and interpersonal processes in play are related to and facilitate important adaptive abilities such as creative thinking, problem solving, coping, and social behavior. These adaptive abilities are important in the general adjustment of the child. Play interventions, to be most effective, should target specific processes in play. Play therapy interventions would be of two general types:

1. Interventions that use play process(es) as a vehicle for change. That is, the play process would be used in the therapy to bring about change. For example, the expression of emotion in play around a traumatic event would be encouraged to enable the emotion to be processed and integrated. The expression of emotion and integration of the emotion would be helpful for children diagnosed with PTSD.
2. Interventions that strengthen play processes. For example, for children with poor ability to organize a story but who have much ex-

pressed emotion that is uncontrolled, a focus on building story-telling and narrative ability could help regulate the emotion.

Often, play interventions would strengthen play processes and also use play processes to bring about change.

In order to develop the empirical foundation for this framework for play intervention, there are a series of questions that need to be empirically investigated:

1. What are the processes that occur in play, and how are they inter-related?
2. What are the empirical correlates of these play processes that are important in children's adjustment and adaptive functioning?
3. Can we demonstrate a causal relationship between specific play processes and adaptive functioning?
4. What is the developmental course of each of these processes?
5. What intervention techniques facilitate change in these play processes?

Child development research in the pretend play area has investigated questions 2 and 3—correlates of and effects of pretend play. Much of the research in the play area has not investigated specific processes in play. Rather, research has treated pretend play as one global entity or has focused on the cognitive process of fantasy/make-believe. My own research program has investigated both cognitive and affective processes.

The review in the next chapter focuses on questions 2 and 3 and summarizes the research on play in the area of child development.

The Role of Play in the Development of Adaptive Abilities

This chapter reviews the research literature in child development that investigates play and important areas of adaptive functioning for children: creativity, coping, and social behavior. It focuses on the correlates of play and the evidence that play facilitates adaptive functioning. This chapter is organized around the criteria that play relates to or facilitates. Specific play processes that are involved will be delineated as much as possible.

PLAY AND CREATIVITY

> You see a child play and it is so close to seeing an artist paint, for in play a child says things without uttering a word. You can see how he solves his problems. You can also see what's wrong. Young children, especially, have enormous creativity, and whatever's in them rises to the surface in free play. (Erik Erikson, 1994, May)

In this quote, Erikson comments on the similarity between the play of a child and the creative process of the adult. He also implies that play is a window through which you can learn about the emotional processes of the child. Play is a diagnostic tool that tells us about the child. Erikson highlights two of the most important functions of play in this quote. One major function of play is creative expression. A second major function of play is to resolve problems. These two functions of play and the cognitive and affective processes involved in them are intertwined and have implications for the area of creativity.

Many of the processes that occur in play are involved in creativity. Much of the research on play and child development has investigated creativity because of the theoretical link between pretending and the creative imagination. Sawyer (1997) conceptualized pretend play in young children as improvisational. Improvisation is an important feature of adult creativity. Sawyer stated that play is unscripted yet has loose outlines to be followed.

In order to theorize about the links between play and creativity, one must be specific about the types of processes involved in creative thinking. Cognitive and affective processes that are expressed and developed in play are important in creativity. In the field of creativity, a distinction is usually made between the creative product and the creative process (Golann, 1963; Mackinnon, 1962). The creative product is the output of the individual which can be judged as to the amount of creativity. There is a consensus in the field that a product must meet two criteria to be judged as creative. A product must be novel (original, new) and must be good (adaptive, useful, aesthetically pleasing). Experts within the various disciplines are the usual judges of the novelty and goodness of a creation. For a truly creative product to be produced in most fields, the knowledge base of the field must be mastered before old ideas can be integrated in new ways (Wallas, 1926). This puts children at a great disadvantage and makes it unlikely that they will contribute to a discipline in new ways. However, if age norms are considered as a reference point, as is usually the case in assessing children, then we can talk about novel and good creative products for a particular age group. A 9-year-old's solution to a problem can be judged on criteria of adaptiveness and originality for that age group. Also, the concept of everyday creativity is very relevant to children. Richards (1993) defined everyday creativity as real-life creativity at work or at leisure. Children are creative in a number of daily activities, including play.

The creative process refers to the many processes that are involved in the creative act. Cognitive, affective, and personality processes are all involved in a creative act. Individuals who are high on some of these creative processes will have a higher likelihood of producing a creative product. Individual differences in these processes can be identified in children, and many of these processes are expressed and developed in pretend play.

Creativity, Play, and Cognitive Processes

D. Singer and J. Singer (1990) suggested areas of cognitive development that are facilitated by pretend play activities. Play helps the child to (a) expand vocabulary and link objects with actions, (b) develop object constancy, (c) form event schemas and scripts, (d) learn strategies for problem solving, (e) develop divergent thinking ability, and (f) develop a flexibility in shifting between different types of thought (narrative and logical).

Two major categories of cognitive processes important in creativity are divergent thinking and transformation abilities. Both of these processes were identified by Guilford (1968) as being important in and unique to creative problem solving. Divergent thinking is thinking that goes off in different directions. For example, a typical item on a divergent thinking test would be, "How many uses for a brick can you think of?" Guilford thought the key concept underlying divergent production abilities was variety. Wallach (1970) stated that divergent thinking is dependent on the flow of ideas and the "fluidity in generating cognitive units" (p. 1240). Divergent thinking involves free association, broad scanning ability, and fluidity of thinking. Divergent thinking has been found to be relatively independent of intelligence (Runco, 1991). Transformation abilities enable the individual to reorganize information and break out of old ways of thinking. They enable the individual to transform or revise what one knows into new patterns or configurations. Transformation abilities involve the ability to break out of an old set and see a new way to solve a problem.

Other cognitive processes that are important in, but not unique to, creative problem solving are: sensitivity to problems and problem finding (Getzels & Csikszentmihalyi, 1976); task persistence and trying alternative problem solving approaches (Weisberg, 1988); breadth of knowledge and wide range of interests (Barron & Harrington, 1981); insight and synthesizing abilities (Sternberg, 1988); and evaluative ability (Guilford, 1950; Runco, 1991).

Research has supported a relationship between play and a number of these creative cognitive processes (Dansky, 1980; Fein, 1981; D. Singer & J. Singer, 1990). Although most of the studies are correlational in design, well-designed experimental studies and longitudinal research suggest that causal inferences can be made. Saltz, Dixon, and Johnson (1977) found that fantasy play facilitated cognitive functioning on a variety of measures. They theorized that fantasy play is related to cognitive development because of the involvement of representational skills and concept formation. J. Singer and D. Singer (1976) concluded that the capacity for imaginative play is positively related to divergent thinking, verbal fluency, and cognitive functioning in general. Sherrod and Singer (1979) proposed that fantasy play and cognition is a transactional system—each facilitates the other.

Early research on play and creative problem solving investigated play and insight ability. In a series of studies, Sylva, Bruner, and Genova (1976) concluded that play in children 3 to 5 years of age facilitated insight in a problem solving task. In one study, they had three groups of children. One group played with the objects which were later used in the problem solving task. A second group observed the experimenter solve the problem. A third control group was exposed to the materials. Significantly more children in the play and observation groups solved the problem than in the control group. The play group was more goal oriented in their efforts on the task and was more likely to piece together the solution than the other groups.

Vandenberg (1978) refined the experimental methodology of the Sylva, Bruner, and Genova studies and used a wider age group, 4 to 10 years of age. The experimental group played with the materials to be used in the problem solving task, and the control group was asked questions about the material. Children were also given hints to the solution. The play group did significantly better on one of the two insight tasks following the intervention. Six- and 7-year-olds benefited most from the play experience. Vandenberg concluded that the relationship between play and insightful tool use was mediated by age and task characteristics.

Smith and Dutton (1979) compared the effects of play, training, and two control groups on two insight tasks in 4-year-olds. The play and training groups did significantly better than the controls on the first task. The play group did significantly better than all other groups on the second task, which required motivated effort. There were more motivated problem solvers in the play condition than in the other conditions.

Vandenberg (1980), in a review of the insight and play studies, concluded that all of these studies had the consistent finding that play facilitated insightful tool use and enhanced motivated task activity. Variables of task type and difficulty and age were mediating factors. Vandenberg pointed up the similarity between play and creativity. In both play and creativity, one is creating novelty from the commonplace and has a disregard for the familiar.

There is a substantial body of studies that has found a relationship between play and divergent thinking. D. Singer and J. Singer (1990) viewed play as a way of practicing divergent thinking ability. D. Singer and Rummo (1973) found a relationship between play and divergent thinking in kindergarten boys. Pepler and Ross (1981) found that play was related to divergent thinking. Feitelson and Ross (1973) found that thematic play facilitated creative thinking. Experience with a divergent thinking task facilitated performance on divergent thinking tasks in a study by Pepler (1979). In that study, performance on the divergent thinking task could be predicted from the expression of symbolic and representational play. Hughes (1987) studied 4- and 5-year-olds and reported that manipulative play with objects facilitated divergent thinking, but only for the number of nonstandard responses on the Alternate Uses Test. Johnson (1976) found that social make-believe play was related to divergent thinking. Dunn and Herwig (1992) on the other hand, found no relationship between dramatic play and divergent thinking, but they did find a negative relationship between non-social play and divergent thinking. Clark, Griffing, and Johnson (1989) found a relationship between divergent thinking in preschool males. Shmukler (1982–1983) carried out a longitudinal study that found that preschool imaginative predisposition and expressive imagination in play related to later imagination and creativity. Shmukler believed that imaginative play reflects a general capacity for creative thinking.

Wallach (1970) stressed the importance of the relationship between divergent thinking and fantasy. Subjects who scored well on divergent thinking tests produced novel stories on the TAT (Maddi, 1965) and engaged in daydreaming activity (J. Singer, 1973). Wallach (1970) proposed that breadth-of-attention deployment is the underlying variable involved in divergent thinking tasks. As Kogan (1983) pointed out, breadth-of-attention deployment refers to a scanning of the environment and memory in an associational manner. Both creativity and fantasy may share breadth-of-attention deployment. From a cognitive perspective, this variable could also account for the play–creativity link.

In several important experimental studies, play facilitated divergent thinking in preschool children (Dansky, 1980; Dansky & Silverman, 1973). In particular, Dansky and Silverman found that children who played with objects during a play period gave significantly more uses for those objects than did control subjects. In the later study, Dansky (1980) found that make-believe play was the mediator of the relationship between play and divergent thinking. Free play facilitated divergent thinking, but only for children who engaged in make-believe play. Also, in this second study, play had a generalized effect in that the objects in the play period were different from those in the test period. These two studies are important because they are experimental studies that show a direct effect of play on divergent thinking.

Dansky's (1980) study was criticized by Smith and Whitney (1987). In a carefully executed study, they failed to confirm the hypothesis that play would enhance divergent thinking in preschool children. One of the major differences between their study and Dansky's was the use of a different examiner to administer the divergent thinking task after the play task. They attributed the experimental effect found in Dansky's study to unconscious experimenter bias during testing. However, another possibility is that the introduction of a new examiner between the play task and the divergent thinking task interfered with the experimental set being induced by the play. Thus, there would be no experimental effect of play on problem solving. Another important point is that there have been a number of correlational studies (Lieberman, 1977; Russ & Grossman-McKee, 1990; D. Singer & Rummo, 1973) that have found a relationship between play and creativity that did use different examiners for the play and creativity tasks. Nevertheless, Smith and Whitney raised an important note of caution about controlling for experimenter bias as much as possible in play and creativity studies.

Fisher (1992) conducted a meta-analysis of 46 studies in the play and child development area up to 1987. He investigated the impact of play on cognitive, affective-social, and linguistic processes. Both correlational and experimental studies were included. In general, he found a modest effect size (ES) of .347. The largest effect size was for divergent thinking and perspective-taking criteria (ES = .387 and .392, respectively). He concluded that play does result in improvement in children's development. The strongest effect size was for cognitive abilities important in creative thinking. Fisher also found that play impacted basic language acquisition.

Dansky's (1980) theoretical rationale for hypothesizing that play would facilitate divergent thinking was that the process of free combination of objects and ideas involved in play is similar to the elements involved in creative thinking. Dansky (1980) speculated that the free symbolic transformations inherent in pretend play helped create a temporary cognitive set toward the loosening of old associations. These ideas are consistent with the work of Sutton-Smith (1966, 1992). Sutton-Smith stressed the role of play in the development of flexibility in problem solving. Play provides the opportunity to explore new combinations of ideas and to develop new associations for old objects. The object transformations that occur in play help develop the capacity to see old objects in new ways. The capacity to see old objects and ideas in new ways should also aid in developing transformation abilities; that is, the ability to break out of an old set and see a new solution to a problem. Kogan (1983) also suggested that children's play behavior involves a search for alternate modes of relating to the object, a process similar to searching for alternate uses for objects in divergent thinking tasks.

Pellegrini (1992) also identified flexibility as one link between play and creativity. In a study of third- and fifth-grade boys, flexibility in rough-and-tumble play was predictive of a variety of prosocial problem solving responses. Pellegrini proposed that in play, children recombine behaviors and develop flexible strategies. A varied problem solving repertoire aids in social competence. Saracho (1992) found results that also support a link between play and flexibility. She found that field-independent children engaged more in play than did field-dependent children. She concluded from observing the children's play that the field-independent children were exhibiting cognitive flexibility.

Until recently, the research on play and creativity has focused on cognitive variables as the explanatory mechanisms underlying the relationship. As discussed, explanations have included practice with divergent thinking, the recombination of objects and ideas, symbolic transformations, breadth-of-attention deployment, and the loosening of old cognitive sets or cognitive flexibility.

Creativity, Play, and Affective Processes

Emotion and the development of affective processes is being increasingly studied. The importance of emotional intelligence (Mayer & Salovey, 1993) is finally getting its due. Although I do not agree with the "intelligence" analogy, the importance of emotional processes in adaptive functioning is an important principle to be recognized. Children's pretend play facilitates the development of emotional processes. J. Singer (1973) discussed the importance of play in helping children to organize their experience, including their emotional experience.

Affective processes could also account for the relationship between play and creativity. Although the empirical research in the play and creativity area has focused on cognitive variables, there is an increasing theoretical emphasis on affective processes in play and creativity (Russ, 1993; Shaw & Runco, 1994). Affect is emerging as an important variable in the play–creativity link. Play is important in the development of major cognitive and affective processes involved in creativity. The re-discovery of Vygotsky's theory has contributed to this development (see Ayman-Nolley, 1992; Smolucha, 1992; Smolucha & Smolucha, 1992). Also, Fein's (1987) concept of affective symbolic units makes affect a key concept in pretend play and creativity. D. Singer and J. Singer (1990) discussed imaginative play within a cognitive-affective framework. They proposed a cognitive-affect framework as a "central conception from which we can explore the nature of imaginative play and its role in childhood" (p. 29). D. Singer and J. Singer reviewed Tomkin's (1962, 1963) model of affect and suggested that play is reinforcing when it permits expression of positive affect and the appropriate control of negative affect. This formulation is consistent with research by Golomb and Galasso (1995). In a study with preschoolers, they found that when the affective valence of an imagined situation was negative, children would modify the theme to diminish their fear, such as imagining a friendly monster. In a positive affect situation, they would embellish the theme to enhance the pleasure. Golomb and Galasso concluded that children monitor and regulate affect in play so as not to exceed a certain threshold while still having enough emotional involvement to enjoy the play. Shmukler (1982–1983) viewed imaginative play as lying at the cognitive-affective interface and reflecting a general capacity for divergent thinking. Finally, Russ' (1993) model of affect and creativity identified some of the major affective processes that are important in creativity.

Theoretical explanations for the links between affect, play, and creativity have been in existence for some time, although research that tests the theory is relatively recent. There is a growing consensus that the affective components of pretend play and creativity must be studied as systematically as the cognitive components. We are just beginning to look at affect, partly because of the difficulty in measuring affective processes in play. In general, the empirical study of affective expression in children is a young area (Masters, Felleman, & Barden, 1981).

The first major theoretical explanation for the relationship between affect and creativity was that of psychoanalytic theory, which proposed that controlled access to primary process thinking facilitated creativity. Primary process thinking was first conceptualized by Sigmund Freud

(1915/1958) as an early, primitive system of thought that was drive-laden and not subject to rules of logic or oriented to reality. Another way to view primary process thought is as affect-laden cognition. Russ (1987, 1993, 1996) proposed that primary process is a subtype of affect in cognition. Primary process content is material around which the child had experienced early intense feeling states (oral, anal, aggressive, etc.). According to psychoanalytic theory, primary process thinking facilitates creativity (Kris, 1952). Children and adults who have controlled access to primary process thinking should have a broader range of associations and be better divergent thinkers than individuals with less access to primary process. Freud's (1926/1959) formulation that repression of "dangerous" drive-laden content leads to a more general intellectual restriction predicts that individuals with less access to affect-laden cognitions would have fewer associations in general. Thus, children who are more expressive of and open to affective content would develop a richer, more complex store of affect-laden memories. This richer store of memories would facilitate divergent thinking and transformation abilities because it provides a broader range of associations and more flexible manipulation of images and ideas.

Primary process content can be expressed in play. As Waelder (1933) has said, play is a "leave of absence from reality" (p. 222) and is a place to let primary process thinking occur. Play can be important in the development of primary process thought and, in turn, foster creative thinking.

Primary process theory is consistent with Bower's (1981) conceptualization of affect and memory processes (see Russ, 1993, 1996). The work on mood and memory suggests that the search process for associations is broadened by the involvement of emotion. Russ (1993) proposed that if primary process is thought of as mood-relevant cognition, then it could fit into a mood and memory theoretical framework. When stirred, primary process content could trigger a broad associative network. Primary process content would be stored into the memory system when emotion was present. Access to this primary process content would activate emotion nodes and associations, thus broadening the search process.

Feins's (1987) view of affect as intertwined with pretend play and creativity makes an important theoretical contribution. Fein (1987) viewed play as a natural form of creativity. She studied 15 children who were master players and concluded that good pretend play consists of five characteristics:

1. *Referential freedom.* The "as if" concept is important in that one object is treated as if it were another, one person functions as if they were another, time and place is as if it were different. Object substitutions and transformations occur. Fein theorized that transformations occur when a representational template is mapped onto persons and objects in the environment. These representations can be manipulated and are detached from practical

outcomes. The ability to engage in referential freedom begins at 2 years of age.

2. *Denotative license.* The child takes a divergent stance with respect to actual experience. There are pretend events, not just object substitution in an accurate account of events.

3. *Affective relations.* Symbolic units represent affective relationships such as fear of, love for, anger at. Fein (1987) proposed an affective symbol system that represents real or imagined experience at a general level. These affective units constitute affect-binding representational templates. The templates store salient information about affect-laden events. The units are "manipulated, interpreted, coordinated and elaborated in a way that makes affective sense to the players" (p. 292). These affective units are a key part of pretend play. In fact, Fein viewed pretend play as symbolic behavior organized around emotional and motivational issues. Fein implied that this affective symbol system is especially important for creative thinking. She stated that divergent thinking abilities like daydreams, pretend play, or drawing can activate the affective symbol system.

4. *Sequential uncertainty.* The sequence of events in pretend play have a nonlinear quality.

5. *Self-mirroring.* Children are aware of the pretend, non-real quality of the play. The self is observed from a distance through the play.

One of Fein's (1987) major conclusions is that creative processes can not be studied independently of an affective symbol system. An affective symbol system is activated in pretend play and is probably facilitated through pretend play. The concept of affective symbols is consistent with the concept of primary process (Russ, 1996). Primary process content could be stored in the affect symbol system.

Vygotsky (1930/1967) is also a major theoretician in the area of affect, play, and creativity. He presented a rich conceptualization of play and creativity. Smolucha (1992) has translated and integrated Vygotsky's major papers on the topic of creativity. From her review of his work, a major premise in Vygotsky's theory is that imagination develops out of children's play. He stated, "The child's play activity is not simply a recollection of past experience but a creative reworking that combines impressions and constructs from them new realities addressing the needs of the child" (1930/1967, p. 7). Through play, children develop combinatory imagination (i.e., the ability to combine elements of experience into new situations and new behaviors). Combinatory imagination is significant because it can contribute to artistic and scientific creativity. Vygotsky thus viewed creativity as a developmental process. By adolescence, play evolves into fantasy and imagination which combines with thinking in concepts (Ayman-Nolley, 1992). Imagination has two parts in adolescence: objective and subjective. Objective imagination creates new ideas and understand-ings of reality. Subjective imagination includes emotion and serves the emotional life. Impulse and thinking are combined in the activity of creative thinking.

Morrison (1988) placed cognitive-affective development within an interpersonal framework. The cognitive integration of affect occurs within safe interactions with parents. Representations of self and others are fused with affect. In play, the child reconstructs past experience and explores definitions of the self. Old metaphors are constantly reworked. In this way, the child develops reflective thought. Conflicts from early interpersonal experience can be a major source of creative thinking in that the metaphors of early experience are reworked in creative acts. Santostefano (1988) also stressed the importance of play in metaphor construction. The process of constructing and negotiating metaphors is creative and can lead to later creativity.

Russ (1993) reviewed the affect and creativity literature and proposed five categories of affect that emerged as important in the creative process. The question of whether or not these five categories are truly separate dimensions of affect needs to be systematically investigated. In Russ' model of affect and creativity, these affective processes are related to specific creative cognitive processes (see Fig. 2.1). The links between the processes are based on theory and the empirical literature. Two broad affective processes are access to affect-laden thoughts and openness to affect states.

Access to affect-laden thoughts is the ability to think about thoughts and images that contain emotional content. Affective fantasy in daydreams and in play are examples of affect-laden thoughts. Thoughts involving emotional themes such as aggressive and sexual ideation illustrate this kind of blending of affect and cognition.

The psychoanalytic concept of primary process thinking is also an example of this kind of emotion-laden thinking (see Dudek, 1980; Kris, 1952; Rothenberg, 1990). Fein's (1987) affective symbols are types of affect-laden thoughts, as well.

Openness to affect states is the ability to feel the affect itself. Comfort with intense affect, the ability to experience and tolerate anxiety, and passionate involvement in a task are examples of openness to affect states.

Two other, more specific affective processes that are important in creativity are affective pleasure in challenge and affective pleasure in problem solving. The capacity to enjoy the excitement and tension in the challenge (Runco, 1994) and the capacity to take deep pleasure in problem solving (Amabile, 1990) are important in the creative process (see Feist, in press, for a discussion of this literature).

Finally, cognitive integration and modulation of affect is important in producing good and adaptive products. Cognitive control of affect is essential for the critical evaluation of ideas and products (Arieti, 1976; Kris, 1952).

Affective Processes   **Cognitive Abilities Involved in Creativity**

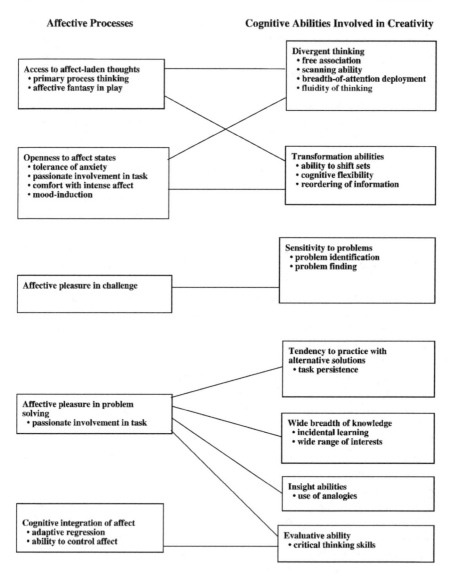

FIG. 2.1.   A model of affect and creativity.

Russ (1987, 1993) developed the Affect in Play Scale (APS) to meet the need for a standardized measure of affect in pretend play. This scale is described in detail in chapter 4. Play sessions are 5 minute standardized puppet play sessions that are individually administered. The play task utilizes two neutral-looking puppets, one boy and one girl, and three small blocks that are laid out on a table. The instructions are standardized and direct the child to play with the puppets any way they like for 5 minutes. The play session can be considered to be a free-play period. The play task and instructions are unstructured enough that individual differences in the use of affect in pretend play can emerge. The APS is appropriate for children from 6 to 10 years of age. The play session is videotaped so that coding can occur at a later time.

The APS measures the amount and types of affective expression in children's pretend play. It also measures cognitive dimensions of the play, such as quality of fantasy and imagination. Conceptually, APS taps three of the five categories of affect in fantasy proposed by Russ to be important in creativity: affect states, affect-laden thoughts, and cognitive integration of affect. The other two types of affect categories, pleasure in challenge and pleasure in problem solving, are not directly tapped by the APS. However, the comfort in play rating measures the child's enjoyment in and involvement in the task. Enjoyment in the play task could be analogous to pleasure in problem solving. This idea remains to be empirically tested. Russ' conceptualization of affect and creativity guided the development of the scale. In addition, both Holt's (1977) Scoring System for Primary Process on the Rorschach and J. Singer's (1973) play scales were used as models for the development of the scale. Details of the instructions and scoring system for the APS can be found in Russ (1993) and in the Appendix.

The major affect scores for the scale are frequency of affect units expressed, variety of affect categories expressed (11 possible categories), and intensity of affect expression. There are also global ratings (1–5 scale) for comfort, quality of fantasy, and imagination. An affective integration score combines frequency of affect and quality of fantasy. Research findings using the APS are presented throughout this book.

Empirical Findings

There is some evidence linking affect, play, and creativity. Also, research in the fantasy and creativity area and the mood-induction and creativity area is relevant to the play and creativity area.

Lieberman's (1977) work supports a relationship between affect in play and divergent thinking. She focused on the variable of playfulness which included the affective components of spontaneity and joy. She found that playful kindergarten children did better on divergent thinking tasks than non-playful children. D. Singer and J. Singer (1990) also found that positive affect was related to imaginative play. Christie and Johnson (1983) concluded that there is a relationship between playfulness and creativity. J. Singer and D. Singer (1981) found that preschoolers rated as high-imagination players showed significantly more themes of danger and power than children with low imagination.

In a series of studies by Russ and her students using the Affect in Play Scale (APS), affect in play did relate to creativity. Russ and Grossman-McKee (1990) investigated the relationships among the APS, divergent thinking and primary process thinking on the Rorschach in 60 first- and second-grade children. As predicted, affective expression in play was significantly, positively related to divergent thinking, as measured by the Alternate Uses Test. All major scores on the APS were significantly correlated with divergent thinking, with correlations ranging from .23 between comfort and divergent thinking to .42 between frequency of affective expression and divergent thinking. All correlations remained significant when IQ was partialed out; IQ had low correlations with the APS. The fact that intelligence did not relate to any of the play scores is consistent with the theoretical model for the development of the scale and is similar to the results of Singer (1973). Also, there were no gender differences in the pattern of correlations between the APS and divergent thinking. Russ and Grossman-McKee also found a relationship between the amount of primary process thinking on the Rorschach and the APS scores. Children who had more primary process responses on the Rorschach had more affect in their play and had higher fantasy scores than children with less primary process on the Rorschach. This is an important finding because it shows that there is some consistency in the construct of affective expression across two different types of situations. It is consistent with findings of Dudek and Verreault (1989), who found that creative fifth- and sixth-grade children gave significantly more total primary process ideation as measured by Holt's system as applied to the Torrance Tests of Creative Thinking. These findings are also consistent with Russ' Rorschach and creativity studies, which found relationships between primary process expression, divergent thinking, and transformation abilities for boys (1982, 1988).

The finding of a relationship between affect in play and divergent thinking (Russ & Grossman-McKee, 1990) was replicated by Russ and Peterson (1990; Russ, 1993) who used a larger sample of 121 first- and second-grade children. Once again, all of the APS scores were significantly positively related to the Alternate Uses Test, independent of intelligence. Again, there were no gender differences in the correlations. Thus, with this replication, we can have more confidence in the robustness of the finding that a relationship exists between affect in pretend play and creativity in young children.

An important question about the APS is whether it is indeed measuring two separate dimensions of play—an affective dimension and a cognitive dimension—or is measuring one dimension—an affect in fantasy dimension. The results of two separate factor analyses with the scale suggest two separate dimensions. Russ and Peterson (1990) carried out a principal component analysis with oblique rotation. It yielded two separate factors as the best solution. The first and dominant factor appeared to be a cognitive factor. Imagination, organization, quality of fantasy, and comfort loaded on this first factor. The second factor appears to be an affective factor. Frequency of affective expression, variety of affect categories, and intensity of affect loaded on this second factor. Although separate factors, there was a significant amount of shared variance ($r = .76$), suggesting that the factors also overlap. A study by D'Angelo (1995) replicated the finding of two factors, one cognitive and one affective, with a sample of 95 first-, second-, and third-grade children. This is an important finding because it lends support to the idea that cognitive expression and affective expression in play are related, but separate processes. Future studies with the play scale should explore the use of factor scores on the cognitive and affective factors as predictors of creativity.

Another interesting finding in D'Angelo's study (1995) was a significant relationship between the APS and J. Singer's (1973) imaginative play predisposition interview. Good players on the APS reported that they prefer activities that require using imagination. A study by Goldstein (2002) also found significant relationships between affect and fantasy scores on the APS and the imaginative play predisposition interview. For example, in a sample of 75 children, frequency of affect in play was positively related to imaginative play predisposition, $r = .42$ ($p < .001$).

Russ, Robins, and Christiano (1999) carried out a follow-up study of the first and second graders in the investigation of Russ and Peterson (1990). Those children were fifth- and sixth-graders for the follow-up. Thirty-one children agreed to participate in the follow-up study. This was a longitudinal study that explored the ability of the APS to predict creativity over a 4-year period (5 years in some cases, because the study took 2 years to complete). The major finding of the study was that quality of fantasy and imagination on the APS was predictive of divergent thinking over a 4-year period. The correlation between variety of affect and divergent thinking did not reach significance, possibly because of the small sample size. In this study, we also administered an adapted version of the play task to the older children. We altered the instructions so that they were asked to put on a play with the puppets. We then scored the task based on the scoring criteria for the APS. The results showed good stability in the dimensions being measured by the APS. For example, the size of the correlation between the two frequency of affect scores was $r = .33$, ($p < .05$); between the two variety of affect scores was $r = .38$, ($p < .05$); and between the two frequency of positive affect scores was $r = .51$, ($p < .01$.) In general, the size of the correlations is quite respectable for a period of 4 and 5 years and lends support for enduring, stable constructs of affective expression in fantasy that are predictive over time of creative thinking. These findings also suggest an enduring quality to the affective and cognitive dimensions of the APS over a 5-year period. These findings are consistent with those of Hutt and Bhavnani (1972), who found that creative inventiveness in pre-school play related to later divergent thinking. Clark, Griffing, and Johnson (1989) also found a relationship between divergent thinking and play in preschoolers, which was predictive of divergent thinking over a 3-year period.

Russ and Cooperberg (2002) followed this longitudinal sample into the eleventh and twelfth grades. Forty-nine of the original 121 children participated in the study. Children's play as measured by the APS was positively related to later creativity as measured by the Alternate Uses Test. Both mean quality of fantasy $r = .28$ ($p < .05$) and imagination $r = .30$ ($p < .05$) were positively related to fluency scores on the Alternate Uses Test. Quality of fantasy and imagination accounted for 9% of the variance in future creativity scores.

In a recent study with a different sample of 47 first- and second-grade children, Russ and Schafer (2002) explored the relationship between APS and divergent thinking. In this study, we used three emotion-laden words and three neutral words for the divergent thinking task. Frequency and variety of affect in play significantly related to divergent thinking for the emotion-laden words (not the neutral words) and to originality of response to both the emotion-laden and non-emotion-laden words. Most of these correlations did not remain significant when IQ was partialed out. This was one of the few studies in which IQ did relate to the APS.

In the Russ and Schafer study, we also investigated the relationship between APS and access to emotion in memory. We hypothesized that children who could express affect in play would also be able to express emotion and think about emotion in other situations. Children were asked nine questions about their experiences. For example, "Tell me about a time when you felt mad," and "Tell me about your first day in school." The results showed a significant relationship between variety of affect in play and amount of affect in the memories $r = .32$ ($p < .05$) and between quality of fantasy and amount of affect in the memories $r = .46$ ($p < .001$). These correlations remained significant after IQ and word count were partialed out. Thus, children who were better players (greater variety of affect and better quality of fantasy) expressed more emotion when talking about their memories. We might speculate that, over time, the child who uses play well will be more open to affect themes and emotions. This openness to affect should effect the storage of material in memory and retention of and access to those memories. More emotion could be included in those memories, and the child would have a richer store of affect symbols (Fein, 1987) to use.

Fantasy and affect in play using the APS has related to creativity in children from 6 to 10 and has predicted creativity over time. What about affect in play in preschool children? To investigate this question, Seja and Russ

(1999b) adapted the APS for use with younger children. We used a variety of toys and props and did some alteration of the scoring (see chapter 4). In a study with 33 children from 4 to 5 years of age, frequency and variety of affect in play was significantly related to creativity and originality on a divergent thinking task. All play scores were significantly related to teachers' ratings of daily play behavior. Even at this young age, cognitive and affective processes in play were related to creative thinking ability.

Mood Induction Research.   The research in the area of mood-induction and creativity is relevant to the question of whether expressing affect in pretend play would facilitate creative problem solving. Most of the research in the area of mood-induction and creativity is with adults. The mood-induction paradigm provides a way of altering affect states so that the effect on cognitive processes can be observed. In a series of studies, Isen found that induced positive affect facilitated creative thinking. Isen (1985) found that positive affect increased divergent associations to neutral words, and Isen, Daubman, and Nowicki (1987) found that positive affect, induced by a comedy film, resulted in more creative problem solving than control conditions. Induction of a negative mood state had no effect on creativity. Jausovec (1989) also found that induced positive affect facilitated performance on an analogical transfer task, thought to be important in creative thinking. He also found that negative mood induction had no effect. Both Isen et al. (1987) and Jausovec (1989) hypothesized that the negative mood-induction method that was used (a Holocaust film) may have been too extreme. In a study by Adaman (1991), a milder form of negative mood-induction that used sad music did facilitate divergent thinking in college students. Also, Vosburg and Kaufmann (1999) found that mild negative affect facilitated creativity on creativity tasks. The only published study with children found that induced positive affect in eighth-grade children facilitated creative problem solving (Greene & Noice, 1988). We can conclude that careful experimental work has shown that some positive affect states facilitate transformation abilities, remote associations, and analogical transfer (see Feist, in press; Isen, 1999, for a review).

Positive and Negative Affect

One of the interesting questions in the affect and creativity area has to do with the differential effects of positive and negative affect on creativity. Both the play and mood induction research suggest that positive affect relates to and facilitates creative cognitive processes. Lieberman's (1977) finding that spontaneity and joy in play related to divergent thinking, D. Singer and J. Singer's (1990) finding that positive affect related to imaginative play, and Krasnor and Pepler's (1980) notion that intrinsic motivation (a pleasurable state) is part of pretend play are all consistent with the mood induction research findings. The mood induction research has found mixed results about the question of negative affect facilitating creativity. However, in play and fantasy research, negative play themes are related to creativity. Themes of danger and power occurred in high-imagination players (J. Singer & D. Singer, 1981), negative primary process themes related to creative thinking (Dudek & Verreault, 1989; Russ, 1982, 1988; Russ & Grossman-McKee, 1990), and both positive and negative themes in affect in play related to divergent thinking (Russ, 1993; Russ & Grossman-McKee, 1990; Russ & Peterson, 1990). Theoretically, both positive and negative affect should facilitate creativity. Richards (1990), Russ, (1993), and Feist (in press) have proposed a curvilinear relationship between affect and creativity. Positive and negative affect may facilitate creativity when they are of low to moderate levels. At those levels, such as in well-controlled play, where the child is in charge of the pacing of the material, negative affect may trigger memories and associations important to the creative process. Because the child is in charge of the material in good pretend play, negative affect may not be so negative. Negative themes such as fear and aggression may not be accompanied by negative mood states. D. Singer and J. Singer (1990) stated that controlled expression of negative affect is reinforcing. Krasnor and Pepler (1980) thought that all pretend play involved mainly positive emotions. On the other hand, Morrison's (1988) idea of reworking old metaphors in play involves dealing with negative affect. Chuck Jones, the cartoonist, has stated that, in the creative process, one must be open to and face down anxieties and fears (Goleman, Kaufman, & Ray, 1992). Joy arrives when the issue has been resolved, in the art. Vandenberg (1988) states that play derives its thrill from the anxiety within it. Since safety is a prerequisite for play, threats and taboos can be explored.

An important question is whether expression of affect in play will immediately impact creativity. Russ and Kaugars (2000–2001) conducted a study with first- and second-grade children that manipulated affect in play and investigated the effects on creativity. Eighty children were randomly assigned to one of four groups: a happy puppet play group; angry puppet play group; free play with puppets group; or puzzle group. The main finding, contrary to prediction, was that there was no effect for experimental condition on divergent thinking. The experimental manipulation of affect was effective for the angry play group but not for the happy play group. There was no facilitation of divergent thinking for any group. Because the experimental manipulation did not work for the happy play condition, the hypothesis remains untested for positive affect in play. The experimental manipulation did work for negative affect, but it did not increase divergent thinking. This finding is not consistent with the results of correlational research that found relations between negative themes in play and creativity. Perhaps the affect in fantasy in play is more trait-like than state-like and manipulations in one-trial studies will have no effect on dependent variables. Christie (1994) has cautioned against brief one-trial studies in the play intervention area.

An interesting finding in the Russ and Kaugars study was that self-reported experience of feeling emotion during the puppet play was associated with original responses on the divergent thinking task. Children who experienced more emotion gave more original responses. This finding is consistent with the findings in the mood induction literature.

Play and Creativity: Summary of Findings

Research has found that play relates to and facilitates (a) insight ability and (b) divergent thinking ability. Both of these cognitive processes are important in creativity. Play has been found to predict divergent thinking in longitudinal studies.

When affect in play is focused on, affect in play relates to divergent thinking ability. No study has found that inducing affect in play facilitates creativity.

The play situation is a place where children can develop modes of expression of both positive and negative affect. In this safe arena, children can call up a variety of pretend mood states, memories and fantasies, and primary process themes. Negative affect can be expressed, worked through, and mastered. Children can practice with free associations and divergent thinking. Over time, this practice could alter cognitive structures, increase metaphors, help develop a rich store of affect symbols (Fein, 1987), and result in increased divergent thinking and transformation abilities.

In summary, pretend-play ability is related to many of the cognitive and affective processes important in creativity. Although much of the research is correlational, there are well-designed experimental studies that have found facilitative effects of play on creative thinking and longitudinal studies that suggest causality. One might speculate that, over time, engaging in pretend play helps the child become more creative in the following ways:

1. Practice with the free flow of associations that is part of divergent thinking.
2. Practice with symbol substitution, recombining of ideas, and manipulation of object representations. These processes are part of transformation ability and insight ability.
3. Express and experience positive affect. Positive affect is important in creativity. Also, the positive affect in play could be the precursor of the passion and intrinsic motivation so often noted in creative individuals.

4. Express and think about positive and negative affect themes. Emotional content and primary process content are permitted to surface and be expressed through play. Over time, the child develops access to a variety of memories, associations, and affective and non-affective cognition. This broad repertoire of associations helps in creative problem solving.
5. Develop cognitive structure that enables the child to contain, integrate, and modulate affect.

We can speculate that, over time, the child who uses play well develops the habit of being open to affect themes and emotions. This openness to affect should effect the storage of material in memory and retention of and access to those memories. Also, the child would have a richer store of affect symbols to use in creative production as an adult.

Play, Creativity, Coping, and Adjustment

An important question is whether creative ability is a resource in other areas of functioning. Does creative problem solving apply to problems of daily life? Does it relate to adaptive functioning? Richards' (1993) concept of everyday creativity proposes that individuals do apply creative problem solving ability to real-life problems. Also, the cognitive and affective processes important in play and creativity should be facilitative of other types of adaptive functioning as well. For example, openness to affect and the ability to integrate affect should be adaptive resources in many ways.

Creative problem solvers should be better copers because they bring their problem solving skills to everyday problems. Good divergent thinkers should be able to think of alternative solutions to real-life problems. There is some empirical support for this concept. Russ (1988) found a relationship between divergent thinking and teacher's ratings of coping in fifth-grade boys. Similarly, Carson, Bittner, Cameron, Brown, and Meyer (1994) found a significant relationship between figural divergent thinking and teacher's ratings of coping. Russ, Robins, and Christiano (1999) found that divergent thinking was significantly related to quality of coping responses in a self-report scale.

Looking specifically at play and coping ability, Christiano and Russ (1996) found a positive relationship between play and coping and a negative relationship between play and distress in 7- to 9-year-olds. Children who were "good" players on the Affect in Play Scale implemented a greater number and variety of cognitive coping strategies (correlations ranging from .52 to .55) during an invasive dental procedure. In addition, good players reported less distress during the procedure than children who expressed less affect and fantasy in play. Consistent with these findings, a recent study by Perry and Russ (1998) found that fantasy in play was positively related to frequency and variety of self-reported coping strategies in a group of homeless children. Also, a study by Goldstein and Russ (2000–2001) found that fantasy and imagination in play, were positively related to the number and variety of cognitive coping attempts in thinking about what to do in a situation that required impulse control of aggression. Finally, in the Russ et al. (1999) longitudinal study, fantasy in play significantly predicted self-reported coping over a 4-year period. Children who had higher quality of fantasy in play could think of more things to do in stressful situations. All of these studies that linked play and coping used different types of coping measures and involved different experimenters. In the recent follow-up study by Russ and Cooperberg (2002), APS predicted coping in high school students over a 10-year period. Variety of affect $r = .24$ ($p < .05$), quality of fantasy $r = .34$ ($p < .05$), and imagination $r = .34$ ($p < .05$) were all positively related to future use of problem-focused coping as measured by the ACOPE, a self-report scale.

Also, there is some empirical work that suggests that play is related to adjustment. D. Singer and J. Singer (1990) concluded that imaginative play in children is related to academic adjustment and flexibility of thought. They also found that toddlers and preschoolers who engage in make-believe play were better adjusted across different situations. Burstein and Meichenbaum (1979) found that children who voluntarily played with stress-related toys prior to surgery demonstrated less distress and anxiety following surgery than children who avoided the toys. One might speculate that those children were accustomed to using play to deal with stress and problems. In a study of 4- to 11-year-olds, Kenealy (1989) investigated strategies that children use when they are feeling depressed and found that 50% of the children's responses included play strategies.

In a study of urban children from 4 to 5 years of age, Rosenberg (1984) found that the quality of fantasy play for children playing in dyads was positively related to measures of social competence and ego resilience (Block-Q sort). Frequency of positive themes and relationship themes in the play was also related to ego resilience and social competence. In general, children with behavior problems and attachment problems had fewer positive and negative themes in play, with the exception of diffuse hostility. Similarly, D'Angelo (1995) found that ego-resilient children showed better play (APS) than undercontrolled or overcontrolled children as measured by the Child Behavior Checklist.

Grossman-McKee (1989) found, using the Affect in Play Scale with first- and second-grade boys, that boys who expressed more affect in play had fewer pain complaints than boys with less affect in play. Good players were also less anxious on the State-Trait Anxiety Inventory for Children (Spielberger, 1973). The conclusion from this study was that the ability to express affect in play was associated with less anxiety and less psychosomatic complaints. A study by Goldstein (2002) also found a negative relationship between quality of fantasy in play and state anxiety on the STAIC.

An interesting finding in the Russ and Cooperberg (2002) longitudinal study was a negative relationship $r = .31$ ($p < .05$) between negative affect in play (APS) and depression (Beck Depression Inventory). Expression of negative affect in play was related to depression 10 years later. In other studies, negative emotion in play has been related to adaptive functioning such as creativity and coping. However, this longitudinal study suggests that negative affect in play could also be an early indicator of depression. Other personality characteristics and the cognitive integration of this negative affect and its intensity are only some of the complex factors that would be involved in predicting depression. However, this longitudinal study reminds us that characteristics of individuals that can be a resource in one area can be a risk-factor in another area.

Negative affect in play also emerged as a predictor of behavior problems in a study by Von Klitzing, Kelsey, Emde, Robinson, and Schmitz (2000). In a study of play narratives of 652 children, they found that aggressive themes in the play narratives of girls was related to externalizing and internalizing problems for girls. Aggressive themes did not predict behavior problems for boys. They concluded that one possibility for the gender differences was that aggressiveness in girls' narratives might imply more deviance than aggressiveness in boys' narratives. Boys had significantly more aggressive themes in play than did girls in their sample. This gender difference in amount of aggression in play is consistent with results of our studies with the APS. Boys consistently express more aggressive themes than girls. The APS is a free-play task, whereas the structured MacArthur Story Stem Battery was used in the Von Klitzing et al. study. Another important finding in the Von Klitzing et al. study was that, for both boys and girls, when aggressive themes were expressed in an incoherent narrative, it was associated with more behavior problems.

In summary, correlational studies found relationships between measures of divergent thinking and coping ability. The ability to generate a variety of ideas on a creativity test relates to the ability to generate ideas about coping with problems and to the ability to cope. Pretend play has been found to relate to different measures of coping with different populations. It is possible that the reason for the link between play and coping is the divergent thinking ability important in both functions. This hypothesis that divergent thinking is a mediator in the play–coping link remains to be empirically tested.

Play also related to different measures of adjustment by different researchers. No study has found a causal relationship between play and coping ability or play and adjustment. Although most of the relationships between play and coping and adjustment have been positive, there is some emerging evidence that negative affect in play could be indicative of internal distress or psychopathology. Gender differences in the expression of negative affect in play is emerging as an important consideration.

PLAY, EMOTIONAL UNDERSTANDING, AND SOCIAL DEVELOPMENT

Pretend play involves cognitive and affective processes that should be important in empathy and social functioning. There is some empirical evidence that play is related to social development. Fisher (1992), in his meta-analysis of play studies, found a modest effect size of .392 for the impact of play on perspective-taking. In the studies he reviewed, perspective-taking was defined as empathic role assumption that is related to cooperative behavior, sociability, and popularity.

Seja and Russ (1999a) discussed the processes that play and perspective-taking may have in common. They hypothesized that children who would be able to express emotion and good quality fantasy in play would be better able to understand emotions in themselves and others than children who expressed less affect and fantasy in their play. In a study with 66 children in the first and second grades, they found that quality of fantasy play was significantly related to two emotional understanding abilities: the ability to describe emotional experiences and the understanding of the emotions of others. These relationships were significant when verbal ability was controlled for. The relationship between fantasy play and understanding others' emotions supports Harris's (1989) proposition that imaginative understanding may enable children to understand other's mental states and affective experiences. This finding is consistent with evidence among preschoolers that individual differences in fantasy have been significantly related to affective and cognitive-perspective taking tasks (Astington & Jenkins, 1995; Youngblade & Dunn, 1995). The ability to understand and vicariously experience others' emotions provides the basis for empathy.

In the Seja and Russ study, frequency of affective expression was not related to the criteria. The cognitive organization of the fantasy and emotion in fantasy were the important variables. Also, play did not relate to understanding of one's own emotions.

The results of this study have important implications for clinical work and suggest that the mere expression of emotion in play is not related to emotional understanding and may not be as useful as play therapists believe. Instead, the integration of affective and cognitive material may be more important in facilitating the development of emotional understanding.

Seja and Russ (1998) examined the relationships among parents' reports of children's daily behavior, children's affect and fantasy in play, and children's emotional understanding among first-grade children in the previous sample. Parents' ratings of children's daily emotional intensity was expected to relate to children's affect expression in play. Results were that children who demonstrated more positive emotion in their daily behavior were more likely to express more emotion overall and more negative emotion in their play than children who expressed less daily positive emotion. Furthermore, children who demonstrated more negative emotion in their daily behavior displayed fewer different types of emotion, less positive emotion, and less emotion overall in their play than children who expressed less daily negative emotion. One implication of these results is that negative emotional themes in play reflect a different variable than the expression of negative emotional states in daily life.

It was also hypothesized that parents' ratings of children's daily emotional intensity would relate to children's emotional understanding. It was found that children who expressed more intense positive emotion in their daily behavior had a better understanding of their own emotions and described more emotional experiences than children with less intense daily positive emotion. Contrary to initial hypotheses, children with more intense negative emotion in daily behavior did not have lower levels of emotional understanding. The results of this study suggest that parents' reports of children's daily behavior may provide important information to clinicians about children's play, emotional development, and adjustment. However, because the sample was small ($n = 23$), the study should be replicated with another sample of children.

Theories of development acknowledge that affect is linked to interpersonal functioning in multiple ways (Emde, 1989; Russ & Niec, 1993; Sroufe, 1989; Strayer, 1987). For example, affective sharing has been related to better quality of infant–parent attachment (Pederson & Moran, 1996; Waters, Wippman, & Sroufe, 1979); regulation of affect has been related to better peer relations and fewer behavior problems (Cole, Zahn-Waxler, Fox, Usher, & Welsh, 1996; Rubin, Coplan, Fox, & Calkins, 1995); openness to affect has been described as providing meaning to interpersonal experience (Sandler & Sandler, 1978), and has also been conceptualized as a key component of empathy (Feshbach, 1987). Given these associations between dimensions of affect and interpersonal functioning, two studies were conducted to investigate the relationship of the Affect in Play Scale with children's interpersonal functioning.

Niec and Russ (1996) investigated relationships among affect and fantasy in play, expression of interpersonal themes in projective stories, and peer and teacher ratings of interpersonal functioning in 49 first- through third-graders. Access to affect in play was predicted to be positively associated with children's expression of interpersonal themes in stories and interpersonal functioning based on the proposition from object relations theory that a "defense against affect is a defense against objects" and leads to an inability to relate with others on anything but a superficial level (Modell, 1980,

p. 266). Children with poor access to affect in play were thus expected to be more likely to have poor peer relationships, while children with good access to affect were expected to have good quality peer relationships.

Children were administered the APS, the Children's Apperceptive Story Telling Test (CAST), and a brief IQ measure (Schneider, 1989). Teachers and peers rated subjects on their likability, disruptiveness, and withdrawal using the Pupil Evaluation Inventory (PEI; Pekarik, Prinz, Liebert, Weintraub, & Neale, 1976). Results found no relationship between the APS and interpersonal functioning. However, relationships were found between the APS and frequency of interpersonal themes on the CAST. Children who were better players in that they expressed a wide variety of affective categories, frequent positive affect, comfort in their play, and high quality fantasy were more likely to project themes involving people and relationships in their stories.

In a study by Niec and Russ (2002), relationships among affect and fantasy in play, internal representations, and capacity for empathy were investigated. Eighty-six children in third and fourth grades completed the APS, the TAT, and the Bryant Index of Empathy for Children (Bryant, 1982; Murray, 1971). Teachers completed ratings of children's empathy and helpfulness for each child. TAT stories were scored using Westen's (1995) Social Cognition and Object Relations Scale (SCORS-Q).

As predicted, quality of fantasy on the APS was related to self-reported empathy. The finding supported the importance of imaginative ability in children's empathic responding and is consistent with the previously discussed Seja and Russ finding (1999a). Children who were able to "put reality aside and imagine the feelings of someone else in a different (make-believe) situation" were likely to be self-described as more empathic to others (Harris, 1994, p. 19).

Access to affect in play did not relate to empathy, perhaps because the APS measures expression of affect-laden themes rather than the experience of emotion so important in empathic understanding.

Neither access to affect nor fantasy in play related to children's representations of relationships on the TAT. This finding helped to answer the question posed by Niec (1994) as to whether access to affect in play would be related to interpersonal representations when content of affect themes (rather than *amount* of affect themes) is assessed. Whereas in the Niec and Russ (1996) study affect and fantasy in play were positively related to frequency of interpersonal themes in projective stories, the Niec and Russ (2002) finding suggests that access to affect may not be related to the qualitative aspects of those representations. It may be that access to affect relates to access to interpersonal representations (i.e., frequency), regardless of the content of those representations (i.e., quality).

It is probable that level of interpersonal representations could be assessed in children's play. Niec has developed a scoring system for interpersonal representations in play. She used the APS task and scored the play narratives with this new system—the Interpersonal Themes in Play System (ITPS). When we recoded the play narratives in the 1998 study with the ITPS, we found that a number of the new play scores did relate to SCORS-Q on the TAT and to empathy measures. Especially promising is the Affect Tone in Play score, which measures the degree to which the play narrative reflects a safe, supportive interpersonal world. Affect Tone in Play significantly related to internal representations on the TAT and to several measures of empathy (Niec, Yopp, & Russ, 2002). This preliminary study suggests that interpersonal schemas can be assessed in play.

In summary, the research evidence to date suggests that the imaginative ability reflected in play and perhaps facilitated through play is related to capacity for empathy and the understanding of emotions. The ability to change roles and take the perspective another could be the theoretical link between play and empathy. The expression of emotion in play has not been shown to be related to empathy, social functioning, or understanding of one's own emotions. However, assessing interpersonal representations in play is an important area for future development.

IMPLICATIONS OF CHILD DEVELOPMENT RESEARCH FOR THE USE OF PLAY IN THERAPY

Research programs on children's play, creativity, emotion, coping, social functioning, and adjustment have not yet had a direct impact on the use of play in psychotherapy. Many of the cognitive and affective processes that have related to play, or have been facilitated by play, in the empirical literature are probably being affected in play therapy, but not in a systematic fashion. One can conclude from the empirical literature that pretend play relates to or facilitates:

1. Problem solving that requires insight ability.
2. Flexibility in problem solving.
3. Divergent thinking ability.
4. The ability to think of alternative coping strategies in dealing with daily problems and the ability to cope.
5. The experiencing of positive emotion.
6. The ability to think about and express both positive and negative affect themes in other situations.
7. The ability to understand the emotions of others and to take the perspective of another.
8. Some aspects of general adjustment.

A causal relationship has been found between play and insight ability and play and divergent thinking. It is theoretically consistent to hypothesize that play facilitates the other abilities as well, but those questions have not been investigated.

It would be useful for the child therapist to be aware of how an individual child could benefit from strengthening these processes and to then develop techniques in the play therapy to focus on them. Many of these processes clearly interact. For example, the research suggests that increasing the amount of positive affect that a child experiences will increase divergent thinking ability. In turn, the generation of different coping strategies should be increased. How to best accomplish the transfer from the therapy setting to the real world is the challenge to the therapist. Thinking of coping strategies and actually doing them are different skills, and many of the self-report coping measures have not been validated with real-life coping criteria. Nevertheless, an awareness of the processes that have been linked to play should help guide the therapist.

A crucial next step for research programs is to identify which specific interventions influence which specific cognitive and affective processes. For example, the results of both the Seja and Russ study (1999a), and the Niec and Russ (2002) study, that fantasy in play related to emotional understanding of others and to empathy, and that affect expression did not, have implications for play therapy. Play is frequently used to communicate about the child's emotional life (Chethik, 1989). Both psychodynamic and person-centered approaches to intervention consider the expression of emotion in play to be an important mechanism of change in child therapy (Russ, 1995). However, the results of these two studies suggest that the mere expression of emotion in play is not related to an understanding of emotions or to empathy. Rather, the quality and organization of the fantasy is the more important factor in relating to these criteria. If the therapist is working with a child for whom one goal of therapy is to improve the child's social functioning, then interventions that foster the fantasy and story-telling in play may be most helpful in developing an imaginative understanding that would help the child to take the perspective of the other (Seja & Russ, 1999a). It is also likely that guided play sessions with puppets or dolls would be more effective in increasing perspective taking than unstructured free play. For other types of problems with different goals, expression of emotions would be more helpful. These are the kinds of questions that need to be empirically investigated.

The next two chapters focus on the play therapy literature. One focus is on whether or not the findings in that literature are consistent with the findings from the child development literature. How do the conclusions from theoretical clinical writings and results from the play therapy research "match-up" with the focused play research findings just reviewed?

3

The Role of Play in Therapy: The Theories

Play has been a part of therapy with children since Melanie Klein and Anna Freud first began using play techniques in child psychotherapy in the 1930s. Play has been utilized in therapy from a variety of theoretical traditions. As of 1992, play in some form was used in child therapy by a majority of clinicians, as reported by Koocher and D'Angelo.

In the child therapy literature, four broad functions of play emerge as important in therapy. First, play is a natural form of expression in children. Chethik (1989) referred to the language of play. Children use play to express feelings and thoughts. Chethik stated that play emerges from the child's internal life and reflects the child's internal world. Therefore, children use play to express affect and fantasy and, in therapy, to express troubling and conflict-laden feelings. The expression of feelings itself, sometimes termed *catharsis*, is thought to be therapeutic (Axline, 1947; A. Freud, 1965; Moustakas, 1953). The therapist facilitates this process by giving permission for feelings to be expressed and by labeling the affect. By labeling the affect, the therapist helps to make the feeling less overwhelming and more understandable. In addition, the child feels more accepted as a whole person by the therapist and, in turn, is thought to become more self-accepting.

Second, the child also uses this language of play to communicate with the therapist. It is essential that the therapist understand these communications, so that the therapeutic relationship can develop (Chethik, 1989). The therapist actively labels, empathizes, and interprets the play, which in turn, helps the child feel understood (Russ, 1995). For many children, this feeling of empathy from the therapist facilitates change in their interpersonal representations and interpersonal functioning. The importance of expression through play and communication with the therapist is thought to be important by both psychodynamic and client-centered or person-centered approaches.

A third major function of play is as a vehicle for the occurrence of insight and working through. The conceptualization of this function of play is a psychodynamic one. Psychodynamic theory views the emotional resolution of conflict or trauma as a major mechanism of change in child therapy. Children re-experience major developmental conflicts or situational traumas in therapy. Many of these conflicts are expressed in play. The play process itself has been thought of as a form of conflict resolution. For example, Waelder (1933) described the play process as one in which the child repeats an unpleasant experience over and over until it becomes manageable. Freedheim and Russ (1992) described the slow process of gaining access to conflict-laden material and playing it out until the conflict is resolved. Erickson (1963) presented the concept of mastery, in which the child uses play to gain mastery over traumatic events and everyday conflicts. During this process, the therapist labels and interprets the play. Although there is controversy in the psychodynamic literature about how much interpretation should occur (A. Freud, 1966; Klein, 1955), there is general agreement that working through and mastery are important mechanisms of change in play therapy.

A fourth major function of play in therapy is that of providing opportunities to practice with a variety of ideas, behaviors, interpersonal behaviors, and verbal expressions. Because play is occurring in a safe environment, in a pretend world, with a permissive, non-judgmental adult, the child can try out and rehearse a variety of expressions and behaviors without concern about real-life consequences. In some forms of play therapy, the therapist is quite directive in guiding the child to try new behaviors. For example, Knell (1993) developed a cognitive behavioral play therapy approach that actively uses modeling techniques and a variety of cognitive behavioral techniques.

It is important to point out that although these major functions of play occur in normal play situations, the therapist builds on these normal functions by enhancing the play experience. The therapist creates a safe environment, gives permission for play to occur, actively facilitates play, and labels the thoughts and feelings expressed. For the psychodynamic therapist, interpretation specifically aids conflict resolution. Because there are so many individual differences in play skills and abilities in children, and differences in theoretical orientations of therapists, there are many different kinds of play therapy techniques that are utilized.

HISTORY OF PLAY THERAPY

The history of play therapy is intertwined with the history of child therapy, and play has been used in different ways in different theoretical approaches (Kessler, 1988). Play was first used in child therapy by therapists in the psychoanalytic tradition. Tuma and Russ (1993) reviewed the psychoanalytic literature in detail. Psychoanalytic techniques were adapted to children by Hug-Hellmuth (1921, 1924), A. Freud (1927), and Burlingham (1932). Play was used to substitute for free association. In addition, the therapist was more responsive and gratifying to the child than the therapist would be with adults, and the child therapist actively worked to develop a positive attachment (A. Freud, 1946). Melanie Klein saw the importance of the communication value of play. She suggested that play for the child was the same as free association for the adult. She advocated active and direct interpretation of the unconscious processes expressed in play. Therefore, the therapist would continually interpret the child's play. A. Freud (1966) also viewed play as a direct expression of fantasy and instincts in a less disguised and more accessible form than in adults. A. Freud (1976) was more cautious in her interpretations of the meaning of the child's play. She was also more respectful of the child's defenses than was Klein, and encouraged greater participation by the child. She thought that it was important that therapy be a positive experience for the child and that the child want to come to therapy.

The psychoanalytic approach has evolved into the psychodynamic approach. Psychodynamic therapists base their interventions and techniques on psychoanalytic principles, but therapy is shorter, less frequent (once a week rather than four or five times a week), has more focused and immediate goals, and is more flexible in incorporating a variety of therapeutic techniques (Tuma & Russ, 1993). Play remains a core part of the therapy process. The use of play in therapy and in child development is a great legacy of the psychoanalytic tradition.

The client-centered and person-centered approaches to child treatment also utilized play. Axline (1947), in her non-directive approach, had the therapist focus on play as a major form of communication for and with the child. The therapist strives to understand and empathize with the child's issues. Interpretation of underlying dynamics or impulses is rare, however. The therapist trusts the child's developmental process and striving for self-development. A wonderful introduction to the use of play in child therapy, for beginning therapists of any theoretical perspective, is Axline's *Dibbs in Search of Self* (1964). Moustakas (1953) was another leading theorist in this area who stressed the importance of expression of feelings in play and the importance of the relationship between the child and therapist. Moustakas discussed the importance of the child and therapist experiencing each other (Moustakas, 1992). Genuineness in the relationship is an important aspect of therapy for Moustakas.

Although not usually associated with cognitive behavior therapy approaches, play has been used as a tool within that framework (Kessler, 1988). Meichenbaum (1974) thought that imagery and fantasy could be used to teach children self-control. He used play as a vehicle for changing thoughts (Goldfried, 1998). More recently, Knell (1993) developed cognitive behavioral play therapy techniques that use principles of modeling and reinforcement.

In addition, play techniques have been used in a variety of more specific approaches such as Gardner's (1971) mutual story-telling techniques, and Levy's (1938) release therapy for children who have experienced trauma. Play is used with a variety of child populations, in short-term and long-term approaches, and by a variety of theoretical approaches. Recent trends in child psychotherapy apply to play therapy as well. Therapy is becoming more specific, more focused, more active, and more theoretically integrated (Freedheim & Russ, 1992; Russ, 1998). These current trends are reviewed in chapter 5.

PROCEDURES AND PRACTICAL CONSIDERATIONS

The concept of play psychotherapy is a bit of a misnomer because most psychotherapy with children is a mix of play and talk (Russ, 1995). Play is a tool that can be used in therapy for a variety of purposes. If and how play is used with a particular child in therapy depends on the child's ability to use play, developmental level, age, ability to verbalize, and the overall treatment approach. In general, play therapy occurs within the context of the overall treatment plan.

In most forms of play therapy, the child and therapist meet individually once a week for 45- to 50-minute sessions. The mutual agreement between the child and the therapist is that the therapist is there to help the child express feelings and thoughts, understand causes of behavior, and form a relationship with the therapist (Freedheim & Russ, 1992). Traditionally, in both psychodynamic and client-centered approaches, the child structures the therapeutic hour by choosing the topics, forms of play, and setting the pace of therapy. In most cases, individual work with the child is only one part of the treatment program. Parent guidance and education, family sessions, and work with the school and community usually occur simultaneously with individual child therapy.

Practical Issues in Using Play in Therapy

A number of practical issues arise in working with children in play therapy. Ideally, a psychological assessment will have been carried out so that the therapist has identified treatment goals and has developed a treatment plan. The therapist should have determined how much play will be utilized in the therapy, as well as the nature of the play to be encouraged. Usually, play approaches should be considered for children from 4 to 10 years of age.

How to Get Started

Many children need help initiating the play process. The therapist usually starts by telling the child that they can play or talk, and shows the child the toys and play materials that are available. Although many children go right to it, many others are reticent. The therapist might tell the child to pick one thing, and start with that or the therapist could pick something for the child. Clay and drawing material are good starters. As a last resort, the therapist might start with something themselves, and have the child join in.

Kinds of Play Materials

Most therapists agree that unstructured play materials that can encourage the use of fantasy and imagination are ideal. Toys that leave much room for individual expression are most appropriate for play therapy. Examples of relatively unstructured toys and material are: clay, crayons, cars, trucks, puppets, dolls, doll houses, and Legos. Games such as checkers do not encourage free expression, and are not ideal for traditional play therapy. I often ask the child for suggestions of other toys that might be useful and encourage them to bring toys in from home. Different children use different media for expression, and it is important to have a variety of items and to individually tailor what is available.

How Much to Engage in Play

One recurring dilemma is how much the therapist should engage in the child's play. The amount of direction and activity by the therapist depends on the general theoretical approach. In more traditional client-centered and psychodynamic approaches, the therapist tries not to play with the child, but rather to observe and comment on the child's play. Many children will eventually become comfortable playing in this way. Some children need more engagement by the therapist. With those children, the therapist tries to follow the lead of the child. The therapist might put on one of the puppets and play, but follow the lead of the child in choosing the topic and setting the dialogue.

In more directive approaches, such as cognitive-behavioral play therapy (Knell, 1993), the therapist will play in a very directive fashion. The therapist might put on a play, modeling adaptive coping strategies for an issue that the child is currently dealing with.

How Much to Interpret

An optimal amount of interpretation of the child's play would facilitate the play process and help the child understand his or her thoughts, feelings, and behavior. Too much interpretation will stop the play process. Most therapists today would agree with A. Freud (1976) that the child's defenses should be respected. Timing of interpretations is as important in child therapy as in adult therapy.

How to Set Limits

For play to be a safe mode of expression, limits about how to play are essential. If rules need to be set, then they should be set. Toys cannot be broken and the therapist can not be a target for affective expression. Alternative modes of expression through play should be facilitated. For example, the child can be encouraged to verbalize anger at the therapist or to have the puppets fight it out in a pretend mode.

MECHANISMS OF CHANGE IN THERAPY

How one uses play in the therapy depends on how one conceptualizes the specific mechanisms of change to be used in the therapy. Freedheim and Russ (1983, 1992) identified six major mechanisms of change that occur in individual child psychotherapy. These mechanisms were based on those identified by Applebaum (1978) and Garfield (1980) in the adult literature. Different mechanisms of change are utilized in different types of psychodynamic psychotherapy with different types of childhood disorders. However, there is rarely a pure type of psychotherapy and frequently all of these mechanisms may occur in any one case. These mechanisms of change are thought to be universal and to cut across various theoretical approaches to psychotherapy. They are based on the major functions of play in child therapy. The specific role of play in these mechanisms was discussed by Russ (1995).

Expression, Catharsis and Labeling of Feelings.   Through talk and play, children express feelings and release emotion. This release of emotion has long been though to be therapeutic (Axline, 1947; A. Freud, 1965; Moustakas, 1953). In addition, by labeling affect, the therapist helps to make the feeling less overwhelming and more understandable. Often, the labeling of affect occurs during pretend play. By saying to the child that the puppet is feeling angry, the therapist connects a label to a feeling state. Words help to put feelings into a context for the child, thus making the feelings less overwhelming.

The major therapeutic techniques to encourage expression are giving permission and labeling. Therapists often state that it is understandable that a child would feel a certain way, or that many children feel this way in this situation. Understanding and labeling encourages the expression of thoughts and feelings and puts them in a context.

Corrective Emotional Experience.   The therapist accepts the child's feeling and thoughts. Often, the child's learned expectations are not met, and a corrective emotional experience occurs (Kessler, 1966). For example, the automatic connection between a child's angry feelings toward his or her father and resultant anxiety should gradually decrease as the therapist helps the child accept the feeling and understand the reasons for the anger. The therapist is not punitive, and is accepting of the child's having angry feelings. Often, these feelings are expressed through play. This acceptance of feelings by the therapist leads to a freer expression of thoughts and feelings in the play situation.

Major therapeutic techniques are similar to those for catharsis/expression. The therapist labels expressions and communicates acceptance and understanding of the feeling. Another important technique is to separate feelings and thoughts from behavior. It is okay to feel angry, but not to hit or be destructive.

Insight, Re-Experiencing, and Working Through.   The emotional resolution of conflict or trauma is a major mechanism of change in play psychotherapy. One goal of the therapist when utilizing this mechanism of change is to help the child re-experience major developmental conflicts or situational traumas in therapy. Frequently, play is the vehicle for this working-through process. Cognitive insight into origins of feelings and conflicts, causes of symptoms, and links between thoughts, feelings, and actions is a goal of psychotherapy when underlying conflicts are a major issue (Sandler, Kennedy, & Tyson, 1980; Shirk & Russell, 1996). Verbal labeling of unconscious impulses, conflicts, and causes of behavior helps lend higher order reasoning skills to understanding problems. However, in many cases, especially with young children, cognitive insight does not occur. Rather, emotional re-experiencing, emotional working through, and mastery do occur and result in symptom reduction and healthy adjustment. This is an important point and is an often overlooked mechanism of change in child treatment. Messer and Warren (1995) also stated that the goal of making the unconscious conscious needs to be modified in child play therapy with many children. In Erikson's (1963) concept of mastery, the child uses play to gain mastery over traumatic events and everyday conflicts. Resolving conflicts through play is part of normal child development. Waelder (1933) described the play process as one in which the child repeats an unpleasant experience over and over until it becomes manageable. As he puts it, the child "digests" the event. Freedheim and Russ (1992) described the slow process of gaining access to conflict-laden material and playing it out until the conflict is resolved.

The therapist helps guide the play, labels thoughts, feelings, and events, and makes interpretations to facilitate conflict resolution and the working-through process. Because cognitive insight is not necessary for conflict resolution to occur, the amount of interpretation should be carefully considered by the therapist. This is especially true of interpretation of symbols in the play or of deeply forbidden wishes. Mild interpretations that link feelings and thoughts to behavior and that spell out cause and effect are especially helpful. Most important is helping children to utilize the play so that they can resolve conflicts and master fears and difficult memories. Creating an atmosphere where a child can totally engage in play is especially important.

Problem-Solving Techniques and Coping Strategies. The therapist, in a more directive approach, helps the child think about alternative ways of viewing a situation and generate problem-solving strategies. Role-playing and modeling of coping strategies are used. Practice with a variety of verbal expressions and interpersonal behaviors can occur in a safe, pretend play situation. The therapist suggests ways of coping or helps the child think of other strategies. For example, D. Singer (1993) gives examples of modeling techniques during therapy. Knell (1993) teaches the child new strategies for coping with feelings and situations.

Object Relations, Internal Representations and Interpersonal Development. Many children have developed internal representations that result in problems with self–object differentiation, interpersonal functioning, self-esteem regulation, impulse control, object constancy, and separation of fantasy from reality. In these children, there are major deficits in underlying cognitive, affective, and interpersonal processes. Structure-building approaches are based on conceptualizations by Mahler (1968) and Kohut (1977) and view the therapist as being a stable, predictable, caring, and empathic figure. Development of good object relations and internal representations is a major goal of play therapy with these children. Gilpin (1976) stressed that the role of the therapist is to become an internalized object. The relationship between the therapist and child is probably the most important aspect of therapy in helping this process to occur. Genuine understanding and expression of empathy by the therapist is a major technique that enables the child to develop better internal representations. Play is important here as a form of communication, in that the therapist can empathize with the child's expressions in the play. The major change that occurs is through the relationship with the therapist that facilitates developing interpersonal representations in the child.

Nonspecific Variables. Nonspecific variables function in child therapy as they do in adult therapy. Expectation of change, hope, awareness of parental concern, and no longer feeling so alone are all factors that contribute to change in therapy.

Mechanisms of Change in Different Types of Therapy

Psychodynamic Play Therapy

Different types of therapy emphasize different mechanisms of change. Different techniques are used to foster the different mechanisms. The form of therapy most associated with the psychodynamic approach is insight-oriented therapy, and it is most appropriate for the child with anxiety and internalized conflicts (Tuma & Russ, 1993). This approach is appropriate for children who have age-appropriate ego development, show evidence of internal conflicts, have the ability to trust adults, have some degree of psychological-mindedness, and can use play effectively. Insight-oriented therapy is most often recommended for internalizing disorders including many of the anxiety disorders and depressive disorders. Children with internalizing disorders often experience internal conflicts and have good ego development and good object relations. An insight-oriented approach with a focus on conflict resolution is most appropriate for internalizing disorders. Many children in this broad category are good players and can easily engage in play in the therapy situation.

The goals of insight-oriented therapy are to help the child resolve internal conflicts and master developmental tasks. The major mechanism of change is insight and working through. Through the use of play and interpretation from the therapist, the child "calls forth forbidden fantasy and feelings, works through and masters developmental problems, and resolves conflicts" (Freedheim & Russ, 1983, p. 983). Active interpretation of the child's play, expressions, and resistances is a major technique. For example, the therapist might interpret a child's stealing from mother's purse as an expression of anger at feeling neglected by her after the birth of a baby brother. However, resolution can also occur without cognitive insight having occurred. Emotional re-experiencing and gradual mastery is an important part of the therapeutic process.

Insight and working through can also be helpful for a child with good inner resources who has experienced a specific trauma (such as the loss of as a parent). Altschul (1988) described the use of psychoanalytic approaches in helping children to mourn the loss of a parent. In this application, Webber (1988) stressed that the therapist must first address the question of whether the child can do his or her own psychological work. If not, therapy can be a major aid in the mourning process.

A second major form of psychotherapy is the structure-building approach, which is used with children with structural deficits and major problems in developing good object relations. For children with impaired object relations, self–other boundary disturbances, and difficulty distinguishing fantasy from reality, the therapist uses techniques that foster the development of object permanence, self–other differentiation, and modulation of affect. The major mechanism of change is the building of internal structure and processes such as object relations. Anna Freud (1965) described the development of object relations through a continual process of separation from the significant adult, usually the mother. Mahler (1975) elaborated on the separation-individuation process and described the development of object constancy and object representations. As Blank and Blank (1986) stressed, Mahler's concept of separation-individuation represented a new organizing principle to development. Object relations is not just another ego function, but plays a major role in the organization of intrapsychic processes.

The growing theory on the development of object relations is a new phase in psychoanalytic theory construction (Tuma & Russ, 1993). Good object relations involve well-developed object representations. The child must invest in the mental representation of the loved external object. Children who have inadequately developed object relations have structural deficits that impair a variety of functions. This impairment is evident with psychotic and characterological disorders. Children with severely impaired object relations, such as borderline children, have early developmental problems with a mix of severe dysfunction in the family and in the case of borderline children, perhaps a genetic predisposition. These children require a structure-building psychotherapeutic approach.

In this approach, empathy on the part of the therapist (as a general relationship factor; Kohut & Wolfe, 1978) is a much more important intervention than is interpretation (Russ, 1995). Chethik (1989) provided an excellent discussion of psychotherapy with borderline children and narcissistically disturbed children. He pointed out that many of the therapeutic techniques are supportive in that they "shore up" defenses. The problems characteristic of borderline and narcissistic children are early developmental problems, usually stemming from severe disturbance in the parent–child interaction. Kohut and Wolfe (1978) discussed the failure of empathy from the parent that is a major issue in the faulty parent–child interaction. Because of the frequency of this defect in parent–child relations, empathy from the therapist around the history of empathic failure becomes an important part of therapy. Frequently, help with problem solving and coping is also used with these children. Therapy with these children is usually long-term (1 to 2 years) to be effective.

A third form of psychodynamic therapy is supportive psychotherapy, most appropriate for children with externalizing disorders. These children frequently act-out, have antisocial tendencies, and are impulse-ridden. The broad syndrome of externalizing disorders includes labels of acting-out, antisocial, character disorders, attention deficit disorders, and conduct disorders. Theoretically, psychodynamic theory views these children as having major developmental problems. These children have not yet adequately developed the processes necessary for delay of gratification. In addition, these children are frequently egocentric, demonstrate an absence of shame and guilt, and their ability to empathize with others is impaired. Kessler (1988) has recommended that structured, supportive therapy is more helpful to these children than any other kind of psychodynamic therapy. Therapy focuses on the here and now and on the development of problem-solving skills and coping resources. For example, the therapist might role-play with the child about how to handle teasing at school or how to be assertive with parents.

At this point, given the effectiveness of behavioral and cognitive-behavioral approaches in working with externalizing disorders, it appears that supportive psychodynamic psychotherapy is not the treatment of choice (Russ, 1995). In my opinion, it should only be used as a supplement to other treatment approaches in order to work on a specific issue.

Chethik (1989) has a thorough discussion of the use of play within the psychodynamic approach. As reviewed by Tuma and Russ (1993), he describes four stages of play development within psychotherapy (see Chethik, 1989, pp. 48–66 for a more detailed description):

1. *Initial period of nonengagement.* Setting the stage–developing expectations, structure, and limits. The therapist first defines how play will be used for communication and how the child's internal life combined with play materials will express and replay the child's internal life for them both. "Meaningful play" must be developed, sometimes by varying the structure. This means that the overinstinctualized child (e.g., impulsive, fast to react) may require more structure, whereas the underinstinctualized child (e.g., obsessive, slow to react) may need to be encouraged to express instinctual life in play.

2. *Early phase of affective engagement.* As play develops, the therapist begins to share metaphors that emerge, and the child becomes attached to both the process and the therapist. When this happens, the therapist can then permit regressions by becoming a player in the play (by doing what the child asks him or her to do). The child can then express his or her instinctual life more freely because he or she identifies with the therapist and the therapist's sanctions. The safety the child feels in expressions is further ensured by imposing boundaries (e.g., by keeping forbidden expression in the room or having clean-up time). The unstructured quality, the accepting attitudes, and the boundaries all foster early "regression in the service of the ego." As the child feels more comfortable and masters anxiety, his or her play becomes more open. Those expressions at first avoided defensively are now displayed in full view of the therapist.

3. *Emergence of central fantasies.* As the process intensifies, the child elaborates highly invested fantasies in play. Repetitive play (characterized by the "compulsion to repeat") begins to deal with past traumatic and difficult situations. In the therapy process, however, the past has a changed

outcome: acceptance of the play and interpretations by the therapist permit new solutions, either verbally or through play. Now the situation is in the control of the child.

4. *Period of working through.* Specific symptoms or behaviors often have more than one meaning. A working through period is necessary where a series and variety of interpretations are made to bring about change in a symptom. Symptoms are discussed in different contexts until all the meanings are worked out.

Client-Centered Play Therapy

In client-centered therapy with children, the major intervention of the therapist that results in change is empathic reflection. Gaylin (1999), in a review of client-centered child and family therapy, summarized Rogers' (1957) six conditions for effective psychotherapy:

1. Two persons are in psychological contact.
2. The client is in a state of incongruence (vulnerable or anxious).
3. The therapist is congruent or integrated in the relationship.
4. The therapist experiences unconditional positive regard for the client.
5. The therapist experiences an empathic understanding of the client's frame of reference and endeavors to communicate this experience to the client.
6. The communication to the client of the therapist's empathic understanding and unconditional positive regard is to a minimal degree achieved.

Gaylin stressed that the empathic reflection of the feeling is the method of achieving empathy. Play is the vehicle for expression of the child's experience. Gaylin refers to play as the child's experiential experimentation. This concept is an interesting way to think about play and affect. The child experiments with the expression of different experiences and feeling states. The therapist strives to achieve and express empathic understanding.

In a review by Landreth (1991), the expression of feelings in play is discussed. Landreth cited two dissertations (Hendricks, 1971; Withee, 1975) that investigated the process of play. In both studies clear patterns emerged over time in play therapy. As play therapy progressed, children expressed feelings more directly with more focus and specificity. Children's play became more aggressive in the middle stages of therapy. In the latter stages, children exhibited more dramatic play with the predominant emotion being happiness in the Hendrick's study. In the latter stages in the Wither study, the expression of anger and anxiety was high.

COGNITIVE BEHAVIORAL PLAY THERAPY

As Goldfried has pointed out, play has been used in cognitive-behavioral therapy for various purposes. Meichenbaum (1977) used play as a vehicle for changing thoughts. He used play as the medium in which to conduct self-instructional training.

Play has also been used to develop relaxation and problem solving skills (Schneider, 1974). A major change mechanism in the use of play within a cognitive behavior framework is the corrective emotional experience. Through exposure, either directly or indirectly through imagery, anxiety of feared stimuli is extinguished.

Recently, principles of cognitive-behavioral therapy and play therapy were systematically integrated into one approach. Knell (1993) introduced the concept of Cognitive-Behavioral Play Therapy (CBPT) in which cognitive and behavioral interventions are incorporated within a play therapy paradigm. Play itself is used to resolve problems.

Knell (1993) identified six properties of CBPT:

1. The child is involved in the treatment through play.
2. CBPT focuses on the child's thoughts, fantasies, and environment.
3. CBPT provides a strategy or strategies for developing more adaptive thoughts and behaviors. The child is taught coping strategies for feelings and for situations.
4. CBPT is structured, directive, and goal oriented, rather than open-ended.
5. CBPT incorporates empirically demonstrated techniques, such as modeling.
6. CBPT allows for an empirical examination of treatment.

Knell (1993) also identified similarities and differences between CBPT and more traditional psychodynamic or client-centered approaches. Similarities included: the importance of the therapeutic relationship; communications occur through play; therapy is a safe place; and play provides "clues" to understanding the child.

Differences suggested that in CBPT therapy is more directed and goal oriented; the therapist is involved in choosing play materials; play is used to teach skills and alternative behaviors; interpretations are given by the therapist (similar to psychodynamic but different from client-centered) and praise is a crucial component. It is also more empirically based.

These similarities and differences are true for the "classic" forms of psychodynamic play therapy. However, new forms of psychodynamic play therapy are also being developed that are more goal oriented. For example, Chethik's (1989) focal therapy is focused on specific problems and is of short duration. Messer and Warren (1995) have called for psychodynamic approaches to be adapted to short-term goal oriented frame-works. They state that short-term therapy is a frequent form of psycho-dynamic intervention and that play is a good vehicle for change. Still, Knell's (1993) approach is a thoughtful integration of different theoretical approaches and techniques and is an excellent model for how to integrate treatment approaches.

Bodiford-McNeil, Hembree-Kigin, and Eyberg (1996) have developed a CBPT approach that is focused on a specific population of children. Their short-term play therapy for disruptive children utilizes the principles of CBPT but tailors the approach for disruptive children. Their approach is also set for 12 sessions with very specific goals and objectives per session. For most of the 12 sessions, the first half of the session is task-oriented and the second half is child-directed play. The therapist uses a variety of techniques such as praise, reflection, imitation of play, questions, interpretation, rein-forcement, and contingent attention. The therapist follows the child's lead in the play, but also tries to move it as quickly as possible. By the eighth ses-sion, the parent is included in the process and is coached to facilitate the child's play. Parent's practice their play sessions at home with the child. Par-ents are taught most of the play facilitation skills, but not that of interpreta-tion, which belongs in the domain of psychotherapy. Bodiford-McNeil et al.'s approach integrates techniques from a variety of theoretical approaches and chooses those that are most effective for a specific population—disrup-tive children. It is a good example of developing an integrated approach for a specific population.

BRIDGING PLAY PROCESSES IN PSYCHOTHERAPY AND IN CHILD DEVELOPMENT

How do the play processes that therapists work with "match-up" with the play processes focused on in the child development literature that was out-lined in chapter 1? In trying to bridge the gap between the two literatures, I propose the framework presented in Table 3.1. Different play therapy tech-niques utilize different processes in play to bring about change in the child. Although all play processes may be utilized and effected during therapy, different techniques and mechanisms of change are intended to focus on specific clusters of play processes. This proposed framework could guide focused research studies in the play therapy area. The value in identifying specific play processes that are involved in different therapeutic ap-proaches is that we can better develop intervention studies that evolve from *both* clinical practice and research. And we can investigate the effec-tiveness of targeting specific processes in play.

Looking first at expression and catharsis, therapists give permission, are accepting, and label thoughts and feelings. As the child feels more com-fortable, the story-telling should become fuller and more complete with a

TABLE 3.1

Play Processes in Psychotherapy and Child Development

Mechanism of Change	Play Therapy Techniques	Play Processes Utilized and Effected

Expression/catharis	Permission
	Labeling
	Acceptance
		Cognitive
		  Organization
		  Divergent thinking
		  Fantasy
		Affective
		  Affect states
		  Affect themes
		  Range
		  Enjoyment in play
		  Emotion regulation
		  Cognitive integration

Corrective emotional experience	Permission
	Labeling
	Acceptance
	Understanding
		Cognitive
		  Organization
		  Divergent thinking
		  Fantasy
		Affective
		  Affect states
		  Affect themes
		  Range Enjoyment of play
		  Emotion regulation
		  Cognitive integration

Insight, re-experiencing, working through	Labeling
	Understanding
	Interpretation
	Facilitating play
		Cognitive
		  Organization
		  Divergent thinking
		  Symbolism
		  Fantasy
		Affective
		  Affect states
		  Affect themes
		  Range
		  Emotion regulation
		  Cognitive integration
		Problem solving/Conflict resolution
		  Approach
		  Conflict resolution

TABLE 3.1 (*continued*)

Strengthening interpersonal schema	Empathy
	Caring
	Predictability
		Interpersonal Processes
		  Empathy
		  Internal representations/
		    Interpersonal schema
		  Communication

Learning problem-solving and coping strategies	Modeling
	Active problem solving
	Coping strategies
	Rehearsing
		Cognitive
		  Divergent thinking
		Affective
		  Emotion regulation
		  Problem solving/Conflict
		    resolution
		  Approach
		  Problem solutions

broader range of themes (divergent thinking), and more fantasy. A wider range of affect states and affect themes, both positive and negative, should be expressed. The labeling of the feelings could help with emotion regulation as well, because the feelings are more understandable and less overwhelming. And the child should become more comfortable with play and enjoy play more. Probably the ability for symbolization is not influenced by this particular set of techniques.

The bringing about of a corrective emotional experience uses the same techniques and play processes as the expression mechanism of change. However, the addition of the therapeutic technique of understanding should help the child more with emotion regulation and cognitive integration of affect. By putting the feeling in a context and making it understandable, the child is more able to control it. For example, a 9-year-old girl is first given permission, over time, to be angry with her mother. It is okay to feel anger. Then, the therapist helps her understand why she is angry. Mother keeps intruding in her space, starting fights, and escalating the argument. The therapist conveys that the child's anger is understandable. By gaining an understanding of her anger, she is able to manage it better and develop strategies for staying calm.

All of the cognitive and affective processes could be utilized when insight, re-experiencing and working through is the major focus of therapy. The ability to use fantasy, symbolism, and metaphors would be especially helpful to a child who is playing out conflicts and problems. As the child begins to master fears and resolve conflicts, emotion regulation and cognitive integration should be strengthened. And major changes should occur in conflict resolution/problem solving processes.

Therapy that focuses on the empathic, stable relationship between therapist and child focuses directly on the interpersonal processes in the play. The therapist empathizes with the feelings expressed in the play and very directly deals with the child–therapist relationship. Often, feelings expressed in the play have to do with feelings about parents, and the therapist has opportunity to empathize with the child's unmet needs and the empathic failures of the parents (and of the therapist). When therapy is effective, changes in the child's internal representations, capacity for empathy, and communication ability should be able to be observed in the play.

Finally, when more directive therapeutic techniques are used, such as modeling and teaching of problem solving strategies, there should also be a strengthening of the approach to problem solving and ability to problem solve. It is interesting to speculate how the nature of the problem solving would be different in an active problem solving training therapy versus an insight-oriented therapy. It is probable that the insight-oriented therapy would better help the child resolve internal conflicts and fears and learn how to use play to do so, whereas the more directive problem solving approaches would better help the child think of an array of solutions to problems or to manage internal states. This specific question is important to investigate empirically.

Active problem solving approaches also focus on divergent thinking processes, in that the child is shown or encouraged to develop a variety of problem solving or coping strategies. And emotion regulation would be enhanced by learning emotion management strategies.

CLINICAL CASE EXAMPLES

What follows are two case examples that illustrate how play is used, what techniques are helpful, and what processes are being worked with in different forms of psychotherapy. Hypotheses about how change occurred are discussed. These cases were not studied empirically. However, ideas and concepts that fit the conceptualizations presented here can be tested in future studies.

I present here excerpts of process notes that I wrote following each session. Although the words are not verbatim, since they were from memory, they are fairly accurate as to the events in the session and the interaction between me and the child. Both of these cases are past cases. The second case was from very early in my career, when very detailed process notes were necessary for supervision. I am grateful to my supervisor, the late Doris Gilpin, MD, for her invaluable guidance. Also, details of both case histories have been disguised and altered in minor ways to protect the identities of the families. My commentary on these cases incorporates my conceptualization at the time, but also a re-conceptualization using the play processes framework.

Case Example # 1: Separation Anxiety

John was a 6-year-old boy brought to therapy by his parents. He had been having trouble staying in school for the past year. He would feel sick, go the nurses' office, and often come home. He was brought to therapy in early summer while school was out. During the assessment, it appeared that John had no major developmental problems. He had friends, was generally a happy child, and trusted adults. His teacher described him as a "perfect child" who could use more confidence. On psychological tests, there were indications of general fearfulness and anxiety. There was a history of some illness in his family—at different times, both he and his mother had been in the hospital. Both were in good health at the time of the therapy. He did verbalize that he worried about something happening to his mother while he was at school. The conceptualization of this case was that there were internal conflicts that were underlying the separation anxiety. It was not clear what the conflicts were, but John was anxious and fearful, perhaps about aggressive impulses. It was also possible that past illnesses of John or his mother had been traumatic for him. During the assessment, John was able to use play well. People figures interacted and he used fantasy and symbolism. However, there was no expression of affect. Play therapy was the treatment plan because he did use play well, was anxious about underlying impulses and/or memories, and had no other developmental problems. He was seen in short-term therapy for a total of eight sessions. Parents were also seen in separate sessions and it was stressed that when school began, it was essential that he go every day and not be permitted to come home, unless he was really ill. However, the main focus of the treatment was on helping John to resolve his internal issues.

The goal of therapy was to help John resolve anxiety around internal feelings and impulses. Especially important would be ambivalent feelings related to the parents and his fear of something happening to them. Although this was insight therapy, partly because of his young age, it was not expected that cognitive insight would be an important part of the therapy. John was especially constricted in his expression of aggression in his play. Helping him to feel more comfortable with aggressive impulses and emotion in general were treatment goals. An important point is that John had no problems with acting out or impulse control.

Session # 3

In this early play session, John used the clay and drawing material. He made a number of different animals from the clay that I would comment on.

John first made an alligator.

Therapist (T):   What is that you are making?
Child (C):   An alligator. (Turned it into something else.)
T: Now what is it?
C: A swordfish.
T: Oh, a swordfish. Now what?
C: A turtle.
T: And now?
C: A hippopotamus.

John then tried to make a horse with Legos but could not get it built to his satisfaction. I kept repeating that what he had done was OK and he could use it to play, but he was critical. He then went back to the clay and made something else.

T: What is that?
C: A dinosaur. (He showed it falling off a cliff.) Now it is an angel. (He made a halo for it.) (He then made something else.)
C: This is a person who eats too much. He is so fat he keeps falling over, because he is so heavy.
T: He's so heavy and ate so much food, that he keeps falling.

Then John drew a picture.

T: What's happening there?
C: This is a giant. He is stomping on the city. Everything is on fire.
T: The giant is stomping on everything. Maybe he is mad about something.

John didn't comment on that. I told him I would see him next week and he seemed happy about coming.

John did not express much emotion in this session. It was interesting that he would make aggressive animals (alligator, swordfish) and follow with non-aggressive animals (turtle, hippo). He also turned the dinosaur into an angel. The giant in the drawing was expressing aggression and I used that as an opportunity to comment on it's being mad. I was trying to give permission for John to express aggression in his play and in his verbalizations.

Session # 4

John continued to play with the clay and make animal forms. During the play, we heard an ambulance outside. He looked scared.

T: That's an ambulance outside. You seem scared.

C: (nodded)

T: Do you ever get scared like that at school?

C: Yes. I think something might happen to Mom or Dad.

T: Did you worry about that?

C: Yes.

John then talked about when Mom was in the hospital several years earlier and how scary that was. He also said that when he was sick and had X-rays, that was scary. I empathized with how scary that was, and that it was hard to be in school when you worried about Mom and Dad. I also reassured him that just because you think something might happen, does not mean that it will. It is just a thought.

In this session, I was labeling his feelings and empathizing with his fear. I was also trying to convey that I understood how hard it was to be in school when he had these concerns. I tried to help him differentiate between fantasy and reality.

Session # 5

John went right to the clay and made forms and smashed them. I commented on his smashing them: "You really smashed that one." Then one clay figure would start to smash another; he would play monster and start to attack and then stop. He would abruptly pull back. This happened repeatedly. I tried to support his aggressive play and say things like, "He is going to attack," or "He is really angry," or "He is going to smash him." John then took some puppets and said he would put on puppet show.

The alligator and hippopotamus puppet were trying to eat the man. The man escaped. I commented that they were trying to eat him, but the man escaped. Then John asked me to play with him. I put on a puppet, but followed his lead. He was the boy puppet.

C: His nose is growing, because he told a lie (this occurred in a previous session).

T: Sometimes it's hard not to lie. Kids lie sometimes.

John immediately stopped playing.

In the session, I was commenting on the aggression of the figures. Labeling the actions and feelings was the major technique. The issue of lying and having the puppet's nose grow had come up before. My comment that it was sometimes hard not to lie was an attempt at empathy but also to give permission to talk about what he might lie about. He immediately stopped playing, which indicated that my comment was mistimed, and threatening, or it was off-base. Because this lying had come up (I had not commented the previous time) I thought it was important to try to work with it.

Session # 6

John began by making clay figures. First he made a flower, which he smashed. Then he made a ring, which he put on his finger. Then he made a play set with slides and caves and had clay figures go down the slide. They were having fun. John then moved to the puppets and put on a puppet show.

There was a father puppet and a boy puppet. First, they boy got shocked by an electric wire and fell on the ground. Then a frog came along and said "I'll cook you for supper." Then a snake came and started to eat his hand. Then the father puppet came and chased the creatures away. He took the boy to the hospital. Father talked to the doctors and asked about what they would do. The doctors operated on the boy. The boy got better. Father took him home. Then father and the boy went on a trip. They climbed a mountain and got to the top. They jumped up and down and cheered.

> T: The dad took care of the boy. He took him to the hospital and talked to the doctors. They boy got better. Then they climbed the mountain and were happy and proud.

Then John asked me to put on a puppet show with him. He made cars out of clay and his puppet and my puppet rode on them. The cars went fast and the puppets were having a good time.

Near the end of the hour, I brought up school, because it was starting the next week. He asked me if I knew who his teacher was. I did not. We talked about beginning school and that we would meet and talk about what happened.

The play in this session was important. He was freer in his play than he had been before. There was more positive emotion during the play (going down the slider; riding in the cars). The puppet show was a well-organized, rather detailed story.

The content of the puppet show is revealing. The boy is hurt and being attacked. Father rescues him. The boy gets better in the hospital. Then he and father climb a mountain and have fun. I thought it did reflect resolution of a conflict or trauma. Father would protect him and he and dad could have fun together.

During our final two sessions, John talked about how school was going.

> C: I had one bad day, Monday, but the rest was good.
> T: That's good. But Monday was hard.
> C: Yes.
> T: What made it hard?
> C: Cause I started to miss my Mom, but then I started doing stuff and I felt better.

T: Well you might miss her sometimes. But it's good you were doing a lot. What were you doing that you liked?
C: Music and recess.
T: Anything you did not like?
C: Art.
T: Why not?
C: Because you had to keep getting up and down off the floor—I didn't like that.

Then he began to play with clay. He made a jungle gym with a slide. A figure went down the slide. Then he crushed the whole jungle gym. He built it and crushed it several times. I commented on his building it and crushing it. He became concerned about getting clay under his nails and I said that clay could get messy but that was OK.

Then he built a car with Legos and pretended to drive. His affect was very positive during the play.

During these last sessions, his play was free. He easily crushed what he built and was no longer was hesitant about expressing aggressions. There was also more positive emotion in his play.

He successfully returned to school and there were no incidents about his wanting to come home during the fall. We terminated with the understanding that if there were problems that came up, he would return.

In this case, I think John used both play and verbalization to overcome his fears. The expression of aggressive ideation and feelings in the play was central to conflict resolution. He gradually, with permission from the therapist, expressed aggression in play and became more comfortable with it. Anxiety around aggressive impulses was extinguished. This aggression might have been responsible for his separation anxiety issues. Play helped John understand that aggressive ideation and feelings are different from aggressive action, which has real-world consequences. It is also possible that he was traumatized by his or his mother's hospitalization, and that was the basis of his fear. His talk about his worries about mother and the therapist's reassurance that thoughts could not make things really happen could also have contributed to the change in his behavior. In his play and in his verbalizations with the therapist, John was able to slowly process and integrate negative emotions of aggression and fear. He was able to do this at his own pace in the therapy. Major therapeutic techniques were labeling and reflecting emotion and giving permission for emotion to be expressed. There were very few interpretations in the therapy. For example, I did not say that he could get so angry with his parents that he might think angry thoughts—like they would get sick and die. I might have if he were older, and if the evidence supporting that hypothesis was clearer. John was able to express feelings and resolve issues well enough to reduce the fears about his parents. This is a good example of a child using play to reduce anxiety around separation issues.

Play processes that were affected during play were both cognitive and affective. His stories became fuller, more elaborated, and had meaningful content. His affect expression became much less constricted. He became able to express more negative affect (aggression and fear) as well as more positive affect. In addition, he was fully engaged in the play. John was then able to use the play to re-experience trauma (hospital rescue story), integrate the negative affect, and be taken care of by father. It is probable that his increased comfort with his own aggression contributed to this resolution, but we cannot know for sure.

Case Example # 2: Borderline Child

This case presentation follows the progress of a borderline child using a structure building approach from a psychodynamic conceptualization. Nine-year-old Steve was seen twice a week over a 3-year period. (A brief discussion of this case appears in Russ, 1998, and in Tuma & Russ, 1993.) The reason for referral was hyperactivity in the classroom, lack of friends, and periodic bizarre behavior in the classroom (crawling on the floor and barking like a dog). A full assessment was conducted and the consensus of the diagnostic team was that Steve fell on the borderline-to-schizophrenia continuum. The assessment results were typical of a borderline child. On the structured WISC, Steve did quite well with an overall IQ of 106 and superior vocabulary and abstract thinking skills. The severity of his psychopathology emerged in the interview, play sessions, and less structured projective tests. He expressed intense, aggressive and sexual material in an uncontrolled fashion. There was confusion of time and space. People were viewed as objects and statues, not warm and caring. There was a mechanical, emotionless quality to his descriptions of violence which also emerged in his play. Steve told the examiner that he was scared much of the time and indicated a primitive fear of annihilation (he was afraid of being swallowed by the vacuum cleaner). He was also preoccupied with death, the devil, graveyards, and violence. His fear was primitive in nature and included an experience of panic unlike the anxiety of the more conflict-laden child. In summary, Steve showed the kind of structural deficits and problems with object relations and reality testing typical of a borderline child, at the severe end of the continuum. He had problems with self—other differentiation, separating fantasy from reality, self-esteem regulation, impulse control, and interpersonal functioning. A major goal of therapy was to help Steve internalize the therapist as a stable internal representation, thereby developing better object relations. A second goal of therapy was to help Steve develop better reality testing and differentiation of fantasy and reality. Long-term individual therapy twice a week was carried out. Play was the major form of communication during the first 2 years. Parents were seen by another therapist, and school consultation was part of the treatment plan, as was medication. Although this was a labor intensive therapy, the other treatment option was residential treatment. Out-patient therapy was the treatment of choice with frequent re-evaluations to determine if residential treatment was necessary.

Steve lived with his parents and siblings. Mother was very supportive of his therapy and drove a long distance to bring him. In general, she was supportive and caring, but not very emotionally expressive toward Steve. Although father was very much a presence in the home, we could not engage him in the therapy. An older sibling had a history of severe emotional disturbance.

In this structure building approach, the major mechanism of change is the strengthening of interpersonal schema. Major therapeutic techniques are expressions of empathy and caring. Predictability of the therapist's behavior is also important. Other important mechanisms of change are expression of feelings and corrective emotional experience. Techniques include giving permission to express feelings and thoughts, labeling feelings and conveying acceptance and understanding. Understanding of thoughts and feelings, where they come from, and what power they do and do not have, is especially important for these children. In this case, much time was spent by the therapist establishing cause and effect. Play processes utilized and effected by these techniques are organization of thought, emotional expression, emotion regulation and cognitive integration of emotion, stability of internal representations/interpersonal schema, capacity for empathy, and communication with others (refer back to Table 3.1).

Early sessions with Steve focused on helping Steve to feel safe with the therapist. He hid under the therapist's desk in early sessions. This is an excerpt from session #5. In this early session, Steve's communication is fragmented and the therapist is trying to understand his expressions.

Steve quietly followed me into my office, stopped inside the door and looked at the desk where he had drawn in earlier sessions.

Therapist (T):   It looks like you want to draw today.
Child (C):   (Nodded yes.)

He drew a picture of a tree with a bird in the tree and a rabbit on the ground eating grass.

T: That looks like a tree, a rabbit, and a bird in the tree. Could you tell me about the picture?
C: The bird's eating cherries, the rabbit's eating grass, and they're happy.

T: They're feeling happy and safe.
C: (Nodded yes, then looks very scared.)

I left something out. He drew a dog barking at the rabbit.

T: The dog is barking at the rabbit.
C: The rabbit will go into the tree.
T: Is it safe in the tree?
C: Yes—no one will get him there.
T: Where do you feel safe?
C: At home.
T: It is not as safe here as at home?
C: (No answer—began looking at ball across the room.)
T: You'd like to play with the ball?
C: (Nods.)
T: You can get it, if you like.
C: (Shakes head, no.)
T: Are you afraid to get the ball?
C: (Nods yes.)
T: Would you like me to get it for you?
C: (Nods and smiles.)

I got the ball and gave it to him. He played with it for awhile, balancing it, which I made comments about. Then he began to pretend to cut it up.

T: What are you doing with the ball?
C: I am cutting it up and cooking it (in a whisper).
T: What is the ball?
C: The rabbit I drew.
T: So you are cooking the rabbit? Will you eat him?
C: No. (He put the ball on the floor and made motions of setting it on fire.) "It blew up" (motions of putting out the fire). He began hopping the ball around the table, as if the rabbit was hopping. It hopped close to me, then away from me, close, away, ...
T: The rabbit is afraid to get close to me, yet it wants to.
C: Yes (he touched my arm with the ball).
T: Why is he afraid?
C: He's afraid that you will hurt him.
T: That I will do something that will hurt him?
C: He's asking you to be his friend.
T: I'd like to be.
C: Will you hurt him?
T: I'll try not to. (Rabbit begins hopping around and Steve looks happy.)

T: He looks happy.

C: Yes—here's a medal for being his friend and trying not to hurt him—the rabbit is happy. (Pretended to give me a medal). Then he went through some motions I did not understand.

T: What now?

C: The rabbit is going back into the picture and here comes the bird. (It flew out and shot at me.)

T: He's afraid of me too. He's shooting at me to keep from getting hurt—to keep me from hurting him.

C: Yeah (pretends to be me and shoots the bird). You shot off his wing (bird comes up to me). Will you be my friend?

T: I'd like to be.

C: He's happy—you can have your medal back.

T: He wants to be my friend but is scared of me at the same time. Am I a frightening person?

C: Sometimes.

T: What's scary?

C: He's seen other wild birds that hunters shoot at.

T: He's afraid that I will shoot at him like other hunters.

C: He wants you to protect him from the other hunters.

T: To keep him safe?

C: Yeah.

T: If I can't, I won't be his friend.

C: No, you'll still be his friend

T: It's time to stop now.

C: (He cheers.) I wish I hadn't done that.

T: Why?

C: Cause I don't mean it—I don't want to go back to school.

T: You'd rather stay here?

C: Yes.

As we left the room, he stood behind me. We had talked about that be-fore—he felt safer walking behind me. This time, he smiled, got a gleam in his eye, and bowed with a sweep of his arm for me to go first. It was the first time I had seen him use humor.

Throughout the session, he would frequently just mouth his responses and I would ask him to repeat. During his play, I told him that I could just guess what he was doing but might be wrong and that I could understand better if he told me.

In this session, there are many examples of the therapist encouraging expression of feelings and labeling feelings. I especially tried to give per-mission for the expression of fear and concern about safety. I struggled to understand his play and expressions. I also tried to reflect that he could have mixed feelings about me—wanting to be my friend but being scared of me at the same time. Helping children like Steve to integrate both positive and negative feelings about the same person should help develop stable internal representations.

Because Steve did not have stable internal representations, separations from the therapist were very difficult for him. During the first year of therapy, he asked if he could take the chalk home with him, prior to a vacation by the therapist. When asked why he wanted the chalk, he said he wanted to draw a picture of me on the sidewalk in front of his house so he could remember what I looked like. He needed help maintaining the mental representation. I permitted him to take home the chalk.

In a session 6 months into the therapy, we had recently moved into a playroom for the sessions. In this session, Steve followed me down the stairs saying "yak, yak, yak" and repeated this in the playroom. I placed an eraser, which he had asked me for the previous week, on the blackboard.

> T: Maybe "yak, yak, yak" is an imitation of me when I talk and maybe you are angry with me and didn't want me to say anything.
> C: I will write my answers with the chalk except that it is in broken pieces instead of whole pieces because you dropped the chalk.
> T: There are usually things wrong with what I give you, like the chalk. I had dropped it. I wonder if you felt like I had let you down.

He continued to be quiet, then pulled out some pots and asked me to fill them with water (this had occurred in previous sessions). I filled two, then Steve told me I had filled the wrong pan, he wanted a different one filled. He kept complaining about how I filled them.

> T: What I give you is both good and bad. Maybe it's scary to take things from me. He said "Right, right, and then told me to sit down while he prepared food.

He then closed the flap on the blackboard, so I could not see him, and opened it several times. He was behind it. I heard him doing something and asked him what he was doing. He said he was painting the board.

> T: You must have mixed feelings about my being here and saying things today. The way you keep opening and shutting the door (and hiding).
> C: The reason I am quiet in here is because I don't trust the room yet.
> T: You don't really feel safe to say things in here.
> C: Yes.
> T: Maybe you don't trust me completely either, or feel really safe with me.

Steve came out from behind the board and picked up the eraser I had brought and the chalk, and began drawing on the board. He drew a picture of a girl behind bars. I asked him if that girl was me—he wrote yes on the board. For the remainder of the session, I made comments and he wrote yes or no about what I had said, with some spoken additions.

T: Am I behind bars because you are angry with me?
C: Yes.
T: Are you angry because I left and went on vacation?
C: Yes—I thought about bad things happening to you. (Then he wrote "You don't like me.")
T: Why do you feel that?
C: If you really liked me, you would not have gone on vacation.
T: If I really cared about you, I would not have left and had you feel so angry and frightened and confused.
C: Yeah, I wish you were like this. (He drew a circular design.)
T: You mean like the design? I'm not sure I understand.
C: I wish you were a robot.

He then drew switches and wrote on and off.

T: If I were a robot, you could turn me on and off, and I couldn't leave you when you didn't want me to or make you feel bad.
C: (Nodded yes.)
T: There will be times when I will have to leave on vacation. But I do care about you and like you, and I know how bad and angry it makes you feel when I go away.

The main role of play in this session was as a form of communication. Play was an indirect way to interact with me and express feelings, thoughts, and issues. The play enabled me to reflect, label, and empathize with him and to "make sense" of what he was expressing. Trying to understand and help him understand what was happening was important. He was angry with me because I went away. That was understandable as was his wish that I were a robot. I also (according to my notes) did talk to him about the fact that thinking that bad things would happen to me was only a thought and had nothing to do with what really happened. This was a common theme in the therapy—that when he thought bad things (like my being in an accident) it did not make it happen. The play involving my filling pots with water and his then making food was a common play theme for about 6 months. It enabled issues of nurturance and caring to be discussed as well as feelings of ambivalence about me to be expressed and, in turn, integrated.

Throughout the therapy, expression of empathy was one of the main therapeutic interventions. Empathy around the therapist's empathic failures was especially important. Steve became visibly upset when I was off-base. In one play episode, he acted out a "wacky" school bus driver who would drive too fast and then go too slow. I was off-base a lot, partly because Steve (and children like Steve) communicated in fragmented, confusing ways. There is a lot of guessing on the part of the therapist about what is being expressed.

In another session after a vacation, Steve enacted a helicopter that was trying to rescue a boy from a cliff. The helicopter kept missing the boy and flying off in the wrong direction.

> **T:**   Help is not there.
> **C:**   It's there, but when I don't need it. It's not there when I do.
> **T:**   Like me—I wasn't here when you needed me. Did something frightening happen when I was gone? I wish you could tell me.
> **C:**   Well—I did have three teeth pulled.
> **T:**   Oh—how was it? I know going to the dentist is hard for you.
> **C:**   Nice, but it was painful. He froze my lip but I still bit through it. The knucklehead—it still hurts.

In this session, I commented on the play and tied it to his feelings about me not being here. Empathy around the dentist was important, but so was helping with his feelings about me.

The final year of therapy, when Steve was 11 and 12, involved more talk than play. By this time, he had developed better internal representations and a better sense of what was fantasy and reality. He was able to integrate positive and negative feelings about one individual. He was verbal and coherent in the therapy with logical thought processes being dominant. The next excerpt is from a session after 2 years of therapy. He is telling me about a Halloween party he had held for his friends.

Steve talked about the party and the different events, like bobbing for apples, the hung man, firecrackers, and a fortune teller using a fake fortune-telling kit.

> **T:**   How did you feel about the party?
> **C:**   Well, OK but it was hard work making sure everybody stayed in their own area. I had to tell one kid in the fortune telling line to beat it till it was his turn and he was not supposed to be there then.
> **T:**   So you had to make sure everyone did what they were supposed to do and not be in the wrong place.
> **C:**   And not go behind the ropes with the fireworks.
> **T:**   So no one would get hurt?

C: Yeah—everyone kept calling me. Steve, we need you here; Steve do this: Steve, this kid shouldn't be here. I was running all over the place.

T: You had a lot to do, and to keep under control.

C: When my Mom brought out the hot dogs, there was this little burner with just a few hot dogs at a time. All these kids were standing around this little grill (he laughed).

T: Everyone was hungry at once.

C: Yeah—then Joe and I did our Dracula act—I dressed up in a Dracula costume and pretended to suck his blood behind my cloak, and he played dead. Then we had a prize for the best costume (listed how many votes other people got). I got three but I didn't win.

T: Sounds like part of you hoped you would win.

C: I couldn't win—it was my party.

T: Well, it's understandable that you would still wish you could win.

C: One kid, when he bobbed for apples, he put his head all the way to the bottom—after he rolled up his sleeves and had someone hold his hat—and he got one. I tried but I didn't like it (shuddered).

T: It can be uncomfortable or scary with water around your head.

C: Yeah—I didn't like my head being under water that long—so I said forget it. When I was over, one person stayed and helped me clean up—all was cleaned up in about two hours. I had prepared for two weeks.

T: I know you worked very hard and the party was important to you. And then it was over fast.

C: I walked this person home to the end of the block. Last night was Halloween—I got half a bag of candy. I ran into some tough guys. I went back to get Tom (older brother) to go with me.

T: You felt safer with Tom there.

C: Yeah—he's big, and could show them karate if they tried anything.

T: What about the guys was tough?

C: Well, they said some things.

T: Can you tell me what they said?

C: No—that's private.

T: Some things make it hard for you to tell me some things—like about what they said. What makes it so hard?

C: Forget it.

T: What I might think?

C: Are you done now?

T: Yes, but I hope in the future you feel safe enough to tell me those kinds of upsetting things so we can understand them better.

Steve then began a discussion of a magic show he saw—and described three illusions and how they worked.

> **T:** It seemed like magic—but you know it isn't.
> **C:** Yeah—they were good illusions.

In this session, empathy was still an important therapeutic technique (the hard work at the party; wishing he could win a prize) but the expression of his thoughts and feelings were much more direct than earlier. His description of his party was well organized and clear. He also shows how he mastered or directly dealt with his fears. He pretends to be Dracula, and decides not to bob for apples. He sees the illusions behind the magic show. There are still some things that are private, and that is very appropriate. It is important to respect his privacy. The one person he walked home I did not inquire about. In later sessions, he revealed that this was a girl who he liked and we began to discuss boy–girl issues. During the last few months of therapy, role playing and problem solving around peer relations was a frequent technique.

At the time of termination, Steve was functioning well in school, had friends, and was in general, doing well. He told me that he thought he "could manage" on his own. He told me that he used to think that "this would happen to me." He then drew a picture on the blackboard and erased it, an illustration I think of the primitive fear of annihilation—or loss of self. He said that he still felt that way sometimes, but he knows that will not happen and that he will be alright. Interestingly, this primitive fear is not something we spoke about or worked on directly. We spoke of fear and feelings of safety. But as he thought back to his earlier experiences, he remembered the feeling and expressed it that way.

In this case, the main focus of the therapy was on the relationship with the therapist and the communication of empathy for Steve's experiences. Much of the content of therapy was expressed in the play. In addition, expressing understanding and the idea of cause and effect, that feelings happen for a reason and can effect behaviors, and vice versa, helped Steve organize his thoughts. He did develop better internal representations, which helped him empathize with others and make friends.

The major play processes that were affected in the therapy were cognitive processes. Over time, his play became better organized. His stories and play events made more sense. This improved cognitive organization, and better differentiation of fantasy from reality, helped him modulate and contain the affect. Emotion regulation in the play improved.

Although the major role of play in therapy was as a form of communication so that the therapist could empathize, an important secondary role was as a way to establish a coherent narrative around his feelings and internal world.

These two cases illustrate how play can be used in therapy in different ways with different children. If play measures had been administered at repeated times throughout the therapy, changes in play processes would have been observed. An empirical foundation needs to be established for the play therapy area. The rich clinical writings that exist can be used as a basis for the generation of hypotheses.

Ideally, research in psychotherapy would focus on changes in these specific processes in play along with changes in symptoms, diagnostic classification, and other clinical criteria. We need to learn which specific intervention techniques effect these processes best and whether changes in these play processes effect behavior and well-being. The next chapter reviews the current state of research in child psychotherapy and play therapy.

The Role of Play in Therapy: The Research

In a review of the current state of play therapy research, I made a distinction between psychotherapy outcome research in general and play intervention research (Russ, 1995). The broad category of psychotherapy outcome research makes sense to review in spite of the fact that most of those studies did not focus specifically on play. Play was frequently embedded in the therapy intervention, although not specifically investigated. Therefore, the results of those outcome studies provide an important context in which to think about play. Play intervention studies are studies that investigate a very specific play intervention that uses theoretically relevant outcome variables. Both types of research studies are reviewed in this chapter.

CHILD PSYCHOTHERAPY OUTCOME RESEARCH

In general, the early reviews of child therapy outcome studies concluded that there was little or no support for child therapy. More recent work has concluded that there is support for the effectiveness of child psychotherapy if the research is well designed.

A classic early review by Levitt (1957) concluded that the mean improvement rate for children was not significantly better than the baseline improvement rate of 72.5% for untreated controls. In later work, in a review of 47 reports of outcome studies, Levitt (1963, 1971) concluded that approximately two thirds of treated children in therapy were improved, but again treated children were no better off than untreated controls. Levitt's conclusions were taken seriously by those in the field of child psychotherapy.

A number of researchers responded to Levitt's conclusions (Heinicke & Goldman, 1960; Hood-Williams, 1960). One of the major methodological issues was that so many of the untreated controls were defectors from treatment. Defectors were children who were evaluated and recommended for treatment but who had not entered treatment. Therefore, there may have been a number of confounding variables operating here, to account for the results.

Barrett, Hampe, and Miller (1978) and Hartmann, Roper, and Gelfant (1977) took a closer look at Levitt's reviews and at the research literature in general. They concluded that there was still no solid empirical evidence for the effectiveness of psychotherapy. Barrett et al. (1978) stated that the global nature of the research was a major problem and concluded that most of the research studies were not specific enough or focused enough to enable research questions to be answered. There was too much of a mix of populations, therapeutic approaches, and interventions in these studies. Often, the outcome measures were unrefined or nonexistent. This led to their often quoted conclusion that the question in psychotherapy research should not be "Does psychotherapy work?" but rather "Which set of procedures is effective when applied to what kinds of patients with which sets of problems and practiced by which sorts of therapists?" (1978, p. 428).

A number of other methodological issues important for research in the child therapy area have been identified: namely, the importance of classification according to developmental level (Heinicke & Strassman, 1975), controlling for maturational effects (Koocher & Broskowski, 1977), the need for homogeneous treatment groups (Achenbach, 1978; Hartmann et al., 1977), the need to control for sex and age variables (Cass & Thomas, 1979), and the need for adequate outcome measures given at appropriate intervals (Kazdin, 1990, 1993).

The field of child therapy research has followed these research guidelines and the research studies have become more focused and methodologically sophisticated. In addition, the technique of meta-analysis has enabled the field to arrive at a more systematic evaluation of outcome studies. As Weisz and Weiss (1993) noted, meta-analysis is a technique that enables the pooling and statistical summarizing of the results of outcome studies. The effect size (ES) is the statistical summary of the treatment efficacy across studies. Use of this systematic procedure helps avoid reviewer subjectivity in coming to conclusions.

Weisz and Weiss (1993) reviewed the major meta-analytic studies in the field of child psychotherapy. Casey and Berman (1985) calculated the effect of psychotherapy across 64 studies and found a mean effect size of 0.71. A slightly higher effect size of 0.79 was found by Weisz, Weiss, Alicke, and Klotz (1987) in a review of 163 treatment–control comparisons. Both studies concluded that the average treated child functioned better after treatment than three fourths of the untreated controls. In the Casey and Berman review, effect sizes did not differ as a function of whether play was used. In a recent meta-analyses by Kazdin, Bass, Ayers, and Rodgers (1990), for 64 studies involving treatment versus no-treatment comparisons, the mean effect size was 0.88. Weisz and Weiss (1993) concluded that "the mean effect sizes reported in child meta-analyses are quite comparable to those of adult meta-analyses and that findings in both categories point to quite positive effects of therapy" (p. 46).

As Kazdin (1990) has pointed out, the results of these meta-analyses have contributed to the field in that they offer evidence that psychotherapy is more effective than no treatment with children. This conclusion is more encouraging than the conclusions based on the reviews in the 1950s, 1960s, and 1970s. Although these child therapy outcome studies did not focus on play per se, one might infer that play is an effective form of treatment since it is so frequently part of the therapy process. The Casey and Berman (1985) review found no difference in effectiveness between those studies that used play and those that did not. On the other hand, Kazdin (2000) offered secondary conclusions from the meta-analyses that treatment differences tend to favor behavioral rather than non-behavioral techniques.

Weisz and Weiss (1989, 1993) pointed out that most of the research studies in the meta-analyses involved controlled laboratory interventions. In many of these studies children were recruited for treatment and were not clinic-referred; samples were homogeneous; there was a focal problem; therapy focused on the target problem; therapists were trained in the specific treatment approaches to be used; and the therapy relied primarily on those techniques. In essence, this was good research that followed many of the methodological guidelines for adequate research design. On the other hand, Weisz and Weiss (1993) cautioned that the evidence for the effectiveness of psychotherapy is based on studies that are not typical of conventional clinical practice. Thus the findings may not be generalizable to real clinical work. In a review of studies that involved clinic-referred children and that occurred in clinical settings, Weisz, Donenberg, Han, and Weiss (1995) concluded that there were negligible effects for psychotherapy.

The results of the meta-analysis point to the need for specificity and precision. Weisz and Weiss (1993) concluded that the studies that showed positive results tended to "zoom in" on a specific problem with careful planning of the intervention. Freedheim and Russ (1983, 1992) stated that we needed to become very specific and ask "Which specific interventions affect which specific cognitive, personality, and affective processes? How are these processes related to behavior and practical clinical criteria?" (1983, p. 988). Shirk and Russell (1996) also call for the targeting of specific cognitive, affective, and interpersonal processes in child therapy.

Many forms of treatment that use play therapy have not been empirically evaluated. It is urgent that empirical evaluations be carried out. In order to be precise, play intervention should be investigated under controlled conditions.

Recently there has been a strong movement in the field of child psychotherapy to identify empirically supported treatments (Lonigan, Elbert, &

Johnson, 1998). Most of the therapy outcome studies have been efficacy studies that are conducted under controlled conditions that involve random assignment, control groups, and single disorders. Effectiveness studies, on the other hand, are clinical utility studies that focus on treatment outcome in real-world environments such as mental health clinics. Empirically supported treatment reviews have focused on efficacy studies (Kazdin, 2000). These reviews spell out the criteria they have used to evaluate the treatment. Criteria usually include studies that use random assignment to conditions, have specific child populations, use treatment manuals, and use multiple outcome measures with "blind" raters (Kazdin, 2000). There has been some controversy about how stringent the criteria should be before concluding that a treatment has been empirically validated. One approach used by the Task Force on Promotion and Dissemination of Psychological Procedures of the American Psychological Association placed treatments into categories of well-established or probably efficacious treatments (Chambless et al., 1996). This approach, with few exceptions, was adopted by the task force focusing on child therapies (Lonigan et al., 1998). Kazdin (2000) concluded that there are empirically supported treatments for children, but at this point in time, they are relatively few in number. The list is composed mainly of cognitive-behavioral treatments. Kazdin recommended placing treatments on a continuum from 1 to 5, with 1 being treatments that have not been evaluated and 5 being best treatments (more effective than one or more other well-established treatments). Using this kind of scale would distinguish among those studies that have not yet been investigated, those that have been and are promising, and those that have been investigated but were not effective. Play therapy is a treatment that has not yet been evaluated in well-controlled studies.

Previously, in a review of the play therapy research, Phillips (1985) called for a systematic program of research with well-controlled studies. He concluded that the play therapy research that found positive results were those studies of a cognitive-behavioral nature that were carefully designed. Phillips speculated that the specificity of treatment goals and focused methods of the cognitive-behavioral studies partially account for the positive results. He recommended that all forms of play therapy be investigated with the precision of the cognitive-behavioral studies. In general, there are not many play therapy studies in the literature and little exploration of variables that leads to change (Faust & Burns, 1991).

It should be relatively easy to apply the principles of specificity and focus to the play area. Play interventions and the cognitive and affective processes that they effect can be broken down into discrete units in controlled conditions. One model is the one I proposed in chapter 2. The large body of research in the play and child development literature offers a wealth of ideas and research lines that could be followed.

PLAY INTERVENTION STUDIES

As Russ has reviewed (1995), studies exist that have investigated the effect of play on specific types of problems and in specific populations. These studies are a good bridge between empirical laboratory studies of the effect of play on specific processes (like creativity) and more global clinical practice outcome studies. I have labeled these studies *play intervention* rather than *play therapy*, because the focus is highly specific. Usually, they involve only a few sessions with no emphasis on forming a "relationship" with a therapist. On the other hand, these studies differ from specific process research in child development in that they are problem focused and are not as fine-tuned as they would be in laboratory research. They fall in the middle of the continuum with laboratory play research on one end and global therapy outcome research on the other. These play intervention research studies seem to fit some of Weisz and Weiss's (1993) criteria by including children who are not clinic-referred, by having homogeneous samples, and by having a focal problem on which the therapy focused.

Phillips (1985) reviewed two studies that would fall into this play intervention research category. Both involved the use of puppet play to reduce anxiety in children facing surgery. Johnson and Stockdale (1975) measured Palmer Sweat Index level before and after surgery. Puppet play in this study involved playing out the surgery. Johnson and Stockdale found less anxiety for the puppet-play group before and after surgery. The one exception was immediately before surgery, when the increased information may have elevated their anxiety. Cassell (1965) used puppets with children undergoing cardiac catheterization and found that anxiety was reduced before surgery for the puppet-play group compared with the no-treatment control. There were no differences after surgery. The treatment group was less disturbed during the cardiac catheterization and expressed more willingness to return to the hospital for further treatment. Rae, Worchel, Upchurch, Sanner, and Dainiel (1989) investigated the effects of play on the adjustment of 46 children hospitalized for acute illness. Children were randomly assigned to one of four experimental groups:

- A therapeutic play condition in which the child was encouraged to play with medical and nonmedical materials. Verbal support, reflection, and interpretation of feelings were expressed by the research assistant.
- A diversionary play condition in which children were allowed to play with toys but fantasy play was discouraged. The toys provided did not facilitate fantasy, nor did the research assistant.
- A verbally oriented support condition in which children were encouraged to talk about feelings and anxieties. The research assis-

tant was directive in bringing up related topics and would ask about procedures.
- A control condition in which the research assistant had no contact with the child.

All treatment conditions consisted of two 30-minute sessions. The main result of this study was that children in the therapeutic play group showed significantly more reduction in self-reported hospital-related fears than children in the other three groups. There were no differences among the groups for parent ratings. Because this study controlled for verbal expression, one can conclude that the fantasy activity itself resulted in fear reduction.

Another specific problem area that lends itself to focused play intervention research is that of separation anxiety. In an excellent example of a well-designed play intervention study, Milos and Reiss (1982) used play therapy for preschoolers who were dealing with separation anxiety. They identified 64 children who were rated as high-separation-anxious by their teachers. The children were randomly assigned to one of four groups. Three play groups were theme-related: the free-play group had appropriate toys; the directed-play group had the scene set with a mother doll bringing the child to school; the modeling group had the experimenter playing out a separation scene. A control group also used play with toys irrelevant to separation themes (blocks, puzzles, crayons). All children received three individual 10-minute play sessions on different days. Quality of play was rated. The results showed that all three thematic play conditions were effective in reducing anxiety around separation themes when compared to the control group. An interesting finding was that, when the free-play and directed-play groups were combined, the quality of play ratings were significantly negatively related ($r = -.37$) to a post-test anxiety measure. High-quality play was defined as play that showed more separation themes and attempts to resolve conflicts. One might speculate that the children who were already good players used the intervention to master their separation anxiety. Milos and Reiss concluded that their results support the underlying assumption of play therapy, that play can reduce anxiety associated with psychological problems. The finding that quality of play was related to effectiveness of the intervention is consistent with the finding of Dansky (1980), that free play facilitated creativity only for those children who used make-believe well.

A well-designed study by Barnett (1984) also looked at separation anxiety and expanded upon work by Barnett and Storm (1981) in which free play was found to reduce distress in children following a conflict situation. In the 1984 study, a natural stressor, the first day of school, was used. Seventy-four preschool children were observed separating from their mothers and were rated anxious or nonanxious.

These two groups were further divided into play or no-play conditions. The play condition was a free-play condition. The no-play condition was a story-listening condition. For half of the play condition, play was solitary. For the other half, peers were present. The story condition was also split into solitary and peers-present segments. Play was rated by observers and categorized in terms of types of play. Play significantly reduced anxiety in the high-anxious group. Anxiety was measured by the Palmer Sweat Index. There was no effect for low-anxious children. For the anxious children, solitary play was best in reducing anxiety. High-anxious children spent more time in fantasy play than did low-anxious children, who showed more functional and manipulative play. They engaged more in fantasy play when no other children were present. Barnett interpreted these results to mean that play was used to cope with a distressing situation. The findings supported her idea that it is not social play that is essential to conflict resolution, but rather imaginative play qualities that the child introduces into playful behavior. Actually, the presence of peers increased anxiety in the high-anxious group.

These play intervention studies are a few examples of the kind of studies that tell us about how play can be helpful in dealing with specific problems. The results of these studies suggest that play helps children deal with fears and reduce anxiety and that something about play itself is important and serves as a vehicle for change. Results of several studies suggest that the involvement of fantasy and make-believe is involved in the reduction of anxiety. The studies effectively controlled for the variable of an attentive adult. Results also suggest that children who are already good players are more able to use play opportunities to resolve problems when these opportunities arise. Teaching children good play skills would provide children with a resource for future coping with fears and anxiety.

PLAY AND ANXIETY REDUCTION:
POSSIBLE CHANGE MECHANISMS

A fascinating area for future research is the identification of mechanisms that account for the finding that play reduces anxiety. What are the cognitive-affective mechanisms that enable anxiety to be reduced? How does play help negative affect, be it anxiety, sadness, aggression, shame, guilt, or frustration, to be handled? The mechanisms may be different for different emotions. A number of current theorists and researchers provide frameworks that could be applied to the play area.

J. Singer (1995) referred to Tomkins' (1970) concept of "miniaturization." Play is a way that children "cut down the large things around it to manageable proportions ..." (p. 191). By creating manageable situations in a pretend, safe setting, negative emotions can be expressed. J. Singer (1995) proposed that children can then increase positive affect and reduce negative affect through play. This conceptualization fits with the idea that play is one way in which children learn to regulate their emotions.

Strayhorn (2002) discussed the role of fantasy rehearsal in developing self-control. Pretend play can be used for fantasy rehearsal activities. The child can act out the adaptive pattern of thoughts, emotions, and behaviors. Strayhorn stated that fantasy rehearsal helps the child to build up habit strength for the adaptive handling of conflict situations (when two goals compete) during moments of calm and control. Using this framework, a child could reduce fears and anxiety around separation or other issues, by acting out the adaptive ways of handling the separation and feelings around it in a pretend play situation.

Using pretend play to reduce anxiety is also consistent with the framework of emotion regulation in understanding adult anxiety disorders (Mennin, Heimberg, Turk, & Fresco, 2002). They conceptualized Generalized Anxiety Disorders (GAD) of adults as reflecting problems in understanding and modulating emotions. Individuals with GAD use worry and maladaptive behaviors as defensive strategies to control, avoid, or blunt emotional experience. They utilize the concept of experiential avoidance to explain the use of worry and the lack of extinction of the anxiety (Hayes, Strosahl, & Wilson, 1999) and conclude that experiential avoidance is associated with many psychological disorders. Treatments that reduce experiential avoidance are recommended, especially those that help individuals become more comfortable with arousing emotional experience, more able to access and utilize emotional information in adaptive problem solving, and better able to modulate emotional experience and expression. Pretend play in therapy can help children experience and modulate the negative affect in a repetitive and guided situation. The child is helped to engage in the emotions he or she has been defending against.

Jacobsen and colleagues (2002) found that avoidance coping predicted symptom severity in a post-traumatic stress disorder (PTSD) population of adults who had undergone bone marrow transplants. They utilized a social-cognitive-processing model of trauma recovery (Lepore, Silver, Wortman, & Wayment, 1996) to understand the results. Greater use of avoidance coping (denial, escape, avoidance, distortion) would give individuals fewer opportunities to process or habituate to trauma-related thoughts, images, and memories. The lack of processing would interfere with cognitive processing and "there would be less integration of the traumatic experience into new or pre-existing mental schemas and greater likelihood that traumatic material would remain active and capable of precipitating intrusive thoughts and other symptoms of PTSD" (p. 236). This framework should apply to children as well. Play with children should help them process the negative emotions associated with the trauma. This is what child therapists working with PTSD children try to accomplish with play, drawing, and talk (Gil, 1991; Terr, 1990). The research on coping and play has found relationships between affect expression in play and the use of a variety of coping strategies and also active problem solving coping strategies (see chapter 2).

Harris (2000) has conducted a number of careful experimental studies that have investigated pretend play. He views play as helping the child to construct a situation model that is revisable. Children go back and forth between reality and an imagined world. Learning how reality could be different helps children make causal judgments. The play process could help children reduce anxiety by a new cognitive appraisal of the situation.

Pennebaker's work (2002) on the emotional expression writing paradigm is also quite relevant to the play area. Pennebaker's studies randomly assign adults to write either about superficial topics or about important personal topics for 3–5 days, from 15 to 30 minutes per day. His studies have found that the emotional writing group's physical and mental health improves (Pennebaker, 2002; Pennebaker & Graybeal, 2001). The health measures included physician visits, lab tests, and biological markers. Mental health measures included drops in rumination and depression and higher grades among students. Pennebaker offered two possible change mechanisms that account for these results based on analysis of the writing samples. First, the coherence of the narrative that is constructed produces a transformation of the emotional event. A new meaning to the event is developed. A second explanation is that people in the emotional writing group showed a change in how they are thinking about themselves relative to others. In the play situation, children are expressing emotions and developing narratives. In play therapy, the therapist helps tie the narrative to the child's own life and put the play event into a meaningful context. One implication of the Pennebaker findings is that the coherent narrative in which the emotion is placed is important.

These recent conceptualizations of emotion regulation and adaptive functioning and of psychotherapy point to the importance of learning to experience, access, and modulate both positive and negative emotion. Pretend play is a natural activity that can help children accomplish these goals. Although these conceptualizations are consistent with the concepts of the psychotherapy literature, such as mastering emotion, working-through process, or corrective emotional experience (see chap. 3), these recent conceptualizations are more precise as to the actual mechanisms involved. They are, therefore, easier to operationalize and to test, and they focus on specific processes. They provide a variety of frameworks in which to investigate the effect of play on different aspects of emotional processing. What we learn from these studies can then inform the use of play in psychotherapy and in prevention programs.

Conclusions From Child Psychotherapy and Play Intervention Research Literature

From the literature reviewed, we can conclude the following:

1. In general, child psychotherapy is effective. The Casey and Berman (1985) review found no difference in effectiveness between those studies that used play and those that did not. Treatment differences favor behavioral techniques. Approaches that most heavily utilize play techniques have not been empirically validated.
2. When play intervention studies are focused and well controlled, play has been found to reduce fears and anxiety. Fears have been reduced around medical procedures and around issues of separation.
3. Several studies suggest that the imagination and fantasy components of the play are key factors in reducing the anxiety.
4. Play is more effective for children who already have good fantasy play skills.

These research findings are consistent with the psychodynamic theoretical and clinical literature that utilizes play to help with internal conflict resolution and mastery of internal issues, as well as with external traumas and stressful life events. As a result of this conflict resolution and problem solving, anxiety is reduced. Psychodynamic approaches also suggest the use of insight, conflict-resolution approaches for children whose fantasy skills are normally developed and who can use play in therapy.

These research findings are also consistent with cognitive behavioral uses of play where playing out fears and anxieties would result in extinction of inappropriate affective responses. Children who could use fantasy better would be more able to imagine various scenarios, and extinction of fears would be more likely to occur for them than for children with less developed fantasy ability.

We can only speculate as to the reasons for these research findings on play and anxiety, because the underlying mechanisms have not been explored in empirical studies. Recent conceptualizations in related areas of psychology, like emotion regulation, provide frameworks and research paradigms in which to investigate play and different forms of negative affect and psychopathology. Investigating exactly how fantasy play helps reduce anxiety is an important research question for the future.

CONSISTENCIES BETWEEN CHILD DEVELOPMENT
RESEARCH AND PSYCHOTHERAPY THEORY
AND RESEARCH

The major consistency between the child development research reviewed in chapter 2 (conclusions on p. 32) and the child psychotherapy theory is the concept that play helps children solve and cope with problems. The empirical literature supports the notion that play is helpful to children in dealing with problems. Play either relates to or facilitates problem solving ability in the form of greater insight, divergent thinking, and flexibility. Both play ability and problem solving abilities relate to the ability to think of alternative coping strategies. Play ability also relates to the ability to take the perspective of the other person and empathize. In the area of emotion, emotional expression in play relates to less constriction of emotion in daily life and more positive emotion in daily life. In a broad sense, the empirical literature does support the use of play to bring about change. However, the techniques used by play therapists and the actual process of play therapy has not been specifically tied to change in these specific processes. Therefore, there is a huge gap between the research literature that demonstrates that play facilitates development, and the actual practice of play therapy that involves the use of specific techniques to alter characteristics such as depression, self-esteem, or chronic anxiety.

The few empirical studies in the play intervention area that were focused on play with specific problems found that play reduced fears and anxiety. Fantasy appears to be an important factor in the anxiety reduction. This finding is intriguing and is theoretically consistent with an underlying principle of insight-oriented therapy. That is, fantasy play should aid in conflict resolution, which in turn reduces anxiety. Identifying the underlying mechanism that accounts for the finding that fantasy play reduces anxiety is an important task for future researchers. Also, play was more effective for children who already had good fantasy skills. This was found in the Milos and Reis study on separation anxiety and in the Dansky study on creativity. One consistency between the play intervention and child development literature is that play opportunities are most beneficial for children who already play well.

Implications for Play Therapy and for Prevention Programs

When goals are broad, such as facilitating problem solving ability and/or emotional expression, the use of play in prevention programs seems most appropriate. The research evidence does warrant the development of play programs to help children develop cognitive and affective processes.

In child therapy, where goals necessarily are more focused, the research does support the use of play to reduce fear or anxiety. Although the research has focused on medical situations and separation anxiety, other populations struggling with anxiety, such as post-traumatic stress disorders should also be appropriate for play therapy. However, research also suggests that children should have good play skills to begin with, for play therapy to be effective in reducing anxiety. Interestingly, anxiety disorders in general are very effectively treated by cognitive-behavioral approaches (Krain & Kendall, 1999), many of which do not use play. Whether a play intervention, cognitive-behavioral intervention, or integrated approach is optimal needs to be empirically determined.

What about the use of play therapy for problems other than anxiety? The clinical literature supports the use of play with depression (Altschul, 1988) and post-traumatic stress disorder (Terr, 1990). The research literature to date has really not investigated the use of play interventions with these populations and types of problems. These kinds of studies need to be carried out. However, the research findings from a variety of studies in the child and adult areas suggest that other types of negative affect, like sadness or extreme anxiety and fear, should be helped by play intervention.

GUIDELINES FOR FUTURE RESEARCH IN PLAY THERAPY

Research programs in play therapy need to be at both the micro and macro levels. First, laboratory research on play and cognitive and affective processes must continue. Concurrent, longitudinal, and experimental studies on specific dimensions of play and specific cognitive, affective, and personality processes need to be carried out in a systematic fashion. We especially need to identify what dimensions of play most relate to specific processes. For example, does affect expression increase divergent thinking? Does positive affect have a different effect from negative affect? Are there different effects with different age groups and different populations of children?

Second, research needs to be carried out with focused play interventions. Russ (1995) outlined different types of play intervention research:

1. *Specific Play Interventions With Specific Populations and Specific Situations.* Populations experiencing anxiety and fears would be a logical group to work with. The Barnett (1984) study with children who were experiencing the first day of school is a good example of this type of study. There are a variety of natural stressors that could be used to investigate play intervention. Divorce, natural disasters, dental visits, presurgery, and loss of a parent are all situations in which play intervention is used. We need to develop an empirical base for play intervention in these situations.

2. *Refining Specific Play Techniques.* The general question of what kinds of intervention by the therapist best facilitate play needs to be studied empirically. There are many guidelines in the clinical literature about how to

facilitate play, but few are based on empirical work. How do we best encourage affect in play? When is modeling more effective than a less directive approach? When is it less effective? For example, Gil (1991) pointed out that it is frequently important with sexually abused children to be nondirective, so that the child does not feel intruded upon. What kinds of intervention most enhance the working-through process and conflict resolution? These kinds of research questions can be posed in well-controlled experimental studies and in psychotherapy-process research. What kind of techniques improve story-telling, divergent thinking, and use of fantasy? What areas of a child's functioning are effected by these improved play processes? All of the processes in play outlined in chapter 1 could be investigated in this manner. This kind of research is consistent with Shirk and Russell's (1996) call for identifying specific change processes in psychotherapy.

Third, underlying mechanisms that account for the changes facilitated by play need to be investigated. What exactly is the working-through process? How does developing a narrative around a feeling affect the integration of that feeling? Is working-through different from the concept of extinction of anxiety? How does fantasy play reduce anxiety? Can we develop specific play techniques that increase emotion regulation?

Fourth, comparative studies of play intervention and other types of interventions with specific problems and populations need to be carried out to determine optimal forms of treatment.

Fifth, dissemination of research results should inform clinical practice and prevention programs. For example, guidelines about how to best facilitate affective expression in play could be better incorporated into play therapy. Treatment manuals using these guidelines can and should be developed. In prevention programs, preschool teachers could follow guidelines about facilitating different aspects of play.

For research on play interventions to be able to focus on the actual processes in the play, measures of play and the processes that occur in play need to be developed. The next chapter discusses the Affect in Play Scale, one measure for assessing children's play.

5

The Affect in Play Scale

For empirical validation of play intervention to occur, the field needs to develop measures of play and the cognitive and affective processes that occur in play. Although there have been measures of cognitive processes in play (J. Singer, 1973), there is a need for measures of affective processes in play. The need for a reliable and valid scale that measures affective expression in children's fantasy play has been widely recognized (Howe & Silvern, 1981; Rubin et al., 1983; Stern et al., 1992). In order for affective processes to be studied in children, we need standardized measures of expression of affect.

The Affect in Play Scale (APS) was developed to meet the need for a standardized measure of affective expression in children's pretend play. This chapter reviews some of the play measures currently available, but focuses on the reliability and validity of the APS. In developing measures of play, we have to ask the question, "Can we truly capture the private spontaneous fantasy play that most expresses the child's thoughts, feelings, fantasies, wishes, and fears?" The growing number of instruments that attempt to measure play have a growing empirical base that supports their reliability and validity. These measures are capturing important aspects of play, even though they may not capture fantasy play in full force.

A SAMPLE OF PRETEND PLAY MEASURES

Pretend play has been a major tool of child therapists. In play therapy, the child uses play to express feelings, express conflicts, resolve problems, role play, and communicate with the therapist. Three measures appropriate for use with school-age children were developed in the context of assessing therapeutic material: the Play Therapy Observation Instrument, the NOVA Assessment of Psychotherapy (Faust & Burns, 1991; Howe & Silvern, 1981), and the Kernberg scale. As clinical instruments, these measures tap both affective and thematic aspects of children's play, rather than solely cognitive aspects of the play. (For a full review of available measures of play, see Schaefer, Gitlin, & Sandgrund, 1991; Gitlin-Weiner, Sandgrund, & Schaefer, 2000.)

The Play Therapy Observation Instrument (PTOI), originally developed by Howe and Silvern (1981), and adapted by Perry (Perry & Landreth, 1991), was designed to assist in the assessment of a child's functioning, and in treatment planning, and prognosis. Three areas of functioning are assessed with 13 items: (a) social inadequacy, (b) emotional discomfort, and (c) use of fantasy. The social inadequacy subscale includes items such as incoherent or bizarre content, exclusion of the therapist from activities, body stiffness, and responding to interventions with hostility or withdrawal. The emotional comfort subscale includes assessment of the valence of child's mood (i.e., positive vs. negative), as well as themes of aggression, conflict, and anxiety. The use of fantasy subscale includes such items as amount of time spent in fantasy versus reality, the use of characters rather than things in fantasy, number of different fantasy stories, and number of different roles enacted. Brief segments of play therapy interactions are scored from videotapes.

The PTOI has been found to discriminate adjusted from maladjusted children most strongly on the emotional discomfort subscale (Perry & Landreth, 1991). Rosen, Faust, and Burns (1994) used the PTOI with children participating in either psychodynamic or client-centered play therapy and found no significant differences between children's play in the two approaches. Differences were found, however, between scores in the first session and a later session, suggesting that the PTOI may be a useful instrument for detecting changes during the treatment process. Two related limitations of the PTOI are the need for developmental norms and a standardized administration (Perry & Landreth, 1991).

The NOVA Assessment of Psychotherapy (NAP) was also designed to assess the play therapy process and outcome by capturing components of the child's and therapist's behavior during play (Faust & Burns, 1991). This scale was intended for use in both clinical and research settings, with both a long and a short version. In the long version, 17 child behaviors and 12 therapist behaviors are coded in 7-second intervals. These behaviors fall into four categories: (a) child verbal, (b) child nonverbal, (c) therapist facilitating, and (d) therapist channeling. Some of the relevant aspects of the child's play that are coded include valence of affect expressed (i.e., positive or negative), cooperative behavior, and aggressive behaviors. The scale can be scored during live interaction or from videotape. Initial single case studies of the validity and reliability of the scale suggest that, similar to the PTOI, the NAP may be useful for assessing affective and behavioral changes during the treatment process (Faust & Burns, 1991). Kernberg's scale (Kernberg, Chazan, & Normandin, 1998) measures a variety of variables from a psychodynamic perspective. Her scale focuses on the psychotherapy process.

There was a need for a standardized measure of pretend play that is comprehensive in its assessment of the kinds of affect that occur during fantasy expression. The development of the Affect in Play Scale (APS) was an attempt to meet the need for this type of instrument.

THE APS PLAY TASK

The Affect in Play Scale consists of a standardized play task and a criterion-based rating scale. The APS is appropriate for children from 6 to 10 years of age, which includes children in Grades 1 through 3. The complete instructions and criteria for scoring can be found in the Appendix.

The play task consists of two human puppets, one boy and one girl, and three small blocks that are laid out on a table. The puppets have neutral facial expressions. The blocks are brightly colored and of different shapes. The play props and instructions are unstructured enough so that individual differences in play can emerge. The task is administered individually to the child, and the play is videotaped. The instructions for the task are:

> I'm here to learn about how children play. I have here two puppets and would like you to play with them any way you like for five minutes. For example, you can have the puppets do something together. I also have some blocks that you can use. Be sure to have the puppets talk out loud. The video camera will be on so that I can remember what you say and do. I'll tell you when to stop.

The child is informed when there is 1 minute left. If the child stops playing during the 5-minute period, the prompt, "You still have time left, keep going" is given. The task is discontinued if the child cannot play after a 2-minute period.

These instructions are free-play instructions that leave much room for the child to structure the play and present themes and affects that are habitual to him or her. Although the instruction "For example, you could have the puppets do something together" does provide structure, we found that some structure was necessary for many children to be able to carry out the task. These instructions can be altered to elicit different types of affect. For example, to pull for aggression, the instructions would be "Play with them and have the puppets disagree about something," rather than "Play with them anyway you like." The play task described here is appropriate for Grades 1–3 (6–10 years of age). In our experience, many kindergarten children have difficulty with the puppet task. However, the rating criteria could be used in a natural play observation situation for very young children. An adaptation of the APS for young children is discussed later in this chapter.

THE APS RATING SCALE

The Affect in Play Scale measures the amount and types of affective expression in children's fantasy play. The APS measures affect themes in the play narrative. Both emotion-laden content and expression of emotion in the play are coded. The APS also measures cognitive dimensions of the play, such as quality of fantasy and imagination.

Both Holt's (1977) Scoring System for Primary Process on the Rorschach and J. Singer's (1973) play scales were used as models for the development of the Affect in Play Scale. In addition, the work of Izard (1977) and Tomkins (1962, 1963) was consulted to ensure that the affect categories were comprehensive and covered all major types of emotion expressed by children in the 4–10 age group.

There are three major affect scores for the APS:

1. Total frequency of units of affective expression: A unit is defined as one scorable expression by an individual puppet. In a two-puppet dialogue, expressions of each puppet are scored separately. A unit can be the expression of an affect state, an affect theme, or a combination of the two. An example of an affect state would be "This is fun." An example of an affect theme would be "Here is a bomb that is going to explode." The expression can be verbal ("I hate you") or non-verbal (one puppet punching the other). The frequency of affect score is the total number of units of affect expressed in the 5-minute period.

2. Variety of affect categories: There are 11 possible affective categories. The categories are: Happiness/Pleasure; Anxiety/Fear; Sadness/Hurt; Frustration/Disappointment; Nurturance/Affection; Aggression; Oral; Oral Aggression; Anal; Sexual; Competition. The variety of affect score is the number of different categories of affect expressed in the 5-minute period. These 11 affect categories can be divided into subsets of positive (happiness, nurturance, oral, sexual, competition) and negative (anxiety, sadness, frustration, aggression, oral aggression, anal) affect. Also, primary process affect themes can be scored (aggression, oral, oral aggression, anal, sexual, competition). Primary process content includes affect-laden oral, aggressive, and libidinal content around which children experience early intense feeling states. It is a subtype of affect in cognition that is based on psychoanalytic theory (Russ, 1987, 1996).

3. Mean intensity of affective expression (1–5 rating): This rating measures the intensity of the feeling state or content theme. Each unit of affect is rated for intensity on a 1–5 scale.

Quality of fantasy and imagination is also scored. Although other scales (J. Singer, 1973) already tapped this dimension, it was important to include this aspect of pretend play in the scoring system, so that the APS would be comprehensive in its assessment of fantasy play. The fantasy scores are:

- *Organization* (1–5 global rating): This score measures the organization of the play, and considers the quality of the plot and complexity of the story.
- *Elaboration* (1–5 global rating): This score measures the amount of embellishment in the play.
- *Imagination* (1–5 global rating): This score measures the novelty and uniqueness of the play and the ability to pretend.
- *Quality of fantasy:* This score is the mean of the previous three fantasy scores.

In addition, comfort in play is rated on a 1-5 scale. Comfort includes the involvement of the child in the play and his/her enjoyment of the play. Finally, an affect integration score is obtained by multiplying the quality of fantasy score by the frequency of affect score. The affect integration score is needed because it attempts to measure the construct of cognitive modulation of emotion. It taps how well the affect is integrated and controlled by cognitive processes.

To summarize, the nine major scores on the APS are total frequency of affect, variety of affect categories, mean intensity of affect, organization of fantasy, elaboration of fantasy, imagination, overall quality of fantasy, comfort, and affect integration.

The APS measures most of the cognitive and affective processes outlined in chapter 1. The organization and elaboration scores assess organization/story-telling; the imagination score measures divergent thinking, fantasy, and symbolism; frequency of affect score measures expression of affect states and affect themes; variety of affect score measures range of affect; and comfort score measures enjoyment of and involvement in the play task. The affective integration score (a statistical combination of affect and fantasy scores) is an attempt to measure cognitive integration. A separate scale, either rating each unit of emotion on effectiveness of cognitive integration or a global rating of the play sample, is needed. The same is true of a measure of emotion regulation. Russ and Dasari are in the process of developing these scales.

Practically, the APS is easy to administer and takes only 5 minutes. The props, human puppets and blocks, are simple. The scoring system takes time to learn, but then takes about 15–20 minutes per child to accomplish. Although the APS has not been used with clinical populations, we do have a number of studies with means for non-clinical populations. Usually, the mean frequency of affect expression is 11–13 units, with a mean variety of categories of 3–4 (see Table 5.1).

TABLE 5.1

Means and Standard Deviations for the Affect in Play Scale Across Studies

	Study 1a (Russ & Grossman-McKee, 1990)		Study 2b (Grossman-McKee, 1989)		Study 3c (Russ & Peterson, 1990)	
	M	SD	M	SD	M	SD
Frequency of affect	24.7	23.61	13.01	21.40	10.99	10.33
# Categories of affect	4.8	3.07			2.97	2.02
Comfort	2.4	1.6	2.33	1.50	2.96	1.3
Quality of fantasy	2.0	1.3	2.27	.93	2.7	1.29
Imagination	2.03	1.3	1.90	1.1	2.59	1.3

[a] 10-minute play period.
[b] 5-minute play period: boys only.
[c] 5-minute play period.

The scoring manual for the APS is presented in the Appendix. This manual is basically the same as the 1993 version, but it has been refined in several ways. There are now more specifications about how to prompt during the administration of the task. There are more examples for coding the different content categories. Also, the imagination criteria have been revised. The repetition scale has been eliminated.

EXAMPLES OF AFFECT IN PLAY SCALE DIALOGUE

In order to give a sense of the play, excerpts from the first 90 seconds (approximately) of play dialogue for three children are presented here. All of these children are girls in the first or second grade. All express some affect in their play, but there are major differences in the amount of affect expressed. The dialogue is always between the puppets. On the videotapes, we can code the nonverbal expressions and affect tone of the verbal expression. The verbal transcripts presented here cannot fully reflect all of the play dimensions, but do give a sense of how these children differ in affective expression. The type of affect scored is given after each unit of expression. The following excerpts are from Russ, 1993.

Play Transcripts—Puppet Dialogue

Child #1: High Affect/High Quality of Fantasy	*Type of Affect*
"Let's build a tall building. I'll put this top on." (build with blocks)	
"No, I want to."	Aggression
"No, I am."	Aggression
"Hey, I said I was—give me those." (tussle)	Aggression
"I want to."	Aggression
"No, I do." (knock it down)	Aggression
"Oh, no. We'll have to start all over thanks to you."	Frustration/ Disappointment
"It wasn't my fault, it was your fault." (a block fell)	Aggression
"Oh, I better go get that block—it fell down the stairs."	Frustration/ Disappointment
"Now you have to put that on top or I'll tell mom."	Aggression
"Ah—what did I do?"	Anxiety/Fear
"Be my sister."	Nurturance/ Affection
"OK, but we will both build a building—I put two on and you put on one since you get to put on the top."	
"Fair enough."	
"Uh oh." (blocks fell)	Frustration/ Disappointment
"I'll straighten this out."	
"We built a tall building." (with glee)	Happiness/Pleasure
"What should we do now?"	
"I don't know."	
"Let's build a playground."	
"The playground is boring." (with feeling)	Frustration/ Disappointment
"No, it isn't. There are lots of fun things to do there."	Happiness/Pleasure
"I always hit my hand and get scratches and scrapes."	Sadness/Hurt
"Well maybe if you were more careful, that wouldn't happen."	Aggression

Child #2: Moderate Affect/High Quality Fantasy   Type of Affect

"Oh, boo, hoo; boo, hoo. I don't have anyone to play with.   Sadness/Hurt
Boo, hoo. I'll just play with my blocks and maybe that will
make me feel better." (building)

"I'll stack this there and this here and stack this
there—that's about as tall as me."

"Um—that makes me feel better—I'm happy—ha, ha, ha."   Happiness/Pleasure

"Maybe I'll go to my friend Sally's house." (knock)   Nurturance/Affection

"Who is it?"

"It's Rebecca, remember, your friend."
                                                              Nurturance/Affection

"Hi Rebecca, come in."

"Hi Sally. I wanted to know if I can play with you."

"Ok—you can play with me—anytime you want, if I'm   Nurturance/Affection
home." (laugh) "Do you want to go to the playground?"

"Oh sure, Sally, but I don't know how to get there."   Anxiety/Fear

"Oh Rebecca" (with feeling) "I do, you can just follow me.   Nurturance/Affection
We'll play and jump rope ok?"

"OK Sally."

"Here is the playground—I think or this might be a
school."

"Oh what—what day is it—it's Saturday, so we don't have
school—Here's the playground."

"Oh remember, we were going to play Miss Lucy."

"Yes—ready." (play and sing)

Child #3. Lower Affect/Lower Quality of Fantasy Type of Affect

"Hello little girls. Want to play with these blocks?"

"OK- let's build something."

"OK." (build)

"Uh, oh." (Blocks fell over)   Frustration/
                                                              Disappointment

"We'll build it again." (build)

"There."

"Let's make a picnic table.

"There."

"Now let's play—let's build a tunnel."

"OK."

"Let's go under the tunnel."

"Let's build some monkey bars."

"Let's play house—I'll be the mother." (Much of the time was spent building—no verbalization.)

Child #1 had 17 units of affective expression, Child #2 had 7, and Child #3 had 1 in these 90-second periods. The intensity of each affective expression is also scored and is based on the expression of content themes and actual feeling states. Non-verbal expression (punching, patting) is an important component of the intensity rating as is the amount of emotion in the tone of expression.

EMPIRICAL STUDIES

Once the Affect in Play Scale was constructed, pilot studies were carried out to ensure that the task was appropriate for young children and would result in adequate individual differences among normal school populations (Russ, Grossman-McKee, & Rutkin, 1984). By 1984, the basics of the task and scoring system were in place. Early studies resulted in refinement of the scoring criteria and a shortening of the play period (from 10 minutes to 5 minutes). The next step was to develop reliability and build construct validity for the scale. To date, a substantial number of validity studies have been carried out with different populations and different examiners (see Table 5.2).

Reliability

Interrater reliabilities in all of the studies have been consistently good. Because a detailed scoring manual was developed, and raters were carefully trained, interrater reliabilities using a number of different raters have usually been in the .80s and .90s, with some in the .70s. For example, in a study by Russ and Grossman-McKee (1990), based on 15 randomly chosen subjects, Pearson -r correlation coefficients were as follows: total frequency of affect, $r = .90$; variety of categories, $r = .82$; intensity of affect, $r = .53$; mean quality of fantasy, $r = .88$; imagination, $r = .74$; and comfort, $r = .89$. With the exception of intensity of affect, which was therefore not included in the analysis, all of the interrater reliabilities were judged to be good.

TABLE 5.2
Validity Studies of Affect in Play Scale

Authors	Date	Variables Investigated
Grossman-McKee	1989	Pain complaints
Peterson	1989	Self-esteem
Russ & Grossman-McKee	1990	Divergent thinking; primary process
Russ & Peterson	1990	Divergent thinking; coping in school
D'Angelo	1995	Adjustment; imagination
Niec & Russ	1996	Interpersonal themes in story-telling and interpersonal functioning
Christiano & Russ	1996	Coping and distress in dental visit
Russ, Robins, & Christiano	1999	Longitudinal prediction of creativity, coping, and older version of play task
Niec & Russ	2002	Internal representations and empathy
Seja & Russ	1998	Parents' reports of daily emotional expression
Seja & Russ	1999a	Emotional understanding
Perry & Russ	1998	Coping and adjustment in homeless children
Kaugars & Russ	2000	Creativity in preschoolers
Russ & Cooperberg	2002	Longitudinal prediction of creativity, coping, and depression
Goldstein & Russ	2000–2001	Coping
Goldstein	2002	Imagination and anxiety
Russ & Schafer	2002	Divergent thinking and emotion in memories

In a study by Christiano and Russ (1996), interrater reliabilities for 20 participants were: total frequency of affect, $r = .91$; variety of affect, $r = .90$; quality of fantasy, $r = .85$; and comfort, $r = .90$. In a recent study by Seja and Russ (1999a), correlations were: frequency of affect, $r = .83$; quality of fantasy, $r = .80$; organization, $r = .72$; elaboration, $r = .74$; and imagination, $r = .78$.

In two studies, we have investigated the internal consistency of the APS and found it to be good. We compared the second and fourth minutes with the third and fifth minutes of the play period for frequency of affect. In both studies we found, using the Spearman-Brown split-half reliability formula, good internal consistency of $r = .85$ for frequency of affect (Russ & Peterson, 1990; Seja & Russ, 1999a).

Test–retest reliability for the APS needs to be determined. We are in the process of analyzing data for 50 children who were administered the task a second time after a 2–4 week interval.

Validity Studies

The development of construct validity for the APS has been carried out by investigating the relationships between the scores on the APS and criteria that should be related to the constructs of fantasy and affect in fantasy (Anastasi, 1988). By finding relationships between a measure and theoretically relevant criteria, conceptual validity is developed (Weiner, 1977). For the APS, validity studies have been carried out with four major types of theoretically relevant criteria: creativity; coping and adjustment; emotional understanding; and interpersonal functioning (see Table 5.2). Each area is briefly reviewed below. Although some of this theoretical material and some of the studies have already been reviewed in chapter 1, the focus here is on the validity of the APS. A few of the studies are reviewed in more detail in this chapter.

APS and Creativity

One of the most robust findings in the literature is the relationship between pretend play and creativity. Russ (1993, 1999) postulated that pretend play is important in developing creativity because so many of the cognitive and affective processes involved in creativity occur in play. Russ's (1993) model of affect and creativity identified the major cognitive and affective processes involved in creativity, and the relationships among them, based on the research literature.

Divergent thinking is one major cognitive process important in creativity and was a focus of several validity studies with the APS. As defined by Guilford (1968), divergent thinking is thinking that generates a variety of ideas and associations to a problem. Divergent thinking involves free association, broad scanning ability, and fluidity of thinking. It has been found to be relatively independent of intelligence (Runco, 1991).

Two affective processes important in creativity are access to affect-laden thoughts and the ability to experience affect states (Russ, 1993). Both the ability to think about affect-laden fantasy and the capacity to experience emotion are important in creativity. In play, children express affect in fantasy and experience emotion. For example, Fein (1987) concluded that play facilitated the development of an affective symbol system important in creativity. Waelder (1933) viewed play as a place in which primary process thinking can occur. Morrison (1988) conceptualized play as an arena in which children reconstruct past experiences and rework old metaphors.

Pretend play should facilitate the development of divergent thinking for several reasons. The expression of emotion and affect-laden fantasy in play could help develop a broad repertoire of affect-laden associations (Russ, 1993, 1996). This broad repertoire of associations and use of emotion to access these associations should facilitate divergent thinking because the involvement of emotion broadens the search process for associations (Isen et al., 1987). Play should also facilitate divergent thinking because in play children practice divergent thinking skills by using toys and objects to represent different things and by role-playing different scenarios (D. Singer & J. Singer, 1990).

A growing body of research has found a relationship between play and creativity. Most of the research has been correlational in nature and has focused on cognitive processes. A substantial body of studies have found a relationship between play and divergent thinking (Clark, Griffing, & Johnson, 1989; Johnson, 1976; Pepler & Ross, 1981; Singer & Rummo, 1973). In addition, in experimental studies, play has been found to facilitate divergent thinking (Dansky, 1980; Dansky & Silverman, 1973; Feitelson & Ross, 1973; Hughes, 1987) and insight (Vandenberg, 1980). Flexibility in problem solving has also been related to play (Pellegrini, 1992).

A few studies have found a relationship between affective processes in play and creativity. Lieberman (1977) found a relationship between playfulness, which included affective components of spontaneity and joy, and divergent thinking in kindergarten children. Christie and Johnson (1983) also concluded that there was a relationship between playfulness and creativity. D. Singer and J. Singer (1981) found that preschoolers rated as high-imagination players showed significantly more themes of danger and power than children with low imagination.

In the first study with the APS, we were particularly interested in the relationship between the affect scores and creativity. Russ and Grossman-McKee (1990) investigated the relationships among the Affect in Play Scale, primary process thinking on the Rorschach, and divergent thinking in first- and second-grade children. Sixty children individually received the Rorschach, Affect in Play Scale, and Alternate Uses Test. A typical item on the Alternate Uses Test is "How many uses for a newspaper can you think of?" Holt's (1977) Scoring System was the measure for the Rorschach. Primary process thinking was included in the study because it is affect-laden ideation that has been found to be related to a number of creativity criteria

(Russ, 1996; Suler, 1980). The version of the APS used in this study was different than the current version in that the play sessions were 10 minutes in length (rather than 5) and the play was audiotaped, not videotaped, with careful notetaking by the examiner as the play occurred.

A major finding of this study was that affective expression in play was predictive of divergent thinking. The predicted relationships between the play scores and the Alternate Uses test were all significant for that total sample, except for the relationship between frequency of nonprimary process affect and divergent thinking. Divergent thinking was significantly related to frequency of affect [$r(58) = .42, p < .001$], variety of affect categories [$r(58) = .38, p < .001$], comfort [$r(58) = .23, p < .051$], frequency of primary process affect [$r(58) = .41, p < .001$], quality of fantasy [$r(58) = .30, p < .01$], imagination [$r(58) = .35, p < .01$], and integration of affect [$r(58) = .42, p < .001$]. All correlations remained significant when IQ was partialed out, due to the fact that IQ had such low relationships with the play scores (e.g., $r = .09$ with frequency of affect, $r = .01$ with comfort, $r = .08$ with quality, and $r = .12$ with imagination). The fact that intelligence did not relate to any of the play measures is theoretically consistent with the model for the development of the scale and is similar to the results of J. Singer (1973). There were no gender differences in the pattern of correlations.

Also, as predicted, amount of primary process thinking on the Rorschach was significantly positively related to the amount of affect in play. Total frequency of primary process on the Rorschach was significantly positively related to the following play measures: frequency of affect [$r(44) = .34, p < .01$]; variety of affective categories [$r(44) = .44, p < .001$]; frequency of primary process affect [$r(44) = .30, p < .05$]; frequency of non-primary process affect [$r(44) = .26, p < .05$]; comfort [$r(44) = .45, p < .001$] quality of fantasy [$r(44) = .48, p < .001$]; imagination [$r(44) = .47, p < .01$] and the composite integration of affect score [$r(44) = .37, p < .01$]. Percentage of primary process, which controls for general productivity, was also significantly related to most of the play variables, although the correlations were lower than those with total frequency. Percentage of Primary Process was significantly related to frequency of affect [$r(44) = .32, p < .05$]; variety of affective categories [$r(44) = .28, p < .05$]; frequency of primary process [$r(44) = .28, p < .05$]; frequency of nonprimary process [$r(44) = .25, p < .05$]; quality of fantasy [$r(44) = .27, p < .05$]; imagination [$r(44) = .30, p < .05$], and integration of affect [$r(44) = .32, p < .05$].

Primary process thinking on the Rorschach was equally predictive for girls and for boys in the play situation. The relationships between the variables were not affected when intelligence was controlled for. The finding in this study, that primary process expression on the Rorschach was significantly related to affective expression in children's play, is important because it shows that there is some consistency in the construct of affective expression across two different types of situations.

A study by Russ and Peterson (1990) investigated the relationships among the Affect in Play Scale, divergent thinking, and coping in school in first- and second-grade children. The main purpose of this study was to obtain a large enough sample size (121 children) so that a sound factor analysis of the play scale could be carried out for the total sample and separately for boys and girls. A second purpose was to replicate the results of the Russ and Grossman-McKee (1990) study that found a positive relationship between affective expression in play and divergent thinking.

One hundred twenty-one children (64 boys and 57 girls) were individually administered the Affect in Play Scale and a Coping in School scale. In a separate testing session, with a different examiner, they were administered the Alternate Uses Test. The Affect in Play Scale used in this study and subsequent studies was the current version of the scale. The play period was 5 minutes instead of 10 minutes. A video camera was used rather than a tape recorder. Also, some of the affect categories were condensed, because of infrequent occurrence. Displeasure and frustration became one category and sadness and hurt became another category. A new category, competition, was added because of its prevalence in children's play and because it is considered to be a derivative of aggressive content in Holt's system. Finally, there were some minor adjustments in the intensity rating criteria.

The main finding in this study was that the Affect in Play Scale was significantly positively related to divergent thinking. These results replicated the findings of the Russ and Grossman-McKee (1990) study with children of the same age. As in the previous study, there were no gender differences in the pattern of correlations. For the total sample, divergent thinking was significantly related to frequency of total affect [$r(115) = .26$, $p < .01$]; variety of affect [$r(115) = .25$, $p < .01$]; comfort [$r(115) = .37$, $p < .001$]; quality of fantasy, [$r(115) = .43$, $p < .001$]; imagination [$r(115) = .42$, $p < .001$]; primary process [$r(115) = .17$, $p < .05$]; non-primary process [$r(115) = .24$, $p < .01$]; and integration of affect [$r(115) = .30$, $p < .001$]. These relationships remained significant when IQ was partialed out. Based on this study, we can say with more confidence that affective expression in fantasy relates to divergent thinking, independent of the cognitive processes measured by intelligence tests.

It is important to note that in both the Russ and Grossman-McKee (1990) study and the Russ and Peterson (1990) study, the significant relationship between play and divergent thinking occurred in studies where the play task and the divergent thinking task were administered by different examiners. Given Smith and Whitney's (1987) criticism that previous positive results that linked play and associative fluency were due to experimenter effects, these are important findings.

In a recent study with 47 first- and second-grade children, Russ and Schafer (2002) found hypothesized significant relationships between frequency of affect and variety of affect and divergent thinking. In this study we used three emotion-laden objects and three non-emotion-laden objects for the Alternate Uses task. Frequency of affect related to total uses for emotion-laden objects $r = .25$, ($p < .05$), and to originality of response for emotion-laden $r = .32$ ($p < .05$) and non emotion-laden $r = .57$ ($p < .01$) objects. The relationship between variety of affect and divergent thinking followed a similar pattern. Most of these correlations did not remain significant when IQ was partialed out (with the exception of originality of response for non emotion-laden objects and affect).

IQ was related to the APS in this sample, an unusual occurrence in the play studies. So for this sample, play related to creativity, but usually not independent of intelligence.

Play also related to divergent thinking in a preschool sample of children, to be discussed late in this chapter (Kaugars & Russ, 2000). The affect scores especially were related to creativity and to teachers' ratings of make-believe.

Using a different kind of imagination criterion, Goldstein (2002) found significant relationships between play and Singer's imaginative predisposition interview (IPPI). Children with more fantasy and affect in play scored higher on this interview, which assessed preference for imaginative activities (frequency of affect and IPPI $r = .42$ [$p < .001$]; variety of affect and IPPI $r = .35$ [$p < .001$)]; fantasy and IPPI, $r = .27$ [$p < .05$].

APS, Coping, and Adjustment

Theoretically, play ability should be related to coping ability and to broader measures of adjustment. This link should occur for several reasons. First, children use play to solve real-life problems and to resolve internal conflicts (Erikson, 1963; Freud, 1965). Children play out their problems in pretend play, express negative emotions in a controllable way, and practice with different behaviors. Second, the creative problem solving skills developed in play should generalize to problem solving skills in daily life. Creative problem solvers should be better copers because they bring their problem solving skills to everyday problems. The ability to generate a variety of associations and alternative solutions should facilitate coping with daily stressors. There is some empirical support for this concept. Russ (1988) found a relationship between divergent thinking and teacher's ratings of coping in fifth-grade boys. Similarly, Carson et al. (1994) found a significant relationship between figural divergent thinking and teacher's ratings of coping.

Looking specifically at play on the APS and coping ability, Christiano and Russ (1996) found a positive relationship between play and coping and a negative relationship between play and distress in 7- to 9-year-olds. Children who were "good" players on the Affect in Play Scale implemented a greater number and variety of cognitive coping strategies (corre-lations ranging from .52 to .55) during an invasive dental procedure. In addition, good players reported less distress during the procedure than children who expressed less affect and fantasy in play. Also, the Russ and Peterson study (1990) found a relationship between fantasy in play, self-report coping, and teachers' ratings of coping.

Consistent with these findings, a recent study by Perry and Russ (1998) found that fantasy in play on the APS was positively related to frequency and variety of self-reported coping strategies on the Schoolagers Coping Strategies Semi-Structured Interview (Ryan, 1989) in a group of homeless children. This sample of homeless children was primarily African Ameri-can (77%). Because videotaping was not permitted in the shelter, the play was transcribed as it occurred. In this sample, 61 children living in home-less shelters were administered the APS, Schoolager's Coping Strategies Inventory (Ryan, 1989), and adjustment measures. The coping measure was self-report. Quality of fantasy in play significantly positively corre-lated with the frequency of coping responses $r = .42, p < .01$) and with the variety of coping responses $r = .35, p < .01$). These relationships were inde-pendent of age and achievement. Thus, children who had good fantasy skills were able to report a greater number and variety of coping strategies to use when confronted with stressful events.

In a study with first-grade children, Goldstein and Russ (2000–2001) found a significant positive relationship between the imagination score on the APS and children's self-reports of how they would cope with a specific situation. The imagination score related to total frequency of coping re-sponses ($r = .43, p < .001$) and total variety of strategies ($r = .40, p < .001$). These relationships remained significant when IQ was controlled for. In a multiple regression analysis, the APS score accounted for 37% of the vari-ance in the total number of coping attempts and 29% of the variance in types of strategies used after controlling for IQ.

These coping studies used different samples of children, different ex-aminers, and different measures of coping. In these different studies, vari-ous scores on the APS were related to coping ability.

The APS has also been related to more global measures of children's ad-justment. Grossman-McKee (1989), using the Affect in Play Scale with first- and second-grade boys, found that boys who expressed more affect in play had fewer pain complaints than boys with less affect in play. Good players were also less anxious on the State-Trait Anxiety Inventory for Children (Spielberger, 1973). The conclusion from this study was that the ability to express affect in play was associated with less anxiety and less psychosomatic complaints.

Peterson (1989) in a 1-year follow-up on a subsample of 50 of the origi-nal 121 children in the Russ and Peterson study, found that the APS pre-dicted self-esteem on the Self-Perception Profile for Children (Harter,

1985). Also, D'Angelo (1995) found, in a group of inner-city first- and second-grade children, that ego-resilient children had higher APS scores than less resilient children. Also, internalizing children on the Child Behavior Checklist (Edelbrock & Achenbach, 1980) had significantly lower fantasy and affect scores in play than did externalizing and ego-resilient children. Externalizing children had significantly lower fantasy scores (but not affect) than did ego-resilient children.

In the Perry and Russ (1998) study with homeless children, the APS was significantly related to depression in children, but not to anxiety. That is, better players had lower scores on the Children's Depression Inventory.

Goldstein (2002) found, similar to the Grossman-McKee (1989) finding, that good players were less anxious on the state anxiety component of the State-Trait Anxiety Inventory for children ($r = .23$ $p < .05$).

Longitudinal Prediction of the APS

A study by Russ et al. (1999) followed-up the first and second graders in the Russ and Peterson (1990) study which investigated the APS, divergent-thinking, and coping. The children were now in the fifth and sixth grades. Thirty-one of the original 121 children participated. This was a longitudinal study that explored the ability of the APS to predict creativity and coping over a 4-year period. The Alternate Uses Test was the measure of divergent thinking and a self-report School Coping Scale was the measure of coping. In addition, a version of the APS for older children was administered. The same basic task was administered, but the children were instructed to put on a play. In essence, the puppet play task became a story-telling task in the form of a play. The stories were scored with the same criteria as for the APS.

As predicted, quality of fantasy and imagination in early play predicted divergent thinking over time, independent of IQ (see Table 5.3). Variety of affect categories and comfort showed low positive correlations with divergent thinking, but did not reach significance. The APS also significantly predicted coping over time. The fantasy scores predicted the number of different responses generated on the coping measures.

In addition, the APS was predictive of the version of the scale for older children. Most of the APS scores were significantly related to the comparable score on the modified play task (see Table 5.4). The magnitude of the correlations is quite good for longitudinal data. The strongest correlations were for the affect scores: $r = .51$ ($p < .01$) for positive affect; $r = .38$ ($p < .05$) for variety of affect; and $r = .33$ ($p < .05$) for total frequency of affect expressed. These findings suggest that the cognitive and affective processes measured by the APS are stable over time and are important processes in divergent thinking.

TABLE 5.3

Longitudinal Pearson Correlations of Play Scale Variables
at First and Second Grade With Divergent Thinking
and Coping Measures at Fifth and Sixth Grade

Affect in Play Scale	Divergent Thinking		Coping	
	Fluency	Spontaneous Flexibility	Frequency	Quality
Frequency of Affect	.13	.11	.02	−.03
Variety of Affect	.25	.20	.26	.23
Comfort	.24	.17	.20	.22
Mean Quality	.34*	.25	.34*	.33*
Organization	.27	.16	.34*	.28
Imagination	.42**	>.35*	.42**	.45**

Note. $N = 30$. *$p < .05$. **$p < .01$.

Although the APS also predicted coping over time, this finding should be interpreted with caution because the coping measure is a new measure and has not been related to other measures of coping behavior. Also, it is a self-report measure not yet related to behavioral measures of coping. It measures how many different things the child can think of to do when real-life problems occur.

A study by Russ and Cooperberg (2002) followed these children into high school. We were able to recruit 49 of the original 121 children, who were now in the eleventh and twelfth grades. We administered in small groups the adult version of the Alternate Uses test, two self-report coping measure (Ways of Coping–Revised; Adolescent Coping Orientation for Problem Experiences), and the Beck Depression Inventory. The results were that quality of fantasy in early play was significantly related to high school divergent thinking $r = .28$, ($p < .05$), and problem-focused coping on the ACOPE $r = .34$, ($p < .01$). Variety of affect also related to problem-focused coping $r = .24$, ($p < .05$). These relationships remained relatively unchanged when IQ was partialed out. These results support the stability of these play processes over time in that they relate to theoretically relevant criteria over a 10-year period. They also support the validity of the APS in measuring important processes in play.

One noteworthy finding in this study was that the frequency of negative affect in play significantly related to depression on the Beck Depression Inventory $r = .31$, ($p < .05$). Children who had more negative affect in their early play had more symptoms of depression 10 years later. It is important to note that in this population, the mean on the Beck was 6.98. The relationship between negative affect in play and depression could be indicative of a tendency to feel mildly dysphoric rather than show symptoms of clinical depression. Nevertheless, these results suggest that play processes that can be adaptive in one area (creativity) can be maladaptive in another.

Factor Analysis of the APS

An important theoretical question is whether affect in fantasy and the cognitive components in fantasy are separate processes or are one process. The theoretical assumption underlying the play scale was that at least two separate processes are involved—one cognitive and one affective. On the other hand, it is possible that affect and fantasy are so intertwined in play that they cannot be measured separately. In the development of the scale, care was taken to make the scoring criteria of the affect scores separate

TABLE 5.4

Longitudinal Pearson Correlations of Affect in Play Scale Variables at First and Second Grade With Similar Variables of the Modified Affect in Fantasy Task at Sixth and Seventh Grade

Affect in Play Scale *(First and Second Grade)*	*Affect in Fantasy Task* *(Sixth and Seventh Grade)*
	r
Frequency of Affect	.33*
Positive Affect	.51**
Negative Affect	.21
Variety of Affect	.38*
Comfort	.29
Mean Quality of Fantasy	.27
Organization	.31*
Elaboration	.32*
Imagination	.08
Repetition	.08
Affective Integration	.40*

Note. $N = 30$. *$p < .05$. **$p < .01$.

from the cognitive dimensions. For example, the intensity rating of an aggressive expression should not be influenced by the amount of imagination in the play; the scoring of affective expressions themselves should be independent of the quality of the fantasy. Also, the scoring of imagination should not be influenced by the amount of affect in the response. Thus, if only one underlying dimension were identified in a factor analysis, it would probably not be due to an artifact of the scoring system.

Factor analyses have been carried out with three separate samples of the APS with different examiners. All three studies had a large enough sample for a solid factor analysis to be carried out. In all three studies, two separate factors were found to be the best model. These two factors appear to be a cognitive factor and an affect factor.

Looking first at the Russ and Peterson (1990) data set of 121 children, a factor analysis of the total sample was carried out using the principal component analysis with oblique rotation (see Table 5.5). Seven major scores for the Affect in Play Scale were included in the factor analysis.

(Scores that involved statistical combinations of scores were not included in this particular factor analysis.) An oblique solution, using the method default (Cattell & Jaspers, 1967) yielded two separate factors as the best solution. The first and dominant factor appears to be a cognitive factor. Imagination, organization, quality of fantasy, and comfort in play significantly loaded on this first factor. The second factor appears to be an affective factor. Frequency of affective expression, variety of affect categories, and intensity of affect loaded on this second factor. Although separate factors, there is a significant amount of shared variance ($r = .76$), suggesting that the factors also overlap.

TABLE 5.5

Oblique Factor Structure of The Affect in Play Scale for Total Sample

Play Scores	Cognitive	Affective
Frequency of Affect	−.27	.79
Variety of Affect	−.00	.60
Mean Intensity	.12	.40
Comfort	.55	.06
Quality of Fantasy	.62	.04
Organization	.69	−.09
Imagination	.65	−.08

Note. N = 121.

TABLE 5.6

Oblique Factor Structure of the Affect in Play Scale
With Primary Process Affect for Total Sample

| Play score | Cognitive | Affect | |
		Primary Process	Nonprimary Process
Frequency of primary process	−.06	.92	−.09
Frequency of nonprimary process	−.01	−.10	.87
Variety of affect	.16	.39	.48
Mean intensity	.32	.37	.13
Comfort	.67	.06	.11
Quality of fantasy	.75	.06	.10
Organization	.81	.00	−.03
Imagination	.75	−.01	.00

Note. N = 121.

When factor analyses were carried out separately for girls and boys, similar factor structures emerged. For boys, the factor structure replicated that of the total sample. For girls, the only difference from the total sample was that intensity of affect loaded on the cognitive factor.

The important finding here is that affective expression and cognitive expression in fantasy play, though related, also have significant amounts of unique variance, which suggests that there are separate processes involved. Similar two-factor structures were found for the D'Angelo (1995) study with 95 children and the Niec (1998) study with 86 children.

In addition, two principal- component analyses using the affect scores with an oblique solution were performed to examine the affect dimension. When the primary process and nonprimary process scores were used in place of the frequency of affect score, three factors were found. The first was a cognitive factor, the second was primary process affect, and the third was nonprimary process affect (Table 5.6). The second factor analysis, using the positive- and negative-affect scores, also revealed three factors: a cognitive factor, positive affect, and negative affect (Table 5.7). These results suggest that the hypothesized constructs have some conceptual validity.

Separate factor analysis using the oblique solution was then performed on the 11 affect content categories and five different factors were found in the play (Table 5.8). The factors make sense theoretically. On the first factor, oral content and nurturance/affection combined. The second factor was composed of negative-affect themes of aggression, anxiety, sadness, and frustration. The third factor comprised happiness themes, with a low aggression loading. The fourth factor was low competition and high anxiety. The fifth factor was an association of sexual and anal content, which is understandable in that they are both unusual content themes in the play of young children. In this factor analysis of content categories, content clustered according to positive- and negative-affect themes, not primary process and non-primary process themes.

The factor structure of the APS suggests that researchers need to go beyond differentiating between positive- and negative-affect or primary-process and non-primary-process themes. There may be specific clusters of affect content categories that go together in play developmentally, are involved in different ways in the creative process, and work differently for girls than for boys. Different dimensions of positive and negative affect could differentially effect different types of cognitive processes (divergent thinking, metaphor construction, etc.). Also, this research on affect themes is looking at a different dimension of affect than is the research on mood

TABLE 5.7

Oblique Factor Structure of the Affect in Play Scale With Positive and Negative Affect for Total Sample

		Affect	
Play score	Cognitive	Negative	Positive
Frequency of positive affect	−.02	−.12	.84
Frequency of negative affect	−.07	.93	−.07
Variety of affect	.13	.42	.51
Mean intensity	.34	.41	.09
Comfort	.70	.15	.02
Quality of fantasy	.73	.05	.10
Organization	.76	−.09	.06
Imagination	.73	−.02	.00

Note. N = 121.

TABLE 5.8
Oblique Factor Structure of APS Content Categories
in the Affect in Play Scale

	Factor				
Category	1	2	3	4	5
Oral	.806	−.022	.008	.081	.142
Sexual	.024	−.044	.067	.061	.873
Competition	−.048	.349	.124	−.765	.165
Oral aggression	.841	.036	.015	−.042	−.003
Anal	.319	.073	−.12	−.185	.64
Aggression	.017	.548	−.649	.143	−.001
Happiness	.057	.136	.795	.063	−.024
Nurturance	.47	.195	.269	.392	.263
Anxiety	−.027	.463	.238	.536	.083
Sadness	−.025	.693	−.028	−.028	.02
Frustration	.08	.716	.05	−.226	−.048

states. For example, children differentiate how the puppets are feeling in the play from how they themselves are feeling (in an aggressive play condition in a recent experiment, 70% of the children reported feeling an affect state different from the puppets' state). As mentioned earlier, in play where the child is in charge of pacing the material, negative affect may not be so negative. Negative themes like aggression may not be accompanied by negative mood states.

APS and Emotional Understanding

Emotional understanding is the process by which people make inferences about their own and others' feelings and behaviors that in turn influence their thoughts and actions (Nannis, 1988). Theoretical and empirical evidence suggests that there may be two reasons for a relationship between children's play and emotional understanding. First, using imagination in play may relate to the cognitive ability to take the perspective of other people. Second, experiencing and expressing different emotions may be central to both fantasy play and emotional understanding.

The relationship between affect and cognitive processes in fantasy play and emotional understanding was examined in children in the first and second grades (Seja & Russ, 1999a). In this study, consistent, yet modest, relations were found between dimensions of fantasy play on the APS and emotional understanding as measured by the Kusche Affective Interview—Revised (Kusche, Greenberg, & Beilke, 1988). Cognitive dimensions of fantasy play, but not affect expression, were related to facets of emotional understanding. The children who were able to access and organize their fantasy and emotions in play were more likely to recall and organize memories related to emotional events and had a more sophisticated understanding of others' emotions. These relationships remained significant when verbal ability was partialed out. The relationship between fantasy play and understanding others' emotions supports Harris's (1989) proposition that imaginative understanding may enable children to understand others' mental states and affective experiences. A composite fantasy play score accounted for a significant amount of variance in a composite emotional understanding score (5%) when verbal ability was accounted for.

Contrary to initial hypotheses, frequency of affect expression was not related to emotional understanding of oneself and others. The results of this study have important implications for clinical work and suggest that the mere expression of emotion in play is not related to emotional understanding and may not be as useful as play therapists believe. Instead, the integration of affective and cognitive material may be more important in facilitating the development of emotional understanding.

Seja and Russ (1998) examined the relationships among parents' reports of children's daily behavior, children's affect and fantasy in play, and emotional understanding among first-grade children in the previous sample. Parents' ratings of children's daily emotional intensity was expected to relate to children's affect expression in play. Results were that children who demonstrated more positive emotion in their daily behavior were more likely to express more emotion overall and more negative emotion in their play than children who expressed less daily positive emotion. Furthermore, children who demonstrated more negative emotion in their daily behavior displayed fewer different types of emotion, less positive emotion, and less emotion overall in their play than children who expressed less daily negative emotion.

It was also hypothesized that parents' ratings of children's daily emotional intensity would relate to children's emotional understanding. It was found that children who expressed more intense positive emotion in their daily behavior had a better understanding of their own emotions and described more emotional experiences than children with less intense daily positive emotion. Contrary to initial hypotheses, children with more intense negative emotion in daily behavior did not have lower levels of emotional understanding. The results of this study suggest that parents' reports of children's daily behavior may provide important information to clinicians about children's play, emotional development, and adjustment. However, because the sample was small ($n = 23$), the study should be replicated with another sample of children.

APS and Interpersonal Functioning

Theories of development acknowledge that affect is linked to interpersonal functioning in multiple ways (Emde, 1989; Russ & Niec, 1993; Sroufe, 1989; Strayer, 1987). For example, affective sharing has been related to better quality of infant–parent attachment (Pederson & Moran, 1996; Waters, Wippman, & Sroufe, 1979); regulation of affect has been related to better peer relations and fewer behavior problems (Cole, Zahn-Waxler, Fox, Usher, & Welsh, 1996; Rubin et al., 1995); openness to affect has been described as providing meaning to interpersonal experience (Sandler & Sandler, 1978), and has also been conceptualized as a key component of empathy (Feshbach, 1987). Given these associations between dimensions of affect and interpersonal functioning, two studies were conducted to investigate the relationship of the Affect in Play Scale with children's interpersonal functioning.

Niec and Russ (1996) investigated relationships among affect and fantasy in play, expression of interpersonal themes in projective stories, and peer and teacher ratings of interpersonal functioning in 49 first- through third-graders. Access to affect in play was predicted to be positively associated with children's expression of interpersonal themes in stories and interpersonal functioning. This prediction was based on the proposition from object relations theory that a "defense against affect is a defense against objects" and leads to an inability to relate with others on anything but a superficial level (Modell, 1980, p. 266). Children with poor access to affect in play were thus expected to be more likely to have poor peer relationships, while children with good access to affect were expected to have good quality peer relationships.

Children were administered the APS, the Children's Apperceptive Story Telling Test (CAST), and a brief IQ measure (Schneider, 1989). Teachers and peers rated subjects on their likability, disruptiveness, and withdrawal using the Pupil Evaluation Inventory (PEI; Pekarik et al., 1976). Results found no relationship between the APS and interpersonal functioning. However, relationships were found between the APS and frequency of interpersonal themes on the CAST. Children who were better players in that they expressed a wide variety of affective categories, frequent positive affect, comfort in their play, and high quality fantasy, were more likely to project themes involving people and relationships in their stories.

In a study by Niec and Russ (2002), relationships among affect and fantasy in play, internal representations, and capacity for empathy were investigated. Eighty-six children in the third and fourth grades completed the APS, the TAT, and the Bryant Index of Empathy for Children (Bryant, 1982; Murray, 1971). Teachers completed ratings of empathy and helpfulness for each child. TAT stories were scored using Westen's (1995) Social Cognition and Object Relations Scale (SCORS-Q).

As predicted, quality of fantasy on the APS was related to self-reported empathy. The finding supported the importance of imaginative ability in children's empathic responding and is consistent with the previously discussed Seja and Russ finding (1999a). Children who were able to "put reality aside and imagine the feelings of someone else in a different (make-believe) situation" were likely to be self-described as more empathic to others (Harris, 1994, p. 19).

Access to affect in play did not relate to empathy, perhaps because the APS measures expression of affect-laden themes rather than the experience of emotion that is so important in empathic understanding.

Neither access to affect nor fantasy in play related to children's representations of relationships on the TAT. This finding helped to answer the question posed by Niec (1994) as to whether access to affect in play would be related to interpersonal representations when content rather than frequency is assessed. Although in the Niec and Russ (1996) study affect and fantasy in play were positively related to frequency of interpersonal themes in projective stories, Niec's (1998) finding suggests that access to affect may not be related to the qualitative aspects of those representations. It may be that access to affect relates to access to interpersonal representations (i.e., frequency) regardless of the content of those representations (i.e., quality).

The two studies have refined the understanding of the constructs of affect and fantasy as measured by the APS. As expected, access to affect has related to access to interpersonal representations (Niec & Russ, 1996), however, it has not related to peer-, teacher-, or self-reported measures of interpersonal functioning including such dimensions as empathy, helpfulness, likability, disruptiveness, and withdrawal (Niec & Russ, 1996, 2002). Quality of fantasy on the APS has been related to both access to interpersonal representations (Niec & Russ, 1996) and self-reported capacity for empathy (Niec & Russ, 2002). These findings and those of previous validity studies suggest that the APS may tap affective dimensions important in mental flexibility (e.g., creativity, role taking, problem solving), rather than the affective constructs that are important in communication and interpersonal behavior. This understanding is consistent with the theoretical conceptualization of the scale. Further studies that investigate both convergent and discriminant validity of the APS based on this conceptualization will enhance the usefulness of the scale.

PLAY AND EMOTIONAL MEMORIES

An important finding in the Russ and Schafer (2002) study with 47 first- and second-grade children was that APS scores were significantly positively related to the expression of emotion in memory narratives. We had hypothesized that children who could express affect and fantasy in play would be better able to express emotion and think about emotion in other situations. Children received the APS and were asked nine questions about past experiences. For example, "Tell me about a time when you felt mad." We used questions about positive, negative, and neutral experiences. The results were that variety of affect in play related to the amount of affect expressed in the memories ($r = .32$, $p < .05$) and quality of fantasy and imagination related to amount of affect in memories ($r = .46$, $p < .01$). These correlations remained significant after IQ and word count were partialed out. Children who were better players (greater variety of affect and better quality of fantasy and imagination) expressed more emotion when talking about memories. This finding is consistent with the Russ and Grossman-McKee (1990) finding that affect and fantasy in play related to the affect-laden primary process expression on the Rorschach in children. These studies suggest a cross-situational component to accessing and expressing emotion. Children who can express affect and fantasy in play also do so when discussing memories and on a cognitive-perceptual task. This openness to affect is a resource in a variety of areas, like creativity and coping. The child who is open to affect in play also has a richer store of emotion in memory and can express those emotions.

In summary, the validity studies suggest that the affective and cognitive processes measured by the APS are predictive of theoretically relevant criteria. The affective processes are related to criteria of creativity, coping, and adjustment. They are not related to measures of emotional understanding, empathy, or interpersonal functioning. The cognitive fantasy processes are related to all criteria. Both cognitive and affective processes are stable over a 5-year period. A very important point is that, in this age group, the APS is independent of IQ. Thus, these processes are resources for children that are independent of intelligence. Finally, the factor analysis results suggest that the APS measures two processes, one cognitive and one affective. Thus, future studies should continue to use both sets of scores.

MEASURES OF OTHER PLAY PROCESSES

The two other major play processes identified in chapter 1, interpersonal processes and problem solving processes, are important areas in which to develop measures. Larissa Niec has developed a coding system for the APS that measures interpersonal representations (Niec, Yopp, & Russ,

2002). The Interpersonal Themes in Play System (ITPS) has shown promising results in one study in that scores on the ITPS related to the Westin SCORS, Q on the TAT, and to empathy measures. Especially promising is the Affect Tone in Play Score, which measures the degree to which the play narrative reflects a safe, supportive interpersonal world. Affect Tone in Play significantly related to internal representations on the TAT and to several measures of empathy. These findings suggest that interpersonal schema can be assessed in play narratives. Future research in this area will be important.

Problem solving approaches and conflict resolution could also be assessed in play. Ronan (Ronan et al., 1996) developed a well-validated scoring system for the TAT that measures ability to identify, conceptualize, and resolve personal problems. That measure could be adapted to play narratives.

PLAY IN PRESCHOOL CHILDREN

Preschool represents a period of time when children's cognitive and emotional advances intersect and foster the development of fantasy play. Specifically, by 4 and 5 years of age, children are actively engaged in imaginative play that demonstrates the integration of their cognitive skills and emotional expression and understanding.

Advances in children's cognitive development are characterized by the capacity for pretend or symbolic play. Piaget (1967) claimed that symbolic play emerged at 2 years of age, increased over the next 3 or 4 years, and then declined at around 6 years of age. Although Piaget believed that these changes were accompanied by a decrease in less mature forms of thought during a young age and an increase in more mature forms in later age, empirical data does not support this assumption (Singer & Singer, 1990). Pretend play in young children has been defined by the following five criteria:

1. Familiar activities may be performed in the absence of necessary material or a social context.
2. Activities may not be carried out to their logical outcome.
3. A child may treat an inanimate object as animate.
4. One object or gesture may be substituted for another.
5. A child may carry out an activity usually performed by someone else (Fein, 1981; D. Singer & J. Singer, 1990).

Pretend play is evident as children arrange stuffed animals around a box, place blocks and pieces of flattened clay in front of each of them, and announce that they are having a tea party. Thus, when pretending, children can incorporate unique combinations of both reality and fantasy themes into their play with an understanding of their distinction.

Young children's play is filled with emotion. This can be seen in the language and facial expressions children use as well as in the themes they recreate in their play. At around 2 years of age, children begin using emotion words such as *happy, sad, mad,* and *scared* to refer primarily to themselves and eventually to other people. By 3½ years of age children are able to accurately recognize situations that elicit emotional reactions such as happiness, sadness, anger, and fear. During the next 3 years their understanding expands to more complex emotional states such as pride, shame, guilt, surprise, and gratitude. Similarly, at these ages children are learning to identify prototypical expressions of emotions (summary in Thompson, 1989). The themes enacted in play are often elaborated by children's emotional gestures, facial expressions, statements, and voice tones.

Due to the many developmental milestones that are encountered by 4 and 5 years of age, play is often used to assess cognitive and language functioning. For example, play can be used to identify cognitive and developmental disorders with normal and clinical populations (Sigman & Sena, 1993). In addition, various methods of assessing affect and fantasy with preschool-age children have been developed. The following summary represents a sample of several different assessment scales measuring fantasy and/or affect in play that have been used with individual children as young as 4 or 5 years of age. Some of these measures are also appropriate for older children. First, methods of assessing cognitive dimensions of play are reviewed. Second, measures of fantasy and thematic content are presented. Finally, techniques for assessing affect alone in play and both affect and fantasy in play are discussed.

Identifying different types of play is common in many observations of both individual children's play (Barnett, 1984) and children's play in groups (Dansky, 1980; Rubin, Watson, & Jambor, 1978). Young children's play has frequently been separated into four categories: functional (simple, repetitive muscle movements with or without objects), constructive (creating something), dramatic play (substitution of imaginary situations to satisfy one's wishes or needs), and games with rules (Smilansky, 1968). Often a category of make-believe play includes role play, object transformation, verbal communication within the context of role play, and nonverbal interaction during role play (Dansky, 1980).

Measures of Preschool Play

Three measures represent methods of assessing cognitive dimensions of play. The Preschool Play Scale (Bledsoe & Shepherd, 1982) has been developed to measure physical, social, and cognitive aspects of children's play from infancy to 6 years of age. One dimension that observers note is whether the child uses imitation, imagination, dramatization, music, and/or books in free-play situations. The Westby Symbolic Play Scale

(Westby, 1980, 1991) describes changes in children's presymbolic play, symbolic play, and language from 9 months to 5 years of age. A method for coding developmental trends in pretend play, developed by Fenson (1984), identifies behavioral examples of decentration, decontextualization, and integration. Lyytinen (1995) described using this coding paradigm when children 2 to 6 years of age were presented with the following toys in an individual play session: Duplo blocks, dolls, bedroom and kitchen equipment, animals, fences, vehicles, and blocks.

Several methods have been developed to assess fantasy and thematic content in play that are relevant to measuring affect in play. Coding of children's fantasy and nonfantasy play speech has been described by Olszewski (1987) and Olszewski and Fuson (1982). In both of these studies, 3- to 5-year-old children were given materials intended to elicit pretend play themes such as a doll family and home, a farm, and a construction site. Children's speech was transcribed, divided into utterances, and classified as either fantasy or nonfantasy speech.

The Child-Psychoanalytic Play Interview (Marans et al., 1991) is a technique for identifying and tracking specific themes in a child's play during a therapy session with a child analyst. The authors identified 30 thematic categories with descriptors to aid raters in inferring how play behaviors reflect particular themes. Some categories require making inferences about the play content and include topics such as bodily functions, loss of object/abandonment, and fighting and attacking. Other categories describe the preparations children make for play such as listing and labeling characters and assigning characters properties. Marans et al. (1991) described using the interview with children 4 to 6 years of age.

An experimental study by Milos and Reiss (1982) concentrated on the presence of separation anxiety themes in play among children beginning to attend nursery school, aged 2 to 6. A score for quality of play was given on a 5-point scale based on the extent to which the child's play expressed separation themes and a desire to master the problem.

Three measures have been used to assess children's affect and/or affect themes while playing or telling stories. The Kiddie-Infant Descriptive Instrument for Emotional States (KIDIES) is a scale that measures behavioral manifestations of affect in infants and young children during individual play, social play, and separation paradigms (Stern et al., 1992). Frequency and intensity of affect displayed for the face, the voice, and the body/gesture system are scored on a 5-point scale for each of fourteen 2- to 3-minute episodes. The affects that are scored include happiness, sadness, anger, fear, disgust, surprise, distress, soberness, interest in things and persons, regression, aggression, and negativism. Children ranging in age from 2 years, 0 months to 4 years, 11 months have participated in studies using this measure (Stern et al., 1992).

J. Singer (1973) developed a scoring system for observations of 10-minute segments of preschool children's free play and structured play (ages 2 to 5). Imaginativeness, affect, and concentration were rated on a 5-point scale for the entire play session. Eight moods (angry/annoyed, fearful/tense, lively/excited, elated/pleased, sad/down-hearted, ashamed/contrite, contemptuous/disgusted, and fatigued/sluggish) were also evaluated on a 5-point scale considering both the intensity and frequency of mood. Aggression, defined as "the intentional delivery of a harmful stimulus to another person or to personal property" (p. 267), was also coded on a 5-point scale for the play episodes.

The MacArthur Story-Stem Battery (Warren, Oppenheim, & Emde, 1996) asks children to complete story stems that are presented to them with the use of dolls, play furniture, and toys. The narratives reflect a variety of childhood events including looking for a lost dog, stealing candy, and witnessing a parental argument. Children's emotional displays during the story-telling are scored on a 4-point scale for emotions such as distress, anger, sadness, and concern. The presence and absence of content themes including aggression, personal injury, and atypical negative responses are noted. Several factors are considered in scoring the manner of story-telling, including coherence, elaboration, conflict resolution, and investment in the task.

AFFECT IN PLAY SCALE—PRESCHOOL (APS-P)

There is no available measure for preschool children that assesses both affective themes in pretend play and fantasy dimensions in a standardized free play situation. This review suggests that there is a need for a standardized assessment of affect and fantasy play in preschool-age children. Based on our work with the APS with children 6 to 10 years of age, we adapted the APS to be used with children 4 and 5 years of age (Kaugars & Russ, 2000). We believed that it is important to develop a scale, the Affect in Play Scale Preschool (APS-P), that will be sensitive to individual differences in children's play at this younger age. Initially we considered what materials and instructions would be appropriate for younger age groups. One of my graduate students, Astrida Seja Kaugars, took the lead in the development of the preschool version.

Based on the understanding that puppets might be more difficult for young children to manipulate, we selected toys that would be easy to play with and that could elicit symbolic and fantasy play. The chosen items include a hippopotamus, shark, bear, giraffe, lion, zebra, elephant, three plastic cups, a plastic car, and a "hairy" rubber ball. The variety of stuffed and plastic animals are often associated with a range of typically neutral (giraffe) and aggressive (shark) connotations. Similarly, several items were included that could have a variety of uses in children's play, including the plastic cups and "hairy" rubber ball. Pilot testing indicated that children enjoyed playing with the toys and could use them in fantasy play. For example, several children had the animals "eat" the rubber ball and "take a bath" in the plastic cups.

The same format for APS instructions is used in the preschool adaptation of the APS with some age-appropriate variations. First, a warm-up task is used to introduce the toys to each child and establish some rapport with the examiner. The children are asked to name the different toys and some of their characteristics such as the color and number of various items. Second, children are given more explicit directions to "make up a story" with the toys, and they are provided with several examples of what they can have the toys do (i.e., have the toys do something together like play house or go to the store). Finally, the children are not given a 1-minute warning near the end of their play time and instead are just told when to start and stop.

The instructions that the children are given are as follows:

> That's all the toys in the basket. Now we're going to make up a story using the toys on the table. You can play with the toys any way that you like and have them do something together like play house or go the store. Be sure to talk out loud so that I can hear you. The video camera will be on so that I can remember what you say and do. You will have five minutes to play with the toys. I'll tell you when to stop. Now remember to play with the toys and make up a story.

Preschool children are given the same prompts used with the APS for instances when children do not play, do not talk, and stop play early. The identical guideline of stopping after 2 minutes if a child is unable to play is used with younger children.

There are seven primary scores: frequency of affect expression, variety of affect expressions, quality of fantasy, comfort, percentage of no play episodes, percentage of functional play episodes, and percentage of pretend play episodes. The first four scores are modifications of scores originally developed for the APS; categorizations of play activities are based on work by Smilansky (1968).

Frequency of affect expression is the number of 10-second intervals in 5 minutes in which a child expressed affect or an affect theme. For example, one animal hitting another or two animals hugging would be considered examples of affect expression. Both verbal and nonverbal expressions are scored. Different from the APS where each affect expression is noted separately, only the presence or absence of affect in 10-second intervals is coded in the APS-P due to the difficulties encountered in understanding children's language. The variety of affect expressions is the number of different affect categories that are represented in each child's 5-minute play session. The possible categories included the following: nurturance/affection, happiness/pleasure, competition, oral, sexual, aggressive, anxiety/fear, sadness/hurt, frustration/disappointment, oral aggression, anal, and undefined affect expression. The undefined affect expression category was not previously included in the APS. This category includes sound effects and comments that are not understandable but seem to include affect (i.e., *roar, beep beep*, and *vroom*). Quality of fantasy is the mean of the rating of three components: imagination, organization, and elaboration in play. Comfort is the rating of the child's enjoyment and involvement in the play task.

The content of children's play is described by the percentage of three types of activities in 20-second intervals: no play, functional play, and pretend play. This scoring system was based on work by Jones and Glen (1991), who adapted Smilansky's (1968) classification of play. No play is the absence of any interaction with toys. Functional play is defined as simple repetitive muscle movements with objects (i.e., moving a car back and forth or arranging the animals without talking). Pretend play includes using one object to represent another or attributing activities to inanimate objects (i.e., pretending the cup is a bathtub, having the animals talk to one another). The child's predominant activity in each 20-second interval is scored.

We have completed two validity studies with the APS-P. First, we looked at the relationship between play, creativity, social competence, and teacher ratings of play in 33 nursery school children, from 4 to 5 years of age (Seja & Russ, 1999b). Creativity was measured with the Multidimensional Stimulus Fluency Measure (Godwin & Moran, 1990). Interrater reliability was good, and correlations ranged from .82 to .97 and internal consistency (second and fourth minutes and third and fifth minutes) for frequency of affect was good, $r = .88$. The affect scores, frequency and variety, were significantly related to creativity and originality for the creativity measure (Table 5.9). Comfort in play also was significantly related to creativity. Interestingly, in this study, the fantasy scores were not related to creativity. All play scores were significantly related to teachers' ratings of daily play behavior (Table 5.9). Finally, good players were rated by teachers as functioning well with little adult supervision in the classroom.

The second study by Kaugars, Russ, and Singer (2002) used multiple methods to examine relationships among affective processes within an at-risk population of 4-year-old children (116 cocaine-exposed; 120 non-cocaine-exposed) and their current caregivers. Specifically, affect expression in fantasy play and daily behavior, emotional regulation in fantasy play and a frustrating situation, and emotional understanding were assessed. Each child participated in a standardized play situation (APS), identified emotional expressions, and was asked to wait for 6

TABLE 5.9

Correlations Between APS-P and Creativity

	APS-P	
	Frequency of Affect	*Variety of Affect*
MSFM Creativity Scores		
Total Number of Responses	.32	.39*
Total Number of Original Responses	.35*	.37*
Teacher Ratings of Daily Play		
Imagination	.43*	.47**
Use of Make-Believe	.42*	.46**
Enjoyment	.46*	.52**
Expression of Emotions	.34	.42**
Use of Make-Believe in Dramatic Play	.30	.44*

$N = 33$. $* p < .05$. $** p < .01$. MSFM = Multidimensional Stimulus Fluency Measure.

minutes before engaging in a desired activity. There were modest relationships among some of the affective variables in the different tasks. Aspects of children's behavior during a frustrating situation were related to children's fantasy play and emotional understanding (i.e., children who expressed predominately positive emotions vs. neutral emotions during a frustrating situation were more likely to have more fantasy in their play, $U = 756, p < .05$, and higher emotional understanding scores, $U = 705, p < .05$); the intensity of children's positive affect expression in daily behavior was related to children's level of emotional understanding ($r = .16, p < .05$); and emotional understanding was related to both cognitive and affective components of children's play (i.e., greater emotional understanding was related to a greater variety of affect in play, $r = .27, p < .001$, and integration of affect and fantasy in play, $r = .24, p < .001$). This study was a subsample of a sample participating in the longitudinal study of cocaine-exposed children in the laboratory of Lynn Singer (Case Western Reserve University). We are currently analyzing the results for the entire sample.

The results of these studies suggest that the APS-P is measuring constructs that relate to important criteria in this preschool age group. Theoretically, the results suggest that affective dimensions of play are related to important functions in child development.

CLINICAL USE OF THE APS

To date, there have been no studies with the APS and clinical populations. An important next step is to investigate the APS with a variety of such groups. In addition, the scale should be used to assess change in child psychotherapy, especially in those therapies that use play.

The APS should be sensitive to changes in a child's affect expression in play during the therapy process and could be used as a measure of therapy outcome. Changes in the amount of emotional expression and the affect themes are frequently noted by child therapists as therapy progresses. Systematic intervention studies with specifically diagnosed child populations could utilize the APS to assess changes in affect and changes in the organization of fantasy life. For constricted, internalizing children affect expression should increase as a result of effective therapy. We know from the D'Angelo (1995) study that internalizing children are more constricted in their affect expression than other groups. On the other hand, children who have problems with organization of their thinking, such as borderline children and some narcissistic children, should have lower quality of fantasy scores than other children. Successful therapy should result in better organization of their play and better integration of their affect.

The APS could also be used to refine play therapy techniques. The general question of what kinds of intervention by the therapist best facilitates play needs to be studied empirically. There are many guidelines in the clinical literature about how to facilitate play, but few are based on empirical work. How do we best encourage affect in play? When is modeling by the therapist more effective than a more reflective approach? How do we best facilitate modulation of affect? How do we increase organization and fantasy ability? Guidelines from studies investigating these questions could be incorporated into treatment manuals, which are needed in the play therapy area.

For the practicing clinician, the APS could be used for a quick assessment of play skills. Because the use of a video camera may be impractical for many clinicians, we are working on developing validity for the scale when the child's play is rated as it occurs. We did use this approach in the Perry and Russ (1998) study. The APS in this study demonstrated good interrater reliability (based on transcripts) and predicted relevant criteria. More work is needed to refine the scoring system using this approach.

FUTURE DIRECTIONS

Next steps for the development of the APS are:

1. Determine validity with clinical populations and high-risk populations.
2. Continue to refine the scoring system. Of special importance is the addition of an emotion regulation score. Although the combination of the affect and fantasy scores attempt to measure integration of affect, a score that is coded separately may be more valid.
3. Use the APS as a measure of change in child therapy intervention studies.
4. Continue longitudinal studies with the APS.
5. Develop validity of the preschool version of the scale.
6. Develop a version of the APS that can be used without a video camera.

The growing body of validity studies to date suggests that the APS measures processes that are important in child development, predict adaptive functioning in children, and are separate from what traditional intelligence tests measure. The use of the APS in a variety of research programs and clinical settings with a variety of child populations will further the development of the measure. Research with the APS will also tell us about this important resource for children–affect expression in fantasy play.

ACKNOWLEDGMENT

This chapter is adapted from Russ, Niec, & Kaugars (2000), Play assessment of affect—The Affect in Play Scale. In K. Gitlin-Weiner, A. Sangrund, & C. Schaefer (Eds.), *Play diagnosis and assessment* (pp. 722–749). New York: Wiley. Copyright © 2000 by John Wiley & Sons. This material is used by permission of John Wiley & Sons, Inc.

6

Current Trends in the Therapeutic
Uses of Play

The new developments in play therapy are consistent with the trends in child psychotherapy in general. Ollendick and Russ (1999) discussed these, beginning with the sea change in the field of child psychotherapy that occurred in the 1980s and 1990s, to which several factors contributed.

First, the move to managed care changed the climate within which child and family psychotherapists worked. There is now a focus on short-term approaches and efficient treatment strategies. There is an increasing need for the "effectiveness and efficiency" demanded by third-party payers (Koocher & D'Angelo, 1992). Second, the stress on empirically supported treatments—on treatments that are proven to work—has caused all conscientious therapists to re-evaluate their practices by reviewing the scientific evidence for treatment effectiveness. Third, the growing awareness of cultural and contextual variables, such as socioeconomic factors, ethnic minority background, and stability of family environment, has resulted in an increased sophistication in choosing among treatment approaches.

CURRENT TRENDS

Current trends in child psychotherapy reflect changing contexts in the field and increasing sophistication and specialization in research and practice. Ollendick and Russ (1999) identified the first five of these six trends: (a) use of a developmental framework; (b) call for empirically validated or empirically supported treatments; (c) focus on specific problems and populations; (d) integration of treatment approaches; (e) the importance of situational and contextual factors in planning and implementing intervention; and (f) use of short-term psychotherapy. Each of these has implications for play therapy interventions.

115

Developmental Framework

The use of a development framework in conceptualizing childhood disorders and treatment has become increasingly evident in recent years. However, a developmental perspective has always been a hallmark of clinical work with children. For example, psychoanalytic and psychodynamic approaches have long striven to return the child to normal developmental pathways (A. Freud, 1965; Palmer, 1970; Shirk & Russell, 1996). Recently, however, there are new elements in the developmental framework that make it more salient for clinical practice. Campbell (1998), for instance, has emphasized research efforts that apply concepts and findings from normal development to the understanding of developmental processes in at-risk populations. A developmental approach also involves early recognition of pathognomonic signs and the awareness that numerous factors can cause and maintain psychopathology (Vernberg, 1998). In short, it has been recommended that interventions with children should be based on research findings in child development (Vernberg, Routh, & Koocher, 1992). As we build a knowledge base about normative development of play, and of development of the cognitive and affective processes in play, then we can begin to identify when play development has gone awry. Identification of pathognomonic signs in play would strengthen the use of play assessment and diagnosis.

In the 1980s, the impact of a developmental psychopathology framework was felt and has become dominant in conceptualizing childhood disorders (Sroufe & Rutter, 1984; Lease & Ollendick, in press). A developmental psychopathology perspective incorporates general systems theory principles and considers multiple contributors and multiple outcomes in interaction with one another. Sroufe and Rutter (1984) defined developmental psychopathology as the study of "the origins and course of individual patterns of behavioral maladaptation, whatever the age of onset, whatever the causes, whatever the transformations in behavioral manifestation, and however complex the course of the developmental pattern may be" (p. 18). In short, the developmental psychopathology approach is concerned with the origin and time course of a given disorder, its varying manifestations with development, its precursors and sequelae, and its relation to non-disordered patterns of behavior.

Protective processes and variables that place children at risk are viewed in the context of each other rather than in isolation (Cicchetti & Rogosch, 1996), and an organizational perspective is taken on development. Although this conceptualization of disorder is a rich one, the implications for child treatment of a developmental psychopathology perspective are just beginning to be articulated (Toth & Cicchetti, 1999). Much work in this realm remains to be accomplished.

Empirically Supported Treatments

A second trend is the emphasis on defining and using evidence-based treatments in clinical practice. There is a strong, healthy movement to obtain empirical support for the various treatment approaches—although the support for the approaches is variable and incomplete at this time. One of the purposes of this book is to determine how much empirical support exists for play therapy interventions and to outline the needs for future research.

As pointed out in chapter 4, the results of the meta-analytic reviews of child psychotherapy point to the need for specificity and precision in research. Weisz and Weiss (1993) concluded that the studies that showed positive results tended to "zoom in" on a specific problem with careful planning of the intervention. Behavioral and cognitive behavioral approaches tended to fit these criteria better than psychoanalytic, psychodynamic, and client-centered approaches. In a similar vein, Freedheim and Russ (1983, 1992) stated early on that we needed to become very specific with these more traditional approaches and ask, "Which specific interventions affect which specific cognitive, personality, and affective processes? How are these processes related to behavior and practical clinical criteria?" (1983, p. 988). More recently, Shirk and Russell (1996) also called for similar targeting of specific cognitive, affective, and interpersonal processes in child therapy.

Shirk and Russell (1996) identified major cognitive, emotional, and cognitive processes that are involved in change in psychotherapy. By focusing research questions on specific cognitive, affective, and personality processes, we can learn more about mechanisms underlying developmental processes and child psychopathology (Russ, 1998; Shirk & Russell, 1996). Specificity would also enable us to investigate which interventions facilitate the development of these processes and which do not.

Play With Specific Populations

The focus on specificity in research is consistent with the third trend of refining interventions for specific problems and populations of children. Schaefer and Millman (1977) recognized this trend early on. This practice grew out of Barrett et al.'s (1978) call for greater specificity in psychotherapy research. Their oft-quoted conclusion that the question in psychotherapy research should not be, "Does psychotherapy work?" but rather, "Which set of procedures is effective when applied to what kinds of patients with which sets of problems and practiced by which sorts of therapists?" (p. 428) led to more specific research and practice.

As child psychotherapy research has become more specific, so too has child psychotherapy practice. The move within many clinical settings to have specialty clinics for different diagnostic groups, such as childhood depression and anxiety disorders, reflects this change. Kazdin (1990) pointed out that many current reviews focus on specific areas of child dysfunction and treatment options for specific purposes.

For example, Parent–Child Interaction Therapy (PCIT) for oppositional children (Rayfield, Monaco, & Eyberg, 1999) is a specific treatment approach developed for young non-compliant children. Principles of cognitive behavior therapy and of play therapy have been applied to this particular group of children. PCIT is a specific type of parent management training for preschool-age children that targets the parent–child relationship. Unique issues that arise with this specific group can be worked with and integrated into the treatment to develop the optimal treatment approach.

Modifications of basic psychodynamic play therapy techniques have been used with seriously developmentally delayed children. The therapist must assess the overall developmental level of the child and be flexible in altering the traditional approach. Mann and McDermott (1983) discussed play therapy with abused and neglected children. Frequently, these children must be guided and taught how to play. Therapists sometimes use food to help build the relationship with the child and attempt to address the severe unmet dependency needs. Irwin (1983) stressed the importance of teaching poor players how to play, so they can have play experiences available to them.

Gil's work with abused children is an example of adapting play therapy techniques to a specific population. She stressed the importance of the therapist being an active participant in the play and actively facilitating self-expression by using techniques such as presenting the child with cartoon figures in different situations with the child filling in the words or pulling secrets from a secrets bag. For many abused children, post-traumatic play is repetitive, devoid of pleasure and can remain fixed (Gil, 1991). Gil intervenes in this repetitive play by making verbal statements, having the child take a specific role, or encouraging the child to differentiate between the traumatic event and current reality in terms of safety and what has been learned. The goal of interrupting the play is to generate alternatives that can lead to a sense of control, help feelings be expressed, and orient the child toward the future.

Principles of play therapy have also been used in hospital settings. Emma Plank established the Child Life programs in hospitals with the first program in the hospitals of Case Western Reserve University in the 1950s. She used play techniques with hospitalized children to help them work through fears and anxieties that are a natural part of illness and hospitalization (Plank, 1962). Contemporary child life programs continue to use play to help prepare children for medical procedures. Children express fears and anxieties in play and also receive information about medical procedures. Golden (1983) viewed play sessions as helping children to deal with separation issues and fear of equipment and procedures, develop some sense of mastery and competence, and build trust with the hospital.

As reviewed in chapter 4, research with play intervention in hospital settings has found play effective in reducing anxiety in children (Cassell, 1965; Johnson & Stockdale, 1975; Rae et al., 1989). It is important that this kind of research continue. Often, in practice, play is used with hospitalized children but not in a systematic way or guided by research. Also, it may be very helpful for some children, but not for others. Or, it may be very helpful for some medical procedures, but not for others. A crucial question is, "When it is best to use play to give information to the child about the medical procedure in a structured play approach and when it is best to let the child play out fears and anxieties in a free-play environment?"

Integration of Psychotherapy Approaches

A fourth important trend in child psychotherapy is the integration of different theoretical approaches, specific techniques, or both from different schools of therapy. Kazdin (1990) pointed out that the field of child psychotherapy needs to consider combining treatment approaches if optimal results are to be obtained. Because there are so many children with multiple disorders, with a host of etiological factors involved, we need to use the most appropriate combination of intervention techniques. Also, the need for short-term intervention pushes therapists to search for optimal interventions.

Wachtel's (1977) sophisticated approach to integrating psychodynamic and behavioral techniques in a complementary way with adults should apply to the child psychotherapy area as well. For example, the therapist might decide to use both insight and problem solving approaches. Actually, this integration has always been true in child psychotherapy because working with children and families forces one to be pragmatic and to do what works (Russ, 1998).

In a special issue of the *Journal of Clinical Child Psychology* (Volume 27[1], 1998) on Developmentally Based Integrated Psychotherapy With Children: Emerging Models, innovative treatment approaches that integrated different theoretical perspectives and intervention techniques were presented.

For example, Knell's (1999) cognitive-behavioral play therapy is based on cognitive-behavioral principles, but also integrates more traditional forms of play therapy. She weaves together change mechanisms from cognitive behavioral approaches and psychodynamic play therapy. One benefit of this approach is that it can "speed up" the psychotherapy process.

Also, in the special issue, Shirk (1998) described a cognitive-interpersonal framework in targeting changes in interpersonal schema. Shirk defined interpersonal schema as referring to expectations about others' probable responses to the self. Within this cognitive-interpersonal framework, based on attachment theory, he presented a model of intervention that integrates relational, representational, and emotional components of child functioning. The therapeutic relationship is a crucial change process in schema transformation.

In her introductory comments to the special issue, Russ (1998) identified a dilemma that we face in developing integrated psychotherapy approaches, however. On the one hand, we know from the child psychotherapy outcome literature and from Weisz and Weiss's (1993) conclusions from their meta-analysis of child therapy outcome studies that those interventions that "zoom in" (to use Weisz and Weiss's term) on a particular problem in a focused way, with clear guidelines for psychotherapy, are most likely to demonstrate treatment efficacy. On the other hand, when we integrate different approaches and techniques, we lose that precision, at least in the beginning stages of model development. However, what we lose in precision we may gain in beneficial outcomes. Hypothetically, since we would be using the most effective change mechanisms from two or more approaches for different problems and populations, we might expect our integrated approaches to be synergistically effective. Quite obviously, we need time for this experimentation with different combinations of treatment to occur. However, such integrated approaches will need to be put to the test of science and not allowed to rest on their respective laurels. After all, it is possible that integrated approaches will be less effective than those from which they are derived. The combination of elements may prove volatile rather than therapeutic.

Shirk (1999) has identified three different types of treatment integration. One type includes a number of different techniques within one theoretical framework. For example, cognitive-behavior therapy can include a number of techniques. A second type combines techniques from different theoretical approaches. A third type is a theoretical integration of different techniques from different theoretical approaches. Shirk specified Knells' (1999) cognitive-behavioral play therapy as an example of theoretical integration of different techniques. He suggests three principles for integrating treatments:

1. Treatment combinations are likely to be beneficial when the component procedures have been shown to be effective.
2. Treatment coherence is important in that the different components should "hang together" and work in a complementary fashion.
3. Treatment selection should focus on treatments that effect underlying processes that will influence the overt symptoms and diagnosis.

Play therapy lends itself toward integration with other treatment components. Play intervention modules may evolve as effective components in treatment packages (Russ, 1995). Kazdin (1993) discussed the possibility of having different modules of intervention for different problems. This concept would work for the play therapy area. Six to twelve work play modules could be developed for different types of problems. Children who have experienced trauma might benefit from the opportunity to play out the trauma in a focused approach. Constricted children could benefit from play modules directed at increasing affective expression. Play assessment would be used to identify what types of play experiences could be most beneficial.

Situational and Contextual Factors

The field is becoming increasingly aware of the importance of situational and contextual factors in child development and in intervention. The complex interaction of these variables has been emphasized in the developmental psychopathology framework (Cicchetti & Rogosch, 1996). Campbell (1998) emphasized the importance of family and social environmental factors in understanding developmental processes. The importance of understanding cultural factors in working with ethnic minority groups is an important principle. The knowledge base about intervention with minority children is fragmented and the literature regarding service delivery, social contexts, and specific problems are separate and distinct (Vraniak & Pickett, 1993). A comprehensive framework needs to be developed. There are some efforts in this area (Vraniak & Pickett, 1993), but there need to be more empirically based guidelines about how to best intervene in different cultures and contexts.

Short-Term Therapy

Conceptual frameworks exist for adult forms of brief psychodynamic intervention (Budman & Gurman, 1988; Mann & Goldman, 1982), but not for child forms of brief intervention. However, as Messer and Warren (1995) pointed out, short-term therapy (6–12 sessions) is a frequent form of psychodynamic intervention. The practical realities of HMOs and of clinical practice in general have led to briefer forms of treatment. Often, the time-limited nature of the therapy is by default, not by plan (Messer & Warren, 1995). The average number of sessions for children in outpatient therapy is 6 or less in private and clinic settings (Dulcan & Piercy, 1985).

There is little research or clinical theory about short-term psychotherapy with children (Clark, 1993; Messer & Warren, 1995). A few research studies have shown that explicit time limits reduced the likelihood of premature termination (Parad & Parad, 1968) and that children in time-limited psychotherapy showed as much improvement as those in long-term psychotherapy (Smyrnios & Kirby, 1993). The time is right for development of theoretically based short-term interventions for children with systematic research studies. Messer and Warren (1995) suggested that the developmental approach utilized by psychodynamic theory provides a useful framework for short-term therapy. One can identify the developmental problems and obstacles involved in a particular case. They also stressed the use of play as a vehicle of change and, as Winnicott (1971) has said, of development. They suggested that active interpretation of the meaning of the play can help the child feel understood, which in turn can result in lifelong changes in self perception and experience. In other words, the understanding of the metaphors in the child's play could give the child insight, or an experience of empathy, or both. This lasting change can be accomplished in a short time.

Chethik (1989) discussed "focal therapy" as therapy that deals with "focal stress events" (p. 194) in the child's life. Chethik listed events such as death in the family, divorce, hospitalization, or illness in the family or of the child as examples of specific stresses. Focal therapy focuses on the problem and is usually of short duration. The basic principles of psychodynamic therapy and play therapy are applied. The basic mechanism of change is insight and working through. Chethik views this approach as working best with children who have accomplished normal developmental tasks before the stressful event occurs.

In general, brief forms of psychodynamic intervention are seen as more appropriate for the child who has accomplished the major developmental milestones. Lester (1968) viewed problems such as transient regressions, mild exaggerations of age-appropriate behaviors, and acute phobias as most appropriate for brief intervention. Proskauer (1969, 1971) stressed the child's ability to quickly develop a relationship with the therapist, good trusting ability, the existence of a focal dynamic issue, and flexible and adaptive defenses as criteria for short-term intervention. Messer and Warren (1995) concluded that children with less severe psychopathology are more responsive to brief intervention than children with chronic developmental problems. My own view is that the internalizing disorders are most appropriate for brief psychodynamic intervention. The therapist is active, at times directive, and uses all mechanisms of change in the therapy. Insight and working through are essential, but modeling, rehearsal, discussing coping strategies are also part of the therapy. Children with major deficits in object relations and with early developmental problems need longer term structure-building approaches.

Messer and Warren (1995) also stressed the importance of the family and social environment in maximizing the effectiveness of brief intervention. A supportive environment and, often, active engagement of the parents and school are essential for brief intervention to work.

Shelby (2000) described the importance of using developmentally appropriate interventions in brief therapy with traumatized children. In working with traumatized children in Sarajevo, Shelby used play and drawing. She described an experiential mastery technique in which children drew pictures of the thing that frightened them. Children are encouraged to verbalize all their feelings to the drawing.

Filial play therapy (Guerney, 1964; Van Fleet, 1994) combines play therapy and family therapy with a goal of helping parents to hold sessions independently at home. Van Fleet (2000) has used short-term filial play therapy with children with chronic illness. Parents are trained to respond empathically to the child's play.

Bodiford-McNeil, Hembree-Kigin, and Eyberg (1996) have developed a short-term play therapy model based on the empirically validated Parent–Child Interaction Therapy (PCIT). The play therapy model develops the play intervention component of PCIT. This model targets young children with disruptive behavior problems. The therapy consists of 12 sessions, with the first 7 focusing on therapist–child interaction and sessions 8–12 focusing on teaching play therapy skills to the parent. The therapist uses praise, reflection, imitation, description, and enthusiasm in responding to the child's play. The therapist then coaches the parent to use these techniques. Daily play sessions with the parent and child occur at home. The therapist in the therapeutic play also uses techniques of questioning and interpretation. Parents are not encouraged to use these particular play techniques. The play component of the early sessions is 20 minutes of a 60-minute session.

Structured play techniques would be especially useful in short-term therapy, but could also be used in longer term therapy. The MacArthur Story Stem Battery (MSSB), although designed as an assessment tool, can be used to structure the play situation. Kelsay (2002), in an innovative approach, used the MSSB to structure play therapy. The MSSB is a set of story beginnings (i.e., parents are arguing over lost keys) and the child is asked to complete the story. The therapist can choose appropriate story stems tailored to the issues that the child is struggling with. This structured approach could help move the therapy to central issues more quickly.

Structured play techniques have been used with very young children by Gaensbauer and Siegel (1995). They described structured play techniques with toddlers who have experience traumatic events. They conceptualized the mechanisms of change when play is used as being similar to mechanisms of change in older children with PTSD. With these very young children, the therapists actively structure the play to recreate the traumatic event. Gaensbauer and Siegel (1995) outlined three purposes of structured play reenactment. First, play enables the child to organize the fragmented experiences into meaningful narratives. Second, the interpretive work by the therapist helps understand the personal meanings of the trauma. Third, there is desensitization of the anxiety and fear and other negative emotions associated with the trauma.

In their structured play approach, Gaensbauer and Siegel (1995) introduced play materials that represent aspects of the traumatic situation. For example, if the child had been in a car accident, they would use cars, set up the hospital room, and so on. Then they would ask the child to play out "what happens next?" They described a number of case examples where 2- and 3-year-olds reenact the traumatic event in the play. The therapist is very active in acting out the events as well. For example, in the case of a dog bite, the therapist would show the toy dog biting the doll. Sensitive timing is, of course, important in terms of whether to introduce elements of the event and how much to introduce them. In addition, the therapist introduces soothing actions—like the parent comforting the child. Often, the parents are present and engage in the therapeutic play as well and help with soothing behaviors and explanation of events. The parents can make up for their inability to protect the child at the time of the initial trauma. They concluded that the young children they work with, once engaged, "repeatedly return to play vehicles that provide them an opportunity to express their unresolved feelings" (p. 303). The striking thing about this work is that children this young can internally represent and integrate traumatic experiences through play. They stressed that the key element that enables the child to use play adaptively, rather than in a repetitive unproductive fashion, is the "degree to which the affects can be brought to the surface so the child can identify them and integrate them in more adaptive ways" (p. 297).

The need for short-term intervention pushes therapists to search for optimal interventions. What will work most quickly and efficiently with a particular child? Conceptualizing in this way often leads to an integration of treatment approaches and techniques. The therapist decides to use both insight and problem solving approaches. The use of short-term treatment approaches should result in the use of integrated treatment approaches. Play modules and/or play techniques are ideal for short-term integrated approaches. Research programs that investigate which play techniques are most useful for which child populations is essential.

7

Teaching Children to Play

Can play skills be taught and pretend play ability be developed? If we can teach children to be better players, will the improved skills affect real-life functioning and behavior? These are two key questions that deserve major research initiatives. Although there is some research in this area, it has not received the attention and funding initiatives that it deserves.

Given the wealth of research studies and clinical work pointing to pretend play as an adaptive resource for children, it seems obvious that we should try to develop techniques that help children play better. But Sutton-Smith (1994) raised an important cautionary note. It is possible that in our attempts to help children play better, we will end up interfering in the development of play. Especially if therapists become too active and structured, they might interfere with the play process itself. Smith stressed the importance of keeping the "playfulness" in play. This is an important point to consider as we review the play training literature.

FACILITATING PRETEND PLAY

Singer (1994) placed play therapy in the context of Leslie's (1987) theory of mind. Leslie conceptualized that people manipulate meta-representations to make inferences and predictions, to understand the world, and to distinguish fantasy from reality. The manipulation of meta-representations occurs in pretend play. Singer sees the play therapist as helping to develop the child's capacity for play.

Most of the therapeutic work with children's play has not been empirically investigated. Although most child therapists assume that they are helping the child's play develop, there is no empirical support for this assumption. There have been efforts to teach children to play better. Many of these play training or play tutoring programs have been in an academic context, rather than a therapeutic context.

Smilansky's (1968) important research in Israel was one of the first studies to demonstrate that teachers could teach play skills. She worked with kindergarten children in Israel for 90 minutes a day, 5 days a week, for 9 weeks. The children who engaged in socio-dramatic play, with help from their teachers, showed significant cognitive improvement when compared with other groups. The teachers helped the children develop their play by commenting, making suggestions, and giving demonstrations. Smilansky worked with children from low SES backgrounds having noticed that many of these children did not have good play skills.

Play training has been found to be effective with mentally retarded populations. Kim, Lombardino, Rothman, and Vinson (1989) carried out imaginative play training with children with a mental age of 3 years. They had 10 daily sessions of 20 minutes. The trainer modeled thematic play. The children in the training group showed an increase in quantity and quality of imaginative play.

Hellendoorn (1994) carried out an imaginative play program for retarded children and adolescents with a mental age of 2 to 3 years. The program consists of eight play themes, each with six consecutive steps. The trainer models each of the play steps. The steps are:

1. Functional use of play material, normal daily activity, no evidence of pretense.
2. Functional activity directed towards a symbolic person (doll or bear).
3. Introduction of a pretense element in a crucial play material becomes make-believe.
4. Make-believe extended to symbolic persons.
5. Expanding the number of transformations.
6. Relating one play theme to another, designing a play story.

The pace of movement through the steps was determined by the level of the child. A new step was introduced only after the child mastered previous steps. When compared with an untreated control group, the children in the play condition exhibited better play skills on a post-training test. The play skills continued to hold after 3 months. The play skill gains did not generalize to play in daily living environment , however.

Hartmann and Rollett (1994) reported positive results from a play intervention program in Austrian elementary schools. The Viennese Play Curriculum involved teachers instructing children in play 4 hours per week during the school year. Hartmann and Rollett compared experimental classes of low-SES children with comparable control classes. They found that the play intervention group had better divergent thinking ability and were happier in school than the control groups.

One of the methodological problems with the Hartmann and Rollett study, and with many other studies in the play facilitation area, is the lack of adequate control groups. Smith (1988, 1994) has consistently raised this issue in reviewing the play intervention literature. Smith stressed that adequate research design requires the inclusion of a control group that involves experimenter–child interaction of a form other than pretend play. Both verbal stimulation and social interaction must be controlled for. He concluded that when this kind of control group is included in the design, usually both the play group and the control group improve.

Dansky (1999) reviewed the play tutoring literature and found that "more than a dozen studies have shown that play tutoring can increase not just the quantity of play displayed but also the richness and imaginativeness of children's pretense" (p. 404). He described these play tutoring studies as usually involving 8–12 small-group sessions with an adult who models and encourages participation in social interactive pretense. Usually the sessions are spread out over 3 to 6 weeks. The pretend activities usually involve everyday activities or fairy tales. Freyberg (1973) was one of the first to demonstrate that training sessions improved imagination in play that generalized to everyday free play over a 2-month period.

Dansky pointed out, in response to Smith's criticism about control groups, that many of the studies did have adequate control groups that controlled for involvement of the experimenter. For example, Dansky (1980) carried out a study with preschoolers that involved three groups: a sociodramatic play tutoring group, exploration tutoring, and free play group. Both tutoring groups received equal amounts of verbal stimulation and attention from the adult. After a 3-week intervention, the play tutoring group had a greater amount of, complexity of, and imaginativeness of pretense in daily free play. In addition, the play group had more imaginativeness on other measures of imagination. Udwin (1983) also found, in a study with adequate control groups, that a play-tutored group showed more imaginative play, positive affect, and cooperation with peers during free play. Shmukler (1984–1985) also found similar increases in imaginative play in children in a well-controlled play tutoring study. These children also did better on creativity tests than the other groups. Dansky (1999), after reviewing the literature, concluded that there were consistently positive results in studies with adequate control groups. He concluded that play tutoring, over a period of time, did result in increased imaginativeness in play and increased creativity on other measures.

A PROGRAM FOR PARENTS

J. Singer and D. Singer (1999) have developed a video-based program for parents and other caregivers of preschool children. The video and accompanying manual uses play and learning games to strengthen school readiness skills in children from 3 to 5 years old. The tape and manual provide very clear examples and instructions for parents and caregivers that model how to use play to help children use imagination and to learn through play. For example, in a going-to-a-restaurant pretend play situation, the children learn to take on different roles, learn to do things in order (frequency), learn to count, and so on. D. Singer and J. Singer (2002) also wrote a book for parents and teachers that reviews games and activities for imaginative play. A wide variety of games, activities, and materials for children from 2 to 5 are presented and can be used in a variety of situations.

PILOT PROGRAM: PLAY INTERVENTION SCRIPTS

I and two of my students, Melissa Moore and Maureen Williams, have begun a study with first-grade children (6- and 7-year-olds) that is "trying out" different play instructions, prompts, and scenarios to determine if we can improve play skills and increase performance on a variety of outcome variables. In the pilot phase, with 13 children, we tried various instructions and interactions. After observing the children's reactions to different instructions and prompts, we decided to include the following scenarios and prompts.

Group 1 is the fantasy and imagination play group. We want to improve the organization of their fantasy and imagination. We ask the children to make up stories with a beginning, middle, and end for a series of events, and to use their imagination and make up new things. We work with children individually for 30-minute sessions for five sessions over a 4–5 week period. In each session we present four or five events. We have a variety of toys available for the children to use (doll figures, animals, Legos, a very small globe, etc.). The instructions for the fantasy and imagination group are to make up a story about:

- Getting ready for a day at school.
- Getting ready for bed.
- Going to visit a friend after school.
- Buying a dress/shirt.
- Going to the grocery store.
- Going to the library.
- Going to the zoo.
- Going to the moon.
- Living in a city under water.
- Living in a castle.
- Being able to talk to animals.
- Having magic powers.
- Being Superman(girl)/Spiderman.
- Going on a boat to a special place.

We start with the simple stories (go to the zoo) and move to the more imaginative stories (magic powers) over time. During the 30-minute sessions, the play trainer is active with prompts to:

- Have a beginning, middle, and end.
- Show details.
- Have the characters talk.
- Pretend that something is there. (One child could not have milk because there was no milk bottle. I suggested that he pretend the Lego was a milk bottle. He was able to continue with the story and was better able to pretend with objects in later stories.)
- Make up different endings.
- Ask what happens next.

The trainer also repeats what is happening to reinforce the coherence of the narrative, models and participates in the play when necessary, and praises the child.

Group 2 is the affect-in-play group. We are trying to increase the amount and type of affect children express. The toys and conditions (number of sessions, trainers) are the same as for Group 1. In this group, we instruct the children to make up a story with lots of feelings, have the toys and dolls talk, say, and show how they are feeling.

We instruct them to make up a story with:

- Sad feelings:

    Friend moves away.
    Pet runs away.

- Happy feelings:

    Get a new bike.
    Go to zoo.
    Have a birthday party.
    Go sledding.
    Go on a picnic.

- Caring feelings:

    Take a puppy for a walk.
    Make cookies with a parent.
    Give a present to a friend.
    Make a birthday card for parent/friend.

- Scary feelings:

   Get lost on way home from school.
   Hear a scary noise.
   Start a new school.
   Get a shot at the doctors.

- Angry feelings:

   Get into an argument.
   Get teased at school.
   Two children wanting same toy.

- Upset/disappointed feelings:

   Cannot find favorite toy.
   Want to go swimming but it starts to rain.

The prompts from the trainer are to:

- Reflect/label feelings.
- Ask how the dolls are feeling.
- State they are feeling this way because … .
- Ask what happens next.
- Have the toys talk to each other about how they are feeling.

The trainer also models, participates in the play, and praises the expression of feelings. For both groups, we also intersperse in every session having the child make up their own story. We also have a control condition where the child plays with puzzles and coloring books. The trainer has the same amount of interaction as with the other two groups.

We are hypothesizing that the fantasy and imagination play group will have better organization and imagination on play outcome measures and the affect play group will have more affect in play on outcome measures. We are also administering a variety of outcome measures of adaptive functioning. However, it is possible that either set of play instructions will facilitate both fantasy and affect. We have especially noticed with the fantasy and imagination group that as their stories improve they include more affect. This is a subjective impression that awaits the results of the study.

The overall goal for this particular study is to develop standardized play intervention scripts that could be used by parents and teachers to facilitate play skills in early elementary school children—kindergarten through third grade.

This kind of play intervention script could also be used as a foundation for a play therapy manual. Manual-based treatment could be applied to the use of play in therapy. One major difference between play training/facilitation interventions and play therapy is that, in therapy, the goal is to tie the play to the child's life. The therapist might make a simple clarifying statement about the play—"that is how you feel—sad—when your parents argue." Or the therapist might make an interpretation "the little girl feels sad because she thinks she caused the arguing between her parents." Or the therapist might model a healthy reaction to the parents' arguing. But the goal, in a different way, is to help the child deal with what is happening in her life. A play therapy manual would combine both techniques that use the play to help children process emotions and help children to integrate life events in their world.

GUIDELINES FOR FUTURE PLAY INTERVENTION PROGRAMS

The results of the play tutoring and play intervention studies are encouraging. They suggest that we can teach children play skills and that these skills, in turn, influence important functions such as creativity. Play intervention programs should be tried on a larger scale with evaluation components built in. A number of guidelines for these programs have emerged in the literature.

Christie (1994) has suggested the following:

- Use long treatment durations with long-term follow-up. He suggests play interventions of several months or years to ensure that new skills are learned. Also, since the effects of improved play may not be evident immediately, long-term follow-up is essential.
- Use an expanded range of dependent variables.
- Investigate subject × intervention interaction. Age, ability, and use of make-believe are just a few variables that could moderate or mediate the effects of a play intervention program.

Hellendoorn, van der Kooij, and Sutton-Smith (1994) suggested the following guidelines:

- Choose the specific intervention carefully.
- Tune the intervention to specific goals.
- Provide a suitable play environment and adequate feedback.
- "Keep modest" about the effectiveness of play.
- Be alert to the "playfulness" of the intervention and the pleasure it should be evoking.

- Monitor individual children and their special needs, especially in group intervention.
- Use results to formulate more specific criteria for different interventions.
- Be open and creative in your own ways of playing.

Dansky (1999) also stressed the importance of longitudinal research and repeated observations of play in multiple contexts and in different areas. Dansky also pointed to the need to investigate the mechanisms by which play effects change.

I would stress the importance of understanding the mechanisms by which play facilitates child development. Specific play processes should be investigated with affect processes being included. For example, can we increase the range and amount of affect in play in a play tutoring program? What other abilities will be affected by increased affect expression? Will increasing affect in play effect different areas of functioning than will increasing imagination in play, or the organization of the story in play? These are some of the questions currently being investigated in my research program.

Another important research line to investigate systematically is how play changes in play therapy. Play therapy is a natural arena in which to investigate mechanisms of change. Now that we have measures available that can assess play, including them in a repeated measures design during psychotherapy will give us important information about how play changes during therapy with different clinical populations. Using play assessment in psychotherapy process research can help tie therapeutic interventions to changes in play. This kind of research will add to the literature on the effectiveness of specific play intervention techniques with different clinical populations.

8

Future Directions in Research and Practice

What conclusions can we draw from the play and play therapy research and clinical literature? What are the implications for future research? What are the guidelines that emerge for using play in child psychotherapy? What are the next steps for developing play therapy as an empirically supported treatment? These questions are addressed in this chapter. Conclusions and guidelines from previous chapters are discussed and integrated.

PLAY AND CHILD DEVELOPMENT

Play and Creativity

As reviewed in chapters 1 and 2, play relates to a number of areas important in child development. The strongest relationship is between play and creativity. This finding emerged in the Fisher (1992) meta-analysis and is also reflected in the large number of studies in the play and creativity literature. Much of the research is correlational, but there is a substantial body of well-controlled experimental studies that have found facilitative effects of play on creative thinking. Specifically, play relates to and facilitates insight ability and divergent thinking. It is important to identify the specific play processes and mechanisms that account for the link between play and creativity. One might speculate that, over time, pretend play helps the child become more creative in the following ways:

1. Practice with the free flow of associations that is important in divergent thinking.
2. Practice with symbol substitution, recombining of ideas, and manipulation of object representations. These processes are important in insight ability and transformation ability.

3. Express and experience positive affect. Positive affect facilitates creativity. Also, the positive affect in play could be the precursor of the passion and intrinsic motivation so often noted in creative individuals.
4. Express and think about positive and negative affect themes. Emotional content and primary process content is permitted to surface and be expressed through play. Over time, the child develops access to a variety of memories, associations, and affective and non-affective cognition. This broad repertoire of associations aids creative problem solving.
5. Develop cognitive structure that enables the child to contain, integrate, and modulate affect.

Future research should investigate the role of specific play processes and how they facilitate creativity.

Guidelines for Research on Play and Creativity

Guidelines for research in the play and creativity area, as suggested by Russ (1999), are:

- Investigate specific mechanisms and processes that underlie the play and creativity link. For example, how does having easy access to affect-laden fantasy facilitate divergent thinking?
- Increase the focus on affect expression in play and creativity. Of special interest are the differential effects of different types of affect content on different types of creativity tasks. Research suggests that positive and negative affect, and different content themes within those categories, may have different effects on various types of creative cognitive processes. Also, affect states and affect themes in fantasy may function quite differently from one another.
- Carry out longitudinal studies that are necessary to determine how creative processes develop over time and whether early play predicts real-life creativity over the life span.

Play and Other Adaptive Abilities in Child Development

There is a growing number of studies that have found relationships between play and coping. Future research needs to investigate the reason for this link. It is probable that one mediating variable is creative problem solving ability. Play facilitates divergent thinking and insight ability. This problem solving ability is generalized to daily life and problems of daily living. This model of play, facilitating coping ability with creative problem solving functioning as a mediator, needs to be empirically investigated.

A few studies have linked play with measures of adjustment such as anxiety and depression. More research needs to be carried out before we can have definite conclusions in this area. The studies that do exist suggest that good play is related to less anxiety. This finding is consistent with the experimental studies that found that play reduced anxiety. Perhaps children who use play well are resolving their fears in the play situation and have less anxiety.

The finding of a positive relationship between negative affect in play and depression over a 10-year period in my own research is important to investigate further. Although the depression was not in the clinical range, this result suggests that negative affect in play may be an important indicator of dysphoric affect. The proportion of negative to positive affect in play may be important to explore in the future.

In general, a logical hypothesis is that good play ability would be positively related to adjustment. The child who can and does use play to solve problems of daily living and to regulate emotions and work through fears should be using play as a resource. Although there is some empirical support for this relationship, we need much more research in this area to test this hypothesis.

The area of play and interpersonal functioning is a complex one. The finding that cognitive aspects of play related to interpersonal functioning is, as Harris (1994) has theorized, probably due to perspective-taking ability. Children who think more flexibly and divergently should be better able to take the perspective of another. And Niec, Yopp, and Russ's (2002) preliminary findings that interpersonal qualities in the pretend play related to object representations on the TAT suggests that we can capture various dimensions of the child's interpersonal world in the play narrative.

There is no substantial evidence that pretend play itself fosters interpersonal development. My own sense is that attachment, internal representations, capacity for empathy, and altruism develop through relationships with others. Although pretend play may be a medium through which a relationship occurs, as with parents, or other children, or a therapist, the pretend play components themselves are not impacting interpersonal relationships in a major way. I would speculate that, although play aids in perspective—taking and understanding the view of the other, it does not influence the interpersonal schema itself.

PLAY PROCESSES

The play processes that emerge in play should each be investigated thoroughly. I proposed four general categories in chapter 1; cognitive, affective, interpersonal, and problem solving, and I identified specific processes within each. There may be other categories as well. As measures are refined and validated for each process, we will be able to systematically investigate them. A major question is whether each of these processes possesses unique variance or is part of one large play ability factor. Research with the APS suggests that the cognitive and affect categories, though related to one another, also do have separate variance components. And, in various research studies, different components relate to different criteria. This is true of sub-categories as well. For example, the imagination component has had stronger relationships than the organization in play component with the creativity criteria. Also, in the longitudinal studies (Russ & Cooperberg, 2002; Russ et al., 1999) the cognitive components in play predicted divergent thinking over time, whereas the affective components did not. This finding suggests that cognitive abilities of organization and imagination may have more stable relationships with creativity over time than do affective processes. Affect may be more important in divergent thinking when the measures have temporal proximity. Or, affect could be predictive over time if the creativity criteria were ones in which affect is important. For example, affect may play a role in criteria of painting or fiction writing where access to affect images and memories would be an advantage. These are the kind of research questions that await exploration.

In addition to questions of differential prediction of each play process, we also need to determine the longitudinal course of each process. What happens to imagination over time and to the relationship with various correlates?

Finally, we need to investigate techniques that facilitate each play process. How can we increase each ability in a meaningful way? If we do increase play abilities, will we effect important functions such as coping and problem solving? We know from the play tutoring studies reviewed in chapter 7 that researchers have improved play skills in well-controlled studies. We need to carry out similar studies focusing on specific processes. A study currently underway in my research program is developing different sets of techniques that will help children express more affect in play, more imagination in play, and better organization of the play narrative. When these techniques are developed, they can be taught to parents and to play therapists. In essence, play intervention techniques should be able to be put into a manual form for therapists with guidelines about how to integrate them into child therapy. Major research initiatives should occur in this area. Manuals are needed for integrating play into different forms of therapy.

Play Processes and Interventions

We need to learn how to target and work with these play processes in therapy. How these play processes can be used in therapy depends on the play abilities of the child and the type of problem the child is presenting with.

For children with constricted affect in play, and who present with anxiety and fear, a play intervention that focuses on helping the child to express emotion in play, especially negative emotion, should help the child to then use the play to resolve problems. It is important that the child be able to pretend, use imagination, and make up stories. On the Affect in Play Scale, this child would have average or above fantasy organization and imagination scores, but below average frequency and variety of affect scores. Once the negative affect can be expressed in play, then the mechanisms of change can begin to work. Those mechanisms of change could be extinction of anxiety, resolution of an internal conflict by gaining a new understanding or having a situation end in a different way, integrating the trauma into preexisting mental schemas, and so on. The hypothesized mechanisms of change reviewed in chapters 3 and 4 need to be tested. This particular profile, high pretend play ability with low expression of affect, was true of the separation-anxiety case presented in chapter 3. This 6-year-old could pretend, but was constricted in affect expression in play. Once he was able to express more emotion in play, he was able to "get to work" and resolve his fears. This change was brought about quickly (eight sessions). He was an ideal candidate for play therapy.

For the child with a different play profile, high expression of affect but poor cognitive organization ability, the nature of the presenting problem is important to consider before deciding whether to use a play intervention. In a short period of time, it would be difficult to increase the cognitive organization through the play to enable the child to use play in a meaningful way. Other empirically supported treatments should be used. If the child is like the borderline child (Steve) presented in chapter 3, with severe psychopathology needing a longer term intervention, then a play approach should be considered. There is time to develop better cognitive organization by developing play skills. For Steve, even though there was serious cognitive disorganization, he did have the ability to pretend, use metaphors (although primitive), and make-believe. For children who have little or no ability to pretend in play, a play therapy approach does not make sense to use.

These guidelines for targeting and using play processes are really for use in the short-term. In the long-term, play therapy research needs to be carried out to determine the effectiveness of play therapy with specific populations of children.

PLAY AND PSYCHOTHERAPY

The major consistency between the child development research and the child psychotherapy theory is that play helps children solve problems and cope with problems. Play relates to or facilitates problem solving ability in the form of greater insight, divergent thinking, and flexibility.

There is empirical evidence that these abilities relate to the ability to think of alternative coping strategies in daily life. There is some evidence that play relates to aspects of interpersonal functioning and to aspects of adjustment. In a broad sense, the empirical literature does support the use of play to bring about change. And there is solid evidence that we can improve children's play skills. However, the techniques used by play therapists and the process of play therapy have not been guided by this research nor tied to change in these specific play processes. Therefore, there is a huge gap between the research literature and the practice of play therapy. Also, a major factor that works against bridging this gap is that, ultimately, the therapist is focused on altering characteristics such as depression, anxiety, impulsivity, and symptoms in general, not problem solving ability.

The well-done play intervention studies reviewed in chapter 4 found that play intervention resulted in reduced fear and anxiety. These studies focused on medical situations or separation-from-parent situations. Researchers concluded that it was something about the fantasy component in play that accounted for the reduced anxiety. The studies also found that play is more effective for children who already have good fantasy play skills. This finding is consistent with some of the play and creativity studies that found that play facilitated creativity best for children who had good fantasy ability.

Guidelines for Clinical Practice

These play intervention studies have implications for clinical practice. There is empirical evidence that giving children the opportunity to play and to use fantasy will reduce fears and anxiety. One would expect that having a therapist interact with the child and use a variety of therapeutic techniques would result in a stronger effect, but this is an empirical question. Results also suggest that children who already have good fantasy play skills will benefit most from the play intervention. These research findings are consistent with the psychodynamic psychotherapy framework that utilizes play to help children with internal conflicts that result in anxiety or resolve fears evolving from stress and trauma. Psychodynamic approaches also suggest the use of these play approaches for children whose fantasy skills are normally developed and who can use play in therapy.

For the clinician, then, in order to decide whether to use play in therapy, two questions should be answered during the assessment phase:

1. Is anxiety a major part of the clinical picture and symptom formation?
2. Can this child use pretend play? Are play skills developed normally?

In regards to the first question, the research only speaks to anxiety around medical procedures and issues of separation. But I think it is reasonable and makes theoretical sense to extrapolate to other kinds of anxiety issues and situations. Post-traumatic stress disorders are logical to extrapolate to, and the clinical literature (Terr, 1990) suggests that play intervention is very helpful in aiding children to re-work and master the trauma. However, we need research studies to answer this question definitely about what kinds of anxiety are best treated with play interventions.

What about other internalizing disorders, such as depression? Again, we need research studies, but if the child has good play skills, play should be a reasonable vehicle for expression of negative affect and resolving the loss. But other components of the therapy will be important as well.

The second question, "How good are the child's play skills?" can be answered in a brief play observation period in the initial intake hour or during the assessment phase. As reviewed in chapter 5, there are a variety of instruments available for use. But even without a "formal" assessment the clinician can determine if there are examples of pretend in the play, evidence of a story, expression of affect and conflict, and an interest in the play material.

What about the use of play therapy approaches for children who cannot play well? At this point, the research does not support the use of play therapy with children who do not have good play skills. Especially in this era of managed care, when short-term treatment is dominant, play therapy can only be effective in a short period of time if the child can quickly use the intervention and quickly "get to work," so to speak. The issue of using the therapy time to teach the child to play, or teach the parent to teach the child to play, is a different question. For children with poor play skills, and presentation of symptoms of anxiety, other forms of empirically validated interventions are preferable. The one exception may be in the area of severely disturbed children such as the borderline child presented in chapter 3. With these children, when long-term therapy is necessary, play can be a form of communication with the therapist and can be used to help the child establish an understanding of cause and effect and differentiate fantasy from reality.

There may be other reasons to have play intervention programs to teach children to play. These reasons are discussed in a later section in this chapter. But to have a therapy phase to first teach play skills, and then work on the anxiety, is hard to justify when other therapy approaches work quickly and effectively.

Another question that arises is whether an alternative cognitive-behavioral approach should be used with anxiety disorders for good players. Again, the comparative studies need to be carried out, comparing the benefits of cognitive behavioral therapy versus play therapy for children who can use play well.

What about externalizing disorders, with or without play skills? The empirical evidence for the use of play in the Parent Child Interaction Therapy intervention developed by Eyberg and her colleagues for Oppositional Defiant Disorders is very strong. Play is an integral part of this intervention program for very young children. But behavioral techniques are also a major part of the treatment. For other externalizing disorders, there is no empirical evidence that play intervention is effective. Other empirically validated treatments should be used. Although play could be beneficial, we need empirical evidence that this is the case.

For children with borderline psychotic features, or psychotic disorders, in addition to medication, play approaches can be useful in establishing a relationship with the therapist and form of communication with the therapist. Although I am not aware of any empirical work supporting play with these seriously emotionally disturbed children, there is not much support for other therapeutic approaches either. So, until that empirical work is carried out, play therapy with these children seems to be a reasonable alternative.

Interestingly, the play intervention studies support using play for children for whom psychodynamic therapy was originally intended—children struggling with anxiety who have developed normally in most areas, including play skills. This finding should guide where we put our energy in future research.

Future Research Directions:
Towards Empirically Supported Practice

The main conclusions from this review of the empirical literature in child development and play intervention are that:

1. Pretend play helps children solve problems, especially in a creative fashion.
2. Pretend play helps children reduce anxiety and fear.

This literature provides an empirical base for the principles of play therapy. However, there is no empirical support for the practice of play therapy in clinical settings. It is imperative that the field move quickly to the next generation of studies—empirically supported treatment studies. It is logical to carry out evaluation studies with problems and populations for which the empirical evidence suggests that play therapy will work. The research points to evaluating play therapy with children with anxiety disorders and post-traumatic stress disorders. Once play therapy has been shown to be effective with these children, it would then make sense to expand to other disorders like depression, where negative affect plays a major role. Research also suggests that using play to help with problem solving in some way would be most effective (for example, using the play to generate ideas about how to cope with a problem). Focusing on forms of problem solving as the mechanism of change in play therapy should be a fruitful research program.

In order for a systematic program of research to be carried out, research should be at both the macro and micro levels, with continuing interaction between laboratory research and research in clinical settings.

Of prime importance is to:

• Investigate play intervention with situations and populations that have anxiety as a focus. Investigating the effectiveness of play with other types of anxiety disorders and post-traumatic stress disorders are next logical steps. Also, investigating the use of play with specific types of anxiety-producing situations (in addition to medical procedures) and after specific traumas, such as accidents, natural disasters, and loss of a parent, is warranted. Carrying out studies of children who experienced trauma will also investigate the use of play with some types of depression that involves mourning and loss. The field needs to develop an empirical base for the use of play in these areas. Carrying out treatment efficacy studies under controlled conditions that involve random assignment and control groups is essential.

• Refine specific play techniques and develop play therapy manuals. Research needs to investigate the effectiveness of specific techniques in facilitating specific play processes. When is modeling most effective—for which processes and populations? How do we help children better regulate their emotions? Would having children make up stories in their play that included emotion help them regulate affect? There are a myriad of interesting questions to investigate in this area that lend themselves to focused research in the lab. Results could then be tested in clinical treatment groups. The question of refining play intervention techniques is one that bridges the research laboratory and the clinical treatment setting. Research groups could go back and forth between the laboratory and clinical setting. Play therapy manuals need to be developed based on this work. For example, Fein (1995) reported on studies that found that when 4-year-olds were given problem props (toys in which one figure was incompatible with the others), they told better stories than did children with compatible toys. Fein concluded that props facilitate story-telling when they tap children's affective knowledge. Implications for clinical practice is that the therapist can set the stage by providing the right mix of toys.

• Carry out psychotherapy process research with play as a focus. Following the individual case, with repeated measures of play (either in the session or separately) will contribute to our knowledge of how play changes in therapy, what therapeutic interventions effect play, and what changes in the child's functioning play effects.

• Investigate specific mechanisms of change. How does fantasy play reduce anxiety? What exactly is the working-through process in play? Can we break down the working-through process into components, measure it, assess its effectiveness, and teach other children to do it? This is a challenging task, but in my opinion, is one of the most important tasks in terms of potential benefits to children.

It is especially important to learn how the child deals with and integrates negative affect (Kelly, 2002). The therapist helps the child experience, modulate, and integrate negative affect. Recent conceptualizations and research paradigms in the emotion regulation area, reviewed in chapter 4, should be used in developing play research studies. Pennebaker's (2002) research on emotional writing suggests that integrating the emotion into a coherent narrative is an underlying mechanism in the effectiveness of emotional writing. Using a play emotional expression paradigm is a logical way to investigate this phenomenon in children. A number of recent theorists in the emotion area would stress the importance of the narrative that is developed around the emotion as being most important. It is not the expression of the emotion that is important, but the narrative context in which it is placed. The child may do that in his play, or the therapist may do that in their labeling, interpretation, and integration of the affect into events in the child's life. On the other hand, for children who are constricted in affect expression, permission to experience and express an emotion such as anger could extinguish the anxiety associated with it. The expression of the affect would be the key mechanism of change.

• Carry out comparative studies of play therapy and other forms of therapy to determine optimal forms of intervention with specific problems and populations. Play therapy studies should follow the generally accepted criteria in the field using random assignment to conditions, specific child populations, treatment manuals, and multiple outcome measure with "blind" raters (Kazdin, 2000). One of challenges for play therapy will be to demonstrate greater effectiveness than cognitive-behavioral approaches in treating childhood disorders. Having a wide variety of outcome measures will be important in contrasting the benefits of different treatment approaches.

• Investigate the use of play intervention modules with specific problems and populations. These modules could develop from the studies that are refining play intervention techniques. Different kinds of play intervention modules could be used with different kinds of problems. For example, there could be one set of play interventions for separation anxiety and another for post-traumatic stress. These modules could be used with other types of treatment techniques.

PLAY AND PREVENTION

In some ways, the play research in the child development area has more implications for prevention programs than for child psychotherapy. Play emerges as a resource for children which could function as a protective factor under stressful circumstances. Play helps children solve problems and reduce anxiety. The play tutoring programs reviewed in chapter 7 found that, in well-controlled studies, children could be taught to play and these improved skills benefitted them in other ways. Imparting play skills, or improving the skills they already have, could help large groups of children over time. Play techniques could be developed to facilitate the processing and regulating of emotions. Teachers and parents have been able to teach children to play. Based on guidelines by researchers in the area, reviewed in chapter 7, future research on the play intervention area should:

- Refrain from one-shot studies (Christie, 1994). Long-term treatment durations (6–12 sessions) with long-term follow-up should be most effective.
- Take into account important moderator and mediator variables (age; ability to use make-believe).
- Keep the intervention "playful."
- Investigate mechanisms of change.
- Tune the intervention to specific goals.
- Investigate the benefits of teaching play skills to high-risk populations.

Ideal places for play intervention prevention programs would be Head Start settings, kindergarten and early elementary school settings, and parent outreach settings. Training parents and teachers to facilitate play, and evaluating the effectiveness of their efforts, will spur the development of model programs that reach larger numbers of children.

In 1993 I suggested a pilot project that would establish a Play Center as a supplementary experience for children from kindergarten through third grade. This kind of center is consistent with Gardner's (1991) call for a restructuring of the school experience. He described Project Spectrum, an early childhood education program, as having different physical areas for different learning domains. A Play Center would fit with this model. Different types of play opportunities could be available so that individual needs would be accommodated. Teachers and aids could guide and facilitate pretend play.

In conclusion, children's pretend play is an ideal focus for the study of early developmental processes. Play is also an ideal focus for interventions to facilitate development of processes and to bring about change in internal distress and behavioral symptoms. I hope I have stirred interest and excitement and have motivated students and professionals to explore the many interesting questions that need to be addressed. There is a lot to do. We should be doing everything possible to help children make full use of this natural tool of play during their childhood years. It will be good for them and good for society.

Appendix: Affect in Play Scale*

Sandra W. Russ
Case Western Reserve University

The Affect in Play Scale (APS) consists of a standardized play task and a criterion-based rating scale. The APS is appropriate for children 6–10 years of age, which includes children in Grades 1 through 3.

The Affect in Play Scale measures the amount and types of affect expression in children's fantasy play. The scale rates the frequency and intensity of affective expression, variety of affect categories, quality of fantasy, imagination, comfort in play, and integration of affect. Play sessions are 5-minute standardized puppet play periods.

THE APS PLAY TASK

The play task consists of two human puppets, one boy and one girl, and three small blocks that are laid out on a table (see Fig. A.1 for puppets). The puppets have neutral facial expressions. Both Caucasian and African-American versions of puppets are used, depending upon the child population. The blocks are brightly colored and of different shapes. The play props and instructions are unstructured enough so that individual differences in play can emerge. The task is administered individually to the child and the play is videotaped. The instructions for the task are:

> I'm here to learn about how children play. I have here two puppets and would like you to play with them any way you like for five min-

FIG. A.1. Puppets for the Affect in Play Scale.

utes. For example, you can have the puppets do something together. I also have some blocks that you can use. Be sure to have the puppets talk out loud. The video camera will be on so that I can remember what you say and do. I'll tell you when to stop.

The child is told when there is one minute left with the instruction, "You have one minute left."

Prompts and Special Circumstances

1. If the child does not know to put on the puppets, tell the child to put them on. Let the child know when they can start and start timing from that point.
2. If the child does not start to play, prompt the child after 30 seconds by saying "Go ahead, have the puppets do something together." Two prompts of this sort can be given. After two minutes of no play, the task should be discontinued.
3. If the child plays but does not have the puppets talk, prompt with "Have the puppets talk out loud so I can hear" after 30 seconds. Two prompts can be given, spaced about one minute apart.
4. If a child has been playing, but then stops before time is up, prompt with "You still have time left, keep on playing." Prompt a second time if needed with "Keep on playing, I'll tell you when to stop." Most children who already played will be able to continue with prompts. If they cannot, then discontinue after two minutes of no play.
5. Be sure not to give any verbal reinforcement during the child's play. It is important however to be attentive and watch the child and be interested. After the child has finished, say "That was good" or "That was fine."

6. Be sure to stop after five minutes. A wristwatch with a second hand is adequate. Time in an unobtrusive manner.

THE APS RATING SCALE

The APS measures the amount and types of affective expression in children's fantasy play. The APS measures affect themes in the play narrative. Both emotion-laden content and expression of emotion in the play are coded. The APS also measures cognitive dimensions of the play, such as quality of fantasy and imagination.

Both Holt's (1977) Scoring System for Primary Process on the Rorschach and Singer's play scales were used as models for the development of the scoring system. In addition, the work of Izard (1977) and Tomkins (1962, 1963) was consulted to ensure that the affect categories were comprehensive and covered all major types of emotion expressed by children in the 4–10 age group.

There are three major affect scores for the APS:

1. *Total frequency of units of affective expression.* A unit is defined as one scorable expression by an individual puppet. In a two puppet dialogue, expressions of each puppet are scored separately. A unit can be the expression of an affect state, an affect theme, or a combination of the two. An example, of an affect state would be one puppet saying "This is fun." An example of an affect theme would be "Here is a bomb that is going to explode." The expression can be verbal ("I hate you") or non-verbal (one puppet punching the other). The frequency of affect score is the total number of units of affect expressed in the five minute period. If non-verbal activity, such as fighting, occurs in a continuous fashion, a new unit is scored every five seconds.

2. *Variety of affect categories.* There are 11 possible affect categories. The categories are: Happiness/Pleasure; Anxiety/Fear; Sadness/Hurt; Frustration/Disappointment; Nurturance/Affection; Aggression; Competition; Oral; Oral Aggression; Sexual; Anal. The variety of affect score is the number of different categories of affect expressed in the 5-minute period. Affect categories can be classified as positive affect (Happiness, Nurturance, Competition, Oral, Sexual) and negative affect (Anxiety, Sadness, Aggression, Frustration, Oral Aggression, Anal). Another classification is primary process affect (Aggression, Oral, Oral Aggression, Sexual, Anal) and non-primary process affect (Happiness, Sadness, Anxiety, Frustration, Competition, Nurturance).

3. *Mean intensity of affective expression (1–5 rating).* This rating measures the intensity of the feeling state or content theme. Each unit of affect is rated for intensity on a 1–5 scale.

Because scoring intensity is time consuming, we score this only when there is a specific interest in the intensity dimension.

CRITERIA FOR AFFECT CONTENT
AND INTENSITY RATINGS

General Principles

An affect unit is scored when there is an expression of an affect content theme, emotion word, or non-verbal expression of emotion in the play narrative.

All of the affect intensity ratings are based on the expression of affect content themes, emotion words, and non-verbal expressions of emotion. "I like this hot dog" is comprised of both an affective content theme (hot dog–oral) and an emotional expression word (like). It could also be accompanied by non-verbal expression of positive affect (voice tone, clapping). In general, combinations of emotional expression and emotion word and content themes get higher intensity ratings than the theme alone or emotional expression alone. The general criteria for the 1–5 intensity ratings are:

1. Reference to affect content.
2. Reference to affect content with special emphasis, which implies experiencing (such as personal referent).
3. Current experiencing, which includes:
   a. Moderate action alone.
   b. Emotion with conversational voice.
   c. Primary process theme plus mild feeling state.
4. Stronger current experiencing, which includes:
   a. Mild action plus mild feeling state.
   b. Strong action alone.
   c. Strong affect alone.
   d. For primary process categories, unusual and strong emotion or strong theme word.
   e. Primary process theme and moderate affect.
5. Very strong feeling state, which includes:
   a. Action plus strong feeling state.
   b. Extreme primary process theme word.
   c. Extremely strong affect.
   d. Extremely strong action.

In general, affective theme, emotional expression (emotion word, tone, facial expression, etc.) and action are additive components.

SPECIFIC CRITERIA FOR AFFECT CATEGORIES AND INTENSITY RATINGS

Aggression

Expression of anger; fighting, destruction, or harm to another character or object; or reference to destructive objects (guns, knives) or actions (breaking).

1. Reference to aggressive content. (Examples: Here's a toy gun; Here's a knife; This is broken.)
2. Personalized reference to aggressive content; mild bickering. (Examples: "I have a knife;" "I'll break it." "Let's fight; "No—I don't want to do that.")
3. Actual fighting, hitting, tussling; destroying other's property; aggressive dialogue with feeling; angry feeling statement—"I am mad." Example: "I don't want to that—That's stupid" (with feeling); I'll punch you; I don't like you; Let's fight (with feeling).
4. Action plus dialogue; strong feeling state; strong theme word. (Example: Hitting plus "You're stupid"; "I hate you"; "Here is a bomb that is going to explode.")
5. Strong action and strong dialogue; extreme emotional theme. (Examples: "I'll kill you;" "I'm going to beat your brains to a pulp;" actions of shooting or stabbing.)

Nurturance/Affection

Expressions of empathy or sympathy with another character; affection; helping and support.

1. Reference to nurturing, affectionate themes. (Examples: "Sally and John are friends"; "Yesterday my Mom helped me.")
2. Personalized nurturing theme or theme with special emphasis. (Examples: "Are you ok?"; "I'll help"; "Don't forget your sweater"; "Sally and John are best friends.")
3. Nurturing activity; current feeling state of affection. (Examples: "I like you"; "You are my friend"; gift-giving; patting; helping.)
4. Action plus dialogue; strong verbal statement or strong action. (Examples: Hugging; Dancing together; "I really like you"; "You're my very best friend.")
5. Strong action plus strong dialogue; very strong nurturing action or word. (Examples: "I love you"; "I really like you" [while patting or hugging].)

Happiness/Pleasure

Expression of positive affect that denotes pleasure, happiness, having a good time, enjoyment, and contentedness.

1. Reference to content involving happiness, pleasure, satisfaction, general preference statements. (Examples: "This is nice"; "Saturday is the best day of the week.")
2. Reference with special emphasis; personalized; affective content distanced by past/future or third person. Subjective reference to fun and amusement. (Examples: "Johnny looks happy"; "That was fun"; "Oh boy, the circus is in town; That's good.")
3. Current affect experiencing or activity involving happiness, pleasure. Happiness themes plus feeling state. (Examples: "I feel happy" [conversational tone]; "This is fun"; Hand clapping; "I love to get presents"; "I like this" [with strong tone]; "This is fun.")
4. Activity plus affective expression. Strong feeling state; strong action alone (jumping up and down with happy expression). (Examples: I feel happy [with feeling]; "Whee, this is fun"; Singing happily; Dancing happily; "I really like this.")
5. Combination of two of the following: emotional expression, theme, or action (At least one at extreme level or two at strong level). Extreme emotional words also scored. (Examples: "I love this" [with action]; jumping and laughing.)

Anxiety/Fear

Expressions of fear and anxiety. Content such as school anxiety, doctors visits, fears, concern about punishment, and worry. Actions of fleeing and hiding, agitation.

1. Reference to fearful theme. (Examples: "Oh—it's time for school"; "It's time to go to the doctor.")
2. Mild anticipation with hint of negative consequence. (Examples: "Oh, no—I broke the teacher's ruler"; "Uh, oh, I dropped my book.")
3. Fearful theme with mild affect; more direct reference to consequences; withdrawal or fleeing activity. (Examples: "We're going to get in trouble"; "Let's hide from them"; "There's a monster over there"; "I see a ghost.")
4. Clear expression of fear or anxiety; combination of theme and strong affect. (Examples: "I'm scared"; "The monster's coming after me"; "Mom's gonna spank me" [with feeling].)
5. Withdrawal activity plus fear; strong theme plus fearful affect. (Examples: "I'm scared, he'll kill us"; "Don't let him hurt me" [while hiding].)

Sadness/Hurt

Expression of illness, physical injury, pain, sadness, loneliness.

1. Non-personalized reference to sadness/hurt (conversational tone). (Examples: "Sally got hurt yesterday"; "Joe was in the hospital.")
2. Personalized reference to sadness/hurt (conversational) or non-personalized reference with exclamation. (Examples: "Sally was crying yesterday"; "Sometimes I cry.")
3. Current experience of sadness/hurt stated in conversational tone; action of sadness/hurt. (Examples: "That's sad"; "That hurts"; "I'm sad"; "I have a headache"; "Please don't leave me alone.")
4. Statement of sadness/hurt action; stronger verbal statement; more intense sad action (experiencing). (Examples: "Ouch that hurts"; "Boy am I sad"; Whimpering; Whining; "I don't want you to go.")
5. Strong verbal statement of sadness/hurt with action; use of very strong sad/hurt words; or very intense current experiencing of sadness/hurt. (Examples: "I don't want the shot" [while crying]; "This hurts" [while crying]; Moaning in pain.)

Frustration/Disappointment/Dislike

Expressions of disappointment and frustration with activities, objects, and limitations.

1. Reference to frustration/disappointment; non-personalized statement of frustration/disappointment (conversational voice). (Examples: "It fell"; "Math is boring"; "She seems bored.")
2. Personalized statement of frustration/disappointment (conversational tone); current action of frustration/disappointment. (Examples: "I'm not good at building"; "It fell" [with affect].)
3. Current experience of frustration/disappointment (conversational tone); current action of frustration/disappointment. (Examples: "This is hard"; "I'm bored"; "I can't do this"; Making noises like clicking tongue.)
4. Statement of frustration/disappointment with an action; statement of current experience of frustration/disappointment (exclamation); Stronger action. (Examples: "I can't get this" (while knocking down the blocks); "Boy, is this hard"; "This is a rotten day"; "Oh darn, I can't get this.")
5. Stronger statement of frustration/disappointment with an action; very strong experiencing statement; very strong action. (Examples: Slamming down the blocks while saying "I can't do this"; Swearing; "I hate this.")

Competition

Expressions of wanting to win, competitive game-playing, pride in achievement, and striving for achievement.

1. Reference to competitive games. (Example: mentioning cops and robbers, checkers, hide and seek.)
2. Personal reference to competitive games. (Examples: "Let's play tag"; "Let's see who can run the fastest.")
3. Game playing with action; competitive theme with mild affect. (Examples: playing hide and seek; "I want to win"; "Mine is the best.")
4. Action plus affect; strong feeling state. (Examples: Playing tag and saying "I win"; "I'm going to beat you" [with feeling]; Playing tag and saying "Got you".)
5. Action plus strong feeling sate. (Examples: Playing tag and saying "I'm king of the mountain"; Jumping up and down and saying "I win".)

Oral

Expressions of oral content of food, cooking, eating and drinking. Affect expressions are positive about oral content:

1. Reference to oral content of food, cooking, mouth. (Examples: "Here's an ice cream shop"; "This is a new special cheese.")
2. Personalized reference to oral content or content with special emphasis. (Examples: "Let's eat dinner"; "I'll feed you"; "Johnny is hungry.")
3. Current experiencing which includes eating behavior or emotional word in addition to oral content. (Examples: "I like candy"; "I am hungry"; "That food looks good"; "Actual eating behavior.")
4. Eating behavior plus affective content; oral theme word plus moderate affective expression in voice or facial expression. (Examples: "Mmmmm—this is good candy"; "I really like cake.")
5. Strong eating behavior plus strong affective expression. (Example: Wow—this is great [while eating].)

Oral Aggression

Expressions of oral aggressive themes such as biting or food that has negative affect associated with it:

1. Reference to oral aggressive themes. (Examples: Teeth, dentist, poison, Dracula.)

2. Personal reference to oral aggressive theme; more intense theme word; special emphasis. (Examples: "Let's go to the dentist"; "That dog might bite me.")
3. Reference plus mild affect; activity such as vomiting. (Examples: Biting activity; "This food tastes terrible.")
4. Reference plus strong affect; activity plus affect. (Examples: Biting with feeling; "This is poison [yech].")
5. Very strong affect and activity. (Examples: Eating people; Dracula attacks puppet and bites.)

Anal

Expression of anal content including dirt and making a mess:

1. Reference to anal content. (Examples: "This is a mess"; "That's dirty.")
2. Personalized reference to anal content or impersonal reference with special emphasis. (Examples: "I made a mess"; "I'll get dirty"; "Be careful not to make a mess"; "We have to clean up.")
3. Reference to anal content plus mild effect. (Examples: "That's a real mess"; "I don't like dirt"; "This is muddy.")
4. Anal activity plus feeling state; anal theme plus strong feeling state. (Examples: "Yech—this is a mess"; "This is gross"; "Look at his butt.")
5. Strong anal theme word; strong expression of disgust around dirt; inappropriate word. (Examples: "Look—he pooped"; "This is an awful mess.")

Sexual

Expressions of sexual content:

1. Reference to boyfriend or girlfriend. (Example: "That is his girlfriend.")
2. Personalized reference or special emphasis. (Examples: "I'm getting undressed"; "He is my boyfriend"; "She is going on a date.")
3. Mild activity or sexual content with feeling state. (Examples: "I like to kiss"; hugging if sexual overtones.)
4. Sexual activity plus feeling or strong sexual content. (Examples: Kissing; Dancing if sexual overtones; Looking under dress.)
5. Extreme sexual content or strong activity. (Examples: Strong kissing; Blatant sexual joke; Reference to genitals.)

QUALITY OF FANTASY

The quality of fantasy rating is the mean of the following three dimensions of fantasy.

Organization

This rating scale measures the quality of the plot and the complexity of the story:

1. Series of unrelated events, no cause and effect, disjointed.
2. Some cause and effect; series of loosely related events.
3. Cause and effect, organized in a temporal sequence, but no overall integrated plot.
4. More cause and effect, close to an integrated plot.
5. Integrated plot with beginning, middle and end.

Elaboration

This rating scale measures the amount of embellishment in the play. One should consider theme, facial expression, voice tones, character development.

1. Very simple themes with no embellishment. Very few details.
2. Minimal embellishment
3. Much embellishment, in one or two dimensions.
4. Moderate embellishment across many dimensions.
5. Much embellishment across many dimensions- many details, high activity, sound effects, changes in voice, lots of facial expressions and verbal inflection.

Imagination

This rating scaled measures the novelty and uniqueness of the play and the ability to pretend and use fantasy. Ability to transform the blocks and pretend with them.

1. No symbolism or transformations, no fantasy.
2. One or two instances of simple transformations. No novel events. Very few fantasy events in the story.
3. Three or more transformations. Some fantasy and pretend events, such as "Let's play house." Some variety of events. No novel events or events removed from daily experience.
4. Many transformations. Variety of events. Some novel fantasy events. Some fantasy with unusual twists or removed from daily experience such as living in a castle or building a space ship. Other characters in addition to the two puppets are included in the story.
5. Many transformations and many fantasy themes. Novelty of ideas is evident. Fantasy has new twists and often has elements outside of daily experience.

The organization, elaboration, and imagination scores can be utilized separately and also combined into a mean quality of fantasy score for each child.

Comfort

A global rating for the child's comfort in play measures the involvement of the child in the play and the enjoyment of the play. The lower end of the scale rates comfort more than enjoyment and the higher end of the scale weighs pleasure and involvement.

1. Reticent; distressed. Stops and starts.
2. Some reticence and stiffness.
3. OK but not enjoying and involved. Continues to play.
4. Comfortable and involved.
5. Very comfortable, involved and enjoying the play.

Affect Integration Score

The affect integration score is obtained by multiplying the quality of fantasy score by the frequency of affect score. This score taps how well the affect is integrated into cognition.

To summarize, the nine major scores on the APS are total frequency of affect, variety of affect categories, intensity of affect, organization, elaboration, imagination, quality of fantasy, comfort, and affect integration.

Practically, the APS is easy to administer and takes only 5 minutes. The scoring system takes time to learn, but then takes about 15–20 minutes per child. We have found that about 8% of children will not be able to engage in the play task. They are not able to make up a story or play in any way. For those children, we score 0 for frequency and variety of affect and 1 for the fantasy scores. Comfort score is based on what was observed. The inference is that lack of ability to do the task reflects low levels of the construct that the task is measuring.

There is a videotape available for training in administration of the APS.

ACKNOWLEDGMENTS

Anna Grossman-McKee, Zina Rutkin, and Amir Jassani contributed to the development of the scale. Larissa Niec, Astrida Kaugars, and Ethan Schafer contributed to this refinement.

References

Achenbach, T. (1978). Psychopathology of childhood: Research problems and issues. *Journal of Consulting and Clinical Psychology, 46,* 759–776.

Adaman, J. (1991). *The effects of induced mood on creativity.* Unpublished masters thesis, University of Miami, Coral Gables, FL.

Altschul, S. (1988). *Childhood bereavement and its aftermath.* Madison, WI: International University Press.

Amabile, T. (1990). Within you, without you: The social psychology of creativity and beyond. In M. Runco & R. Albert (Eds.), *Theories of creativity* (pp. 61–69). Newbury Park, CA: Sage.

Anastasi, A. (1988). *Psychological testing* (6th ed.). New York: Macmillan Publishing Company.

Applebaum, S. (1978). Pathways to change in psychoanalytic therapy. *Bulletin of Menniger Clinic, 42,* 239–251.

Arieti, S. (1976). *Creativity: The magic synthesis.* New York: Basic Books.

Astington, J. W., & Jenkins, J. M. (1995). Theory of mind development and social understanding. *Cognition and Emotion, 9,* 151–165.

Axline, V. M. (1947). *Play therapy.* Boston: Houghton Mifflin.

Axline, V. M. (1964). *Dibs: In search of self: Personality development in play therapy.* Boston: Houghton Mifflin.

Ayman-Nolley, S. (1992). Vygotsky's perspective on the development of imagination and creativity. *Creativity Research Journal, 5,* 77–85.

Barnett, I. (1984). Research note: Young children's resolution of distress through play. *Journal of Child Psychology and Psychiatry, 25,* 477–483.

Barnett, I., & Storm, B. (1981). Play, pleasure and pain: The reduction of anxiety through play. *Leisure Science, 4,* 161–175.

Barrett, C., Hampe, T. E., & Miller, L. (1978). Research on child psychotherapy. In S. Garfield & A. Bergin (Eds.), *Handbook of psychotherapy and behavior change* (pp. 411–435). New York: Wiley.

Barron, F., & Harrington, D. (1981). Creativity, intelligence, and personality. In M. Rosenzweig & L. Porter (Eds.), *Annual review of psychology,* (Vol. 32, pp. 439–476). Palo Alto, CA: Annual Reviews.

Blank, R., & Blank, G. (1986). *Beyond ego psychology: Developmental object relations theory.* New York: Columbia University Press.

Bledsoe, N. P., & Shepherd, J. T. (1982). A study of reliability and validity of a pre-school play scale. *The American Journal of Occupational Therapy, 36*(12), 783–788.

Bodiford-McNeil, C., Hembree-Kigin, T. L., & Eyberg, S. (1996). *Short-term play therapy for disruptive children.* King of Prussia, PA: The Center for Applied Psychology.

Bower, G. H. (1981). Mood and memory. *American Psychologist, 36,* 129–148.

Bryant, B. (1982). An index of empathy for children and adolescents. *Child Development, 53,* 413–425.

Budman, S. H., & Gurman, A. S. (1988). *Theory and practice of brief therapy.* New York: Guilford Press.

Burlingham, D. (1932). Child analysis and the mother. *Psychoanalytic Quarterly, 4,* 69–92.

Burstein, S., & Meichenbaum, D. (1979). The work of worrying in children undergoing surgery. *Journal of Abnormal Child Psychology, 7,* 121–132.

Campbell, S. (1998). Developmental perspectives. In T. Ollendick & M. Hersen (Eds.), *Handbook of child psychopathology* (3rd ed., pp. 3–35). New York: Plenum Press.

Carson, D., Bittner, M., Cameron, B., Brown, D., & Meyer, S. (1994). Creative thinking as a predictor of school-aged children's stress responses and coping abilities. *Creativity Research Journal, 7,* 145–158.

Casey, R. J., & Berman, J. S. (1985). The outcome of psychotherapy with children. *Psychological Bulletin, 98,* 388–400.

Cass, L., & Thomas, C. (1979). *Childhood pathology and later adjustment.* New York: Wiley.

Cassell, S. (1965). Effect of brief puppet therapy upon the emotional response of children undergoing cardiac catheterization. *Journal of Consulting Psychology, 29,* 1–8.

Cattell, R. B., & Jaspers, J. (1967). A general plasmode for factor analytic exercises and research. *Multivariate Behavior Research Monographs, 67*(3), No. 30-10-5-2.

Chambless, D. L., Sanderson, W. C., Shoham, V., Johnson, S. B., Pope, K. S., Chris-Christoph, R., Baker, M., Johnson, B., Woods, S. R., Sue, S., Beutler, L., Williams, D. A., & McCurry, S. (1996). An update on empirically validated therapy. *The Clinical Psychologist, 49,* 5–18.

Chethik, M. (1989). *Techniques of child therapy: Psychodynamic strategies.* New York: Guilford.

Christiano, B., & Russ, S. (1996). Play as a predictor of coping and distress in children during an invasive dental procedure. *Journal of Clinical Child Psychology, 25,* 130–138.

Christie, J. (1994). Academic play. In J. Hellendoorn, R. Van der Kooij, & B. Sutton-Smith (Eds.), *Play and intervention* (pp. 203–213). Albany: State University of New York Press.

Christie, J., & Johnson, E. (1983). The role of play in social-intellectual development. *Review of Educational Research, 53,* 93–115.

Cicchetti, D., & Rogosch, F. (1996). Equifinality and multifinality in developmental psychopathology [special issue]. *Development and Psychopathology, 8*(4).

Clark, P. J. (1993). Towards an integrated model of time-limited psychodynamic therapy with children. *Dissertation Abstracts International, 54,* 1659–B.

Clark, P., Griffing, P., & Johnson, L. (1989). Symbolic play and ideational fluency as aspects of the evolving divergent cognitive style in young children. *Early Child Development and Care, 51,* 77–88.

Cole, P., Zahn-Waxler, C., Fox, N., Usher, B., & Welsh, J. (1996). Individual differences in emotion regulation and behavior problems in preschool children. *Journal of Abnormal Psychology, 105*(4), 518–529.

D'Angelo, L. (1995). *Child's play: The relationship between the use of play and adjustment styles.* Unpublished dissertation, Case Western Reserve University, Cleveland, OH.

Dansky, J. (1980). Make-believe: A mediator of the relationship between play and associative fluency. *Child Development, 51,* 576–579.

Dansky, J. (1999). Play. In M. Runco & S. Pritzker (Eds.), *Encyclopedia of creativity* (pp. 393–408). San Diego: Academic Press.

Dansky, J., & Silverman, F. (1973). Effects of play on associative fluency in preschool-aged children. *Developmental Psychology, 9,* 38–43.

Dudek, S., (1980). Primary process ideation. In R. H. Woody (Ed.), *Encyclopedia of clinical assessment* (Vol. 1, pp. 520–539). San Francisco: Jossey-Bass.

Dudek, S., & Verreault, R. (1989). The creative thinking and ego functioning of children. *Creativity Research Journal, 2,* 64–86.

Dulcan, M., & Piercy, F. (1985). A model for teaching and evaluating brief psychotherapy with children and their families. *Professional Psychology: Research and Practice, 16,* 689–700.

Dunn, L., & Herwig, J. (1992). Play behaviors and convergent and divergent thinking skills of young children attending full-day preschool. *Child Study Journal, 22,* 23–38.

Edelbrock, C., & Achenbach, T. M. (1980). A typology of child behavior profile patterns: Distribution and correlates for disturbed children aged 6–16. *Journal of Abnormal Psychology, 8,* 441–470.

Emde, R. (1989). The infant's relationship experience: Developmental and affective aspects. In A. Sameroff & R. Emde (Eds.), *Relationship disturbances in early childhood* (pp. 33–51). New York: Basic Books.

Erikson, E. (1963). *Childhood and society.* New York: Norton.

Erikson, E. (1999, May 13). Obituary. *New York Times,* p. C16.

Faust, J., & Burns, W. (1991). Coding therapist and child interaction: Progress and outcome in play therapy. In C. Schaefer, K. Gitlin, & A. Sandgrund (Eds.), *Play diagnosis and assessment* (pp. 663–690). New York: John Wiley & Sons.

Fein, G. (1981). Pretend play in childhood: An integrative review. *Child Development, 52,* 1095–1118.

Fein, G. (1987). Pretend play: Creativity and consciousness. In P. Gorlitz & J. Wohlwill (Eds.), *Curiosity, imagination, and play* (pp. 281–304). Hillsdale, NJ: Lawrence Erlbaum Associates.

Fein, G. (1995). Toys and stories. In A. Pellegrini (Ed.), *The future of play theory* (pp. 151–164). Albany: State University of New York Press.

Feist, G. (in press). Affective states and traits in creativity: Evidence for non-linear relationship. In M. A. Runco (Ed.), *Handbook of creativity research* (Vol. 2). Cresskill, NJ: Hampton Press.

Feitelson, D., & Ross, G. (1973). The neglected factor-play. *Human Development, 16,* 202–223.

Fenson, I. (1984). Developmental trends for action and speech in pretend play. In I. Bretherton (Ed.), *Synthetic play: The development of social understanding* (pp. 249–270). Orlando, FL: Academic Press.

Feshbach, N. D. (1987). Parental empathy and child adjustment/maladjustment. In N. Eisenberg & J. Strayer (Eds.), *Empathy and its development* (pp. 271–291). New York: Cambridge University Press.

Fisher, E. (1992). The impact of play on development: A meta-analysis. *Play and Culture, 5,* 159–181.

Freedheim, D. K., & Russ, S. W. (1983). Psychotherapy with children. In C. E. Walker & M. E. Roberts (Eds.), *Handbook of clinical child psychology* (2nd ed., pp. 978–994). New York: Wiley.

Freedheim, D., & Russ, S. W. (1992). Psychotherapy with children. In C. Walker & M. Roberts (Eds.), *Handbook of clinical child psychology* (2nd ed., pp. 765–781). New York: Wiley.

Freud, A. (1927). Four lectures on child analysis. In *The writings of Anna Freud* (Vol. 1, pp. 3–69). New York: International Universities Press.

Freud, A. (1946). *The psychoanalytic treatment of children.* New York: International Universities Press.

Freud, A. (1965). *Normality and pathology in childhood: Assessment of development.* New York: International Universities Press.

Freud, A. (1966). The ego and the mechanisms of defense. In *The writings of Anna Freud* (Vol. 2). New York: International Universities Press.

Freud, A. (1976). Changes in psychoanalytic practice and experience. In *The writings of Anna Freud* (Vol. 7, pp. 176–185). New York: International Universities Press.

Freud, S. (1958). The unconscious. In S. Strachey (Ed. & Trans.), *The standard edition of the complete psychological works of Sigmund Freud* (Vol. 14, pp. 159–215). London: Hogarth Press. (Original work published 1915)

Freud, S. (1959). Inhibition symptoms, and anxiety. In J. Strachey (Ed. & Trans.), *The standard edition of the complete psychological works of Sigmund Freud* (Vol. 20, pp. 87–172). London: Hogarth Press. (Original work published 1926)

Freyberg, J. F. (1973). Increasing the imaginative play of urban disadvantaged kindergarten children through systematic training. In J. L. Singer (Ed.), *The child's world of make-believe.* New York: Academic Press.

Gaensbauer, T. J., & Siegel, C. H. (1995). Therapeutic approaches to posttraumatic stress disorder in infants and toddlers. *Infant Mental Health Journal, 16*, 292–305.

Gaylin, N. (1999). Client-centered child and family therapy. In S. Russ & T. Ollendick (Eds.) *Handbook of psychotherapies with children and families* (pp. 107–120). New York: Kluwer, Academic/Plenum Publishers.

Gardner, H. (1991). *The unschooled mind.* New York: Basic Books.

Gardner, R. (1971). *Therapeutic communication with children: The mutual storytelling technique.* New York: Aronson.

Garfield, W. (1980). *Psychotherapy: An eclectic approach.* New York: Wiley.

Getzels, S., & Csikszentmihalyi, M. (1976). *The creative vision: A longitudinal study of problem finding in art.* New York: Wiley-Interscience.

Gil, E. (1991). *The healing power of play.* New York: Guilford.

Gilpin, D. (1976). Psychotherapy of borderline psychotic children. *American Journal of Psychotherapy, 30*, 483–496.

Gitlin-Weiner, B, Sangrund, A., & Schaefer, C. (Eds.). (2000). *Play Diagnosis and Assessment.* New York: Wiley & Sons.

Godwin, L. J., & Moran, J. D. (1990). Psychometric characteristics of an instrument for measuring creative potential in preschool children. *Psychology in the Schools, 27*, 204–210.

Golann, S. E. (1963). Psychological study of creativity. *Psychological Bulletin, 60*, 548–565.

Golden, D. (1983). Play therapy for hospitalized children. In C. E. Schaefer & K. J. O'Connor (Eds.), *Handbook of play therapy* (pp. 213–233). New York: Wiley.

Goldfried, M. (1998). A comment on psychotherapy integration in the treatment of children. *Journal of Clinical Child Psychology, 27*, 49–53.

Goldstein, A. (2002). *The effect of affect-laden reading passages on children's emotional expressivity in play.* Unpublished doctoral dissertation, Case Western Reserve University, Cleveland, OH.

Goldstein, A., & Russ, S. (2000–2001). Understanding children's literature and its relationship to fantasy ability and coping. *Imagination, cognition, and Personality, 20,* 105–126.

Goleman, D., Kaufman, P., & Ray, M. (1992). *The creative spirit.* New York: Dutton.

Golumb, C., & Galasso, L. (1995). Make believe and reality: Explorations of the imaginary realm. *Developmental Psychology, 31,* 800–810.

Golumb, C., & Kuersten, R. (1996). On the transition from pretense play to reality: What are the rules of the game? *British Journal of Developmental Psychology, 14,* 203–217.

Greene, T., & Noice, H. (1988). Influence of positive affect upon creative thinking and problem solving in children. *Psychological Reports, 63,* 895–898.

Gross, J. J. (1998). The emerging field of emotion regulation: An integrative review. *Review of General Psychology, 2,* 271–299.

Grossman-McKee, A. (2989). The relationship between affective expression in fantasy play and pain complaints in first and second grade children. *Dissertation Abstracts International, 50.*

Guerney, B. G., Jr. (1964). Filial therapy: Description and rationale. *Journal of Counseling Psychology, 20,* 303–310.

Guilford, J. P. (1950). Creativity. *American Psychologist, 5,* 444–454.

Guilford, J. P. (1968). *Intelligence, creativity and their educational implications.* San Diego: Knapp.

Harris, P. (1989). *Children and emotion: The development of psychological under- standing.* Cambridge, MA: Blackwell Publishers.

Harris, P. (1994). The child's understanding of emotion: Developmental change, and the family environment. *Journal of Child Psychology and Psychiatry, 35*(1), 3–28.

Harris, P. (2000). *The work of the imagination.* Oxford, UK: Blackwell.

Harter, S. (1985). *Manual for the Self-Perception Profile for Children.* Denver, CO: University of Denver.

Hartmann, W., & Rollett, B. (1994). Play: Positive intervention in the elementary school curriculum. In J. Hellendoorn, R. van der Kooij, & B. Sutton-Smith (Eds.), *Play and intervention* (pp. 195–202). Albany: State University of New York Press.

Hartmann, D. P., Roper, B. L., & Gelfant, D. M. (1977). An evaluation of alternative modes of child psychotherapy. In B. H. Lahey & A. E. Kazdin (Eds.), *Advances in clinical psychology* (Vol. 1, pp. 1–37). New York: Plenum.

Hayes, S. C., Strosahl, K. D., & Wilson, K. G. (1999). *Acceptance and commitment therapy: An experiential approach to behavior change.* New York: Guilford.

Heinicke, C., & Goldman, A. (1960). Research on psychotherapy with children: A review and suggestions for further study. *American Journal of Orthopsychiatry, 30,* 483–494.

Heinicke, C., & Strassman, L. (1975). Toward more effective research on child psychotherapy. *Journal of Child Psychiatry, 14,* 561–588.

Hellendoorn, V. (1999). Imaginative play training for severely retarded children. In J. Hellendoorn, R. van der Kooij, & B. Sutton-Smith (Eds.), *Play and intervention* (pp. 113–122). Albany: State University of New York Press.

Hellendoorn, J., van der Kooij, R., & Sutton-Smith, B. (1994). Epilogue. In J. Hellendoorn, R. van der Kooij, & B. Sutton-Smith (Eds.), *Play and intervention* (pp. 215–224). Albany: State University of New York Press.

Hendricks, S. (1971). A descriptive analysis of the process of client-centered play therapy (doctoral dissertation, Worth Texas State University). *Dissertation Abstracts International, 32,* 3689A.

Holt, R. R. (1977). A method for assessing primary process manifestations and their control in Rorschach responses. In M. Rickers-Ovsiankina (Ed.), *Rorschach psychology* (pp. 375–420). New York: Kreiger Publisher.

Hood-Williams, J. (1960). The results of psychotherapy with children. *Journal of Consulting Psychology, 24,* 84–88.

Howe, P., & Silvern, L. (1981). Behavioral observation during play therapy: Preliminary development of a research instrument. *Journal of Personality Assessment, 45,* 168–182.

Hug-Hellmuth, H. (1921). On the technique of child analysis. *International Journal of Psychoanalysis, 2,* 287–305.

Hug-Hellmuth, H. (1924). *New paths to the understanding of youth.* Leipzig-Wien, Germany: Franz Deuticki.

Hughes, M. (1987). The relationship between symbolic and manipulative (object) play. In D. Gorlitz & J. Wohwill (Eds.), *Curiosity, imagination, and play* (pp. 247–257). Hillsdale, NJ: Lawrence Erlbaum Associates.

Hutt, C., & Bhavnani, R. (1972). Predictions for play. *Nature, 237,* 171–172.

Irwin, E. (1983). The diagnostic and therapeutic use of pretend play. In C. E. Schaefer & K. J. O'Connor (Eds.), *Handbook of play therapy* (pp. 148–173). New York: Wiley.

Isen, A. (1985). The asymmetry of happiness and sadness in effects on memory in normal college students. *Journal of Experimental Psychology: General, 114,* 388–391.

Isen, A. (1999). On the relationships between affect and creative problem solving. In S. Russ (Ed.), *Affect, creative experience, and psychological adjustments* (pp. 3–17). Philadelphia: Brunner/Mazel.

Isen, A., & Daubman, K., & Nowicki, G. (1987). Positive affect facilitates creative problem solving. *Journal of Personality and Social Psychology, 52,* 1122–1131.

Izard, E. (1977). *Human emotions.* New York: Plenum Publishing.

Jacobsen, P. B., Sadler, F., Booth-Jones, M., Soety, E., Weitzner, M., & Fields, K. (2002). Predictors of post trauma stress disorder symptomatology following bone marrow transplantation for cancer. *Journal of Consulting and Clinical Psychology, 76,* 235–240.

Jausovec, N. (1989). Affect in analogical transfer. *Creativity Research Journal, 2,* 255–266.

Johnson, J. (1976). Relations of divergent thinking and intelligence test scores with social and nonsocial make-believe play of preschool children. *Child Development, 47,* 1200–1203.

Johnson, P. A., & Stockdale, D. E. (1975). Effects of puppet therapy on palmar sweating of hospitalized children. *Johns Hopkins Medical Journal, 137,* 1–5.

Jones, A., & Glenn, S. M. (1991). Gender differences in pretend play in a primary school group. *Early Child Development and Care, 72,* 61–67.

Kaugars, A., & Russ, S. (2000, March). *Validity of the Affect in Play scale-Preschool version.* Paper presented at the midwinter meeting of the Society for Personality Assessment, Albuquerque, NM.

Kaugars, A., Russ, S., & Singer, L. (2002, March). *Multimethod assessment of affective processes on preschool children.* Paper presented at the meeting of the Society for Personality Assessment, San Antonio.

Kazdin, A. (1990). Psychotherapy for children and adolescents. In M. R. Rosenweig & L. W. Potter (Eds.), *Annual review of psychology* (pp. 21–54). Palo Alto, CA: Annual Review.

Kazdin, A. (1993). Evaluation in clinical practice: Clinically sensitive and systematic methods of treatment delivery. *Behavior Therapy, 24,* 11–45.

Kazdin, A. (2000). *Psychotherapy for children and adolescents.* New York: Oxford University Press.

Kazdin, A., Bass, D., Ayers, W., & Rodgers, A. (1990). Empirical and clinical focus of child and adolescent psychotherapy research. *Journal of Consulting and Clinical Psychology, 58,* 729–740.

Kelly, F. (2002, March). Comments as discussant for symposium: Fantasy play as narrative: Assessment of affective and interpersonal process (L. Niec, Chair). Meeting of the Society for Personality Assessment, San Antonio, TX.

Kelsay, K. (2002, October). *MacArthur Story Stem Battery as a therapeutic tool.* Paper presented at the meeting of the Academy of Child and Adolescent Psychiatry, San Francisco.

Kenealy, P. (1989). Children's strategies for coping with depression. *Behavior Research Therapy, 27,* 27–34.

Kernberg, P., Chazan, S., & Normandin, L. (1998). The children's play therapy incident (CPTI): Description, development, and reliablity studies. *Journal of Psychotherapy Practice and Research, 7,* 196–207.

Kessler, J. (1966). *Psychopathology of childhood.* Englewood Cliffs, NJ: Prentice Hall.

Kessler, J. (1988). *Psychopathology of childhood* (2nd ed.). Englewood Cliffs, NJ: Prentice Hall.

Kim, Y. T., Lombardino, L. J., Rothman, H., & Vinson, B. (1989). Effects of symbolic play intervention with children who have mental retardation. *Mental Retardation, 27,* 159–165.

Klein, M. (1955). The psychoanalytic play technique. *American Journal of Orthopsychiatry, 25,* 223–237.

Klinger, E. (1971). *Structure and functions of fantasy.* New York: Wiley-Interscience.

Knell, S. (1993). *Cognitive-behavioral play therapy.* Northvale, NJ: Aronson.

Knell, S. (1999). Cognitive-behavioral play therapy. In S. Russ & T. Ollendick (Eds.), *Handbook of psychotherapies with children and families* (pp. 395–404). New York: Kluwer Academic Plenum Publishers.

Kogan, N. (1983). Stylistic variation in childhood and adolescence: Creativity, metaphor, and cognitive styles. In P. Mussen (Ed.), *Handbook of child psychology* (Vol. 3, pp. 631–706). New York: Wiley.

Kohut, H. (1977). *The restoration of the self.* New York: International Universities Press.

Kohut, H., & Wolfe, E. R. (1978). The disorders of the self and their treatment: An outline. *International Journal of Psychoanalysis, 59,* 413–424.

Koocher, G., & Broskowski, A. (1977). Issues in the evaluation of mental health services for children. *Professional Psychology, 8,* 583–592.

Koocher, G., & D'Angelo, E. J. (1992). Evolution of practice in child psychotherapy. In D. K. Freedheim (Ed.), *History of psychotherapy* (pp. 457–492). Washington, DC: American Psychological Association.

Krain, A., & Kendall, P. (1999). Cognitive-behavioral therapy. In S. Russ & T. Ollendick (Eds.), *Handbook of psychotherapies with children and families* (pp. 121–135). New York: Kluwer Academic/Plenum.

Krasnor, l., & Pepler, D. (1980). The study of children's play: Some suggested future directions. *New Directions for Child Development, 9,* 85–94.

Kris, E. (1952). *Psychoanalytic exploration in art*. New York: International Universities Press.

Kusche, C. A., Greenberg, M. T., & Beilke, B. (1988). *The Kusche affective interview*. Unpublished manuscript, University of Washington, Seattle, WA.

Landreth, G. (1991). *Play therapy: The art of the relationship*. Bristol, PA: Accelerated Development.

Lease, C. A., & Ollendick, T. H. (in press). Development and psychopathology. In A. S. Bellack & M. Hersen (Eds.), *Psychopathology in adulthood: An advanced textbook*. New York: Pergamon Press.

Lepore, S. J., Silver, R. C., Wortman, C. B., & Wayment, H. A. (1996). Social constraints, intrusive thoughts, and depressive symptoms among bereaved mothers. *Journal of Personality and Social Psychology, 70*, 271–282.

Leslie, A. M. (1987). Pretense and representation: The origins of "theory of mind." *Psychological Review, 94*, 412–426.

Lester, E. (1968). Brief psychotherapy in child psychiatry. *Canadian Psychiatric Association Journal, 13*, 301–309.

Levitt, E. E. (1957). The results of psychotherapy with children: An evaluation. *Journal of Consulting Psychology, 21*, 189–196.

Levitt, E. E. (1963). Psychotherapy with children: A further evaluation. *Behavior Research and Therapy, 1*, 45–51.

Levitt, E. E. (1971). Research in psychotherapy with children. In A. E. Bergin & S. L. Garfield (Eds.), *Handbook of psychotherapy and behavior change: An empirical analysis* (pp. 474–484). New York: Wiley.

Levy, T. M. (1938). Release therapy in young children. *Psychiatry, 1*, 387–390.

Lieberman, J. N. (1977). *Playfulness: Its relationship to imagination and creativity*. New York: Academic Press.

Lonigan, C., Elbert, J., & Johnson, S. (1998). Empirically supported psychosocial interventions for children: An overview. *Journal of Clinical Child Psychology, 27*, 138–145.

Lyytinen, P. (1995). Cross-situational variation on children's pretend play. *Early Child Development and Care, 105*, 33–41.

Mackinnon, D. W. (1962). The nature and nurture of creative talent. *American Psychologist, 17*, 484–495.

Maddi, S. (1965). Motivational aspects of creativity. *Journal of Personality, 33*, 330–347.

Mahler, M. S. (1968). *On human symbiosis and the vicissitudes of individuation*. New York: International Universities Press.

Mahler, M. S. (1975). On human symbiosis and the vicissitudes of individuation. *Journal of American Psychoanalytic Association, 23*, 740–763.

Mann, E., & Goldman, N. (1982). *A casebook in time-limited therapy*. New York: McGraw-Hill.

Mann, E., & McDermott, J. (1983). Play therapy for victims of child abuse and neglect. In C. E. Schaefer & K. J. O'Connor (Eds.), *Handbook of play therapy* (pp. 283–307). New York: Wiley.

Marans, S., Mayes, L., Cicchetti, D., Dahl, K., Marans, W., & Cohen, D. J. (1991). The Child Psychoanalytic Play Interview: A technique for studying thematic content. *Journal of the American Psychoanalytic Association, 39*(4), 1015–1036.

Masters, J., Felleman, E., & Barden, R. (1981). Experimental studies of affective states in children. In B. Lahey & A. Kazdin (Eds.), *Advances in clinical child psychology* (pp. 91–118). New York: Plenum.

Mayer, J. D., & Salovey, P. (1993). The intelligence of emotional intelligence. *Intelligence, 17*, 433–442.

McNeil, C., Bahl, A., & Herschell, A. (2000). Involving and empowering parents in short-term play therapy for disruptive children. In H. Kaduson & C. Schaefer (Eds.), *Short-term play therapy for for children* (pp. 69–104). New York: Guilford Press.

Meichenbaum, D. (1974). *Cognitive-behavior modification.* New York: Plenum.

Meichenbaum, D. (1977). *Cognitive-behavioral modification: An integrative approach.* New York: Plenum.

Mennin, D., Heimberg, R., Turk, C., & Fresco, D. (2002). Applying an emotion regulation framework to integrative approaches to generalized anxiety disorder. *Clinical Psychology, 19,* 85–90.

Messer, S. B., & Warren, C. S. (1995). *Models of brief psychodynamic therapy.* New York: Guilford.

Milos, M., & Reiss, S. (1982). Effects of three play conditions on separation anxiety in young children. *Journal of Consulting and Clinical Psychology, 50,* 389–395.

Modell, A. H. (1980). Affects and their non-communication. *International Journal of Psychoanalysis, 61,* 259–267.

Morrison, D. (1988). The child's first ways of knowing. In D. Morrison (Ed.), *Organizing early experience: Imagination and cognition in childhood* (pp. 3–14). Amityville: Baywood.

Moustakas, C. (1953). *Children in play therapy.* New York: McGraw-Hill.

Moustakas, C. (1992). *Psychotherapy with children: The living relationship.* Greeley, CO: Carron. (Original work published 1959)

Murray, H. A. (1971). *Thematic Apperception Test Manual.* Cambridge, MA: Harvard University Press.

Nannis, E. D. (1988). Cognitive-developmental differences in emotional understanding. In E. D. Nannis & P. A. Cowan (Eds.), *Developmental psychopathology and its treatment: New directions for child development* (No. 39, pp. 31–49). San Francisco: Jossey-Bass.

Niec, L. N. (1994). *Relationships among affect and interpersonal themes in children's fantasy and interpersonal functioning.* Unpublished masters thesis, Case Western Reserve University, Cleveland, OH.

Niec, L. N. (1998). *Relationships among internal representations, affect in play, and interpersonal functioning.* Unpublished doctoral dissertation, Case Western Reserve University, Cleveland, OH.

Niec, L. N., & Russ, S. W. (1996). Relationships among affect in play, interpersonal themes in fantasy, and children's interpersonal behavior. *Journal of Personality Assessment, 66*(3), 645–649.

Niec, L. N., & Russ, S. W. (2002). Children's internal representations, empathy, and fantasy play: A validity study of the SCORS-Q. *Psychological Assessment, 14,* 331–338.

Niec, L. N., Yopp, J. M., Russ, S. (2002). *Children's interpersonal themes in play and interpersonal functioning: Development of the Interpersonal Themes in Play System.* Manuscript submitted for publication.

Ollendick, T., & Russ, S. (1999). Psychotherapy with children and families: Historical traditions and current trends. In S. Russ & T. Ollendick (Eds.), *Handbook of psychotherapy with children and families* (pp. 3–13). New York: Kluwer Academic/Plenum.

Olszewski, P. (1987). Individual differences in preschool children's prediction of verbal fantasy play. *Merrill-Palmer Quarterly, 33*(1), 69–86.

Olszewski, P., & Fuson, K. C. (1982). Verbally expressed fantasy play of preschoolers as a function of toy structure. *Developmental Psychology, 18,* 47–57.

Palmer, J. (1970). *The psychological assessment of children.* New York: Wiley.

Parad, J., & Parad, N. (1968). A study of crisis-oriented planned short-term treatment, Part 1. *Social Casework, 49,* 346–355.

Pederson, D., & Moran, G. (1996). Expressions of the attachment relationship outside of the Strange Situation. *Child Development, 67*(3), 915–927.

Pekarik, F. R., Prinz, R., Liebert, D., Weintraub, S., & Neale, J. (1976). The Pupil Evaluation Inventory: A sociometric technique for assessing children's social behavior. *Journal of Abnormal Child Psychology, 4*(1), 83–97.

Pellegrini, A. (1992). Rough and tumble play and social problem solving flexibility. *Creativity Research Journal, 5,* 13–26.

Pennebaker, J. W. (2002). What our words can say about us: Toward a broader language psychology. *APA Monitor,* January/February, pp. 8–9.

Pennebaker, J. W., & Graybeal, A. (2001). Patterns of natural language use: Disclosure, personality, and social integration. *Current Directions in Psychological Science, 10,* 90–93.

Pepler, D. (1979). *Effects of convergent and divergent play experience on preschoolers problem-solving behaviors.* Unpublished doctoral dissertation, University of Waterloo.

Pepler, D., & Ross, H. (1981). The effects of play on convergent and divergent problem solving. *Child Development, 52,* 1202–1210.

Perry, D., & Russ, S. (1998). *Play, coping, and adjustment in homeless children.* Unpublished manuscript.

Perry, L., & Landreth, G. (1991). Diagnostic assessment of children's play therapy behavior. In C. Schaefer, K. Gitlin, & A. Sandgrund (Eds.), *Play diagnosis and assessment* (pp. 641–660). New York: John Wiley & Sons.

Peterson, N. (1989). *The relationship between affective expression in fantasy play and self-esteem in third grade children.* Unpublished Masters' Thesis, Case Western Reserve University, Cleveland, OH.

Phillips, R. (1985). Whistling in the dark? A review of play therapy research. *Psychotherapy, 22,* 752–760.

Piaget, J. (1967). *Play, dreams, and imitation in childhood.* New York: Norton. (Original work published 1945)

Plank, E. (1962). *Working with children in hospitals.* Cleveland, OH: Case Western Reserve University Press.

Proskauer, S. (1969). Some technical issues in time-limited psychotherapy with children. *Journal of the American Academy of Child and Adolescent Psychiatry, 8,* 154–169.

Proskauer, S. (1971). Focused time-limited psychotherapy with children. *Journal of the American Academy of Child and Adolescent Psychiatry, 10,* 619–639.

Rae, W., Worchel, R., Upchurch, J., Sanner, J., & Dainiel, C. (1989). The psychosocial impact of play on hospitalized children. *Journal of Pediatric Psychology, 14,* 617–627.

Rayfield, A., Monaco, L., & Eyberg, S. (1999). Parent–child interaction therapy with oppositional children. In S. Russ & T. Ollendick (Eds.), *Handbook of psychotherapies with children and families* (pp. 327–343). New York: Kluwer Academic/Plenum.

Richards, R. (1990). Everyday creativity, eminent creativity, and health: Afterview for CRT issues on creativity and health. *Creativity Research Journal, 3,* 300–326.

Richards, R. (1993). Everyday creativity, eminent creativity, and psychopathology. *Psychological Inquiry, 4,* 212–217.

Rogers, C. R. (1957). The necessary and sufficient conditions for psychotherapeutic personality change. *Journal of Consulting and Clinical, 21,* 95–103.

Ronan, G. F., Senn, J., Date, A., Mauer, L., House, K., Carroll, J., & Van Horn, R. C. (1996). Personal problem-solving scoring of TAT responses: Known groups validation. *Journal of Personality Assessment, 67,* 641–653.

Rosen, C., Faust, J., & Burns, W. (1994). The evaluation of process and outcome in individual child psychotherapy. *International Journal of Play Therapy, 3*(2), 33–43.

Rosenberg, D. (1984). *The quality and content of preschool fantasy play: Correlates in concurrent social-personality function and early mother-child attachment relationships.* Unpublished dissertation, University of Minnesota, Minneapolis.

Rothenberg, A. (1990). Creativity, mental health, and alcoholism. *Creativity Research Journal, 3,* 179–201.

Rubin, K., Coplan, R., Fox, N., & Calkins, S. (1995). Emotionality, emotion regulation, and preschoolers' social adaptation. *Development and Psychopathology, 7*(1), 49–62.

Rubin, K., Fein, G., & Vandenberg, B. (1983). Play. In P. Mussen (Ed.), *Handbook of child psychology* (Vol. 4, pp. 693–774). New York: Wiley.

Rubin, K. H., Watson, K. S., & Jambor, T. W. (1978). Free-play behaviors in preschool and kindergarten children. *Child Development, 49,* 534–536.

Runco, M. A. (1991). *Divergent thinking.* Norwood, NJ: Ablex.

Runco, M. A. (1994). *Creative sequelae of tension and disequilibrium.* In M. Shaw & M. Runco (Eds.), *Creativity and affect* (pp. 102–123). Norwood, NJ: Ablex.

Russ, S. (1982). Sex differences in primary process thinking and flexibility in problem solving in children. *Journal of Personality Assessment, 45,* 569–577.

Russ, S. (1987). Assessment of cognitive affective interaction in children: Creativity, fantasy, and play research. In J. Butcher & C. Spielberger (Eds.), *Advances in personality assessment* (Vol. 6, pp. 141–155). Hillsdale, NJ: Lawrence Erlbaum Associates.

Russ, S. (1988). Primary process thinking on the Rorschach, divergent thinking, and coping in children. *Journal of Personality Assessment, 52,* 539–548.

Russ, S. (1993). *Affect and creativity: The role of affect and play in the creative process.* Hillsdale, NJ: Lawrence Erlbaum Associates.

Russ, S. (1995). Play psychotherapy research: State of the science. In T. Ollendick & R. Prinz (Eds.). *Advances in clinical child psychology* (pp. 365–391). New York: Plenum.

Russ, S. (1996). Psychoanalytic theory and creativity: Cognition and affect revisited. In J. Masling & R. Borstein (Eds.), *Psychoanalytic perspectives on developmental psychology* (pp. 69–103). Washington, DC: APA Books.

Russ, S. (1998). Introductory comments to special section on developmentally based integrated psychotherapy with children: Emerging models. *Journal of Clinical Child Psychology, 27,* 2–3.

Russ, S. (1999). Play, affect, and creativity: Theory and research. In S. Russ (Ed.), *Affect, creative experience and psychological adjustment* (pp. 57–75). Philadelphia: Brunner/Mazel.

Russ, S., & Cooperberg, M. (2002). *Play as a predictor of creativity, coping and depression in adolescence.* Manuscript submitted for publication.

Russ, S., & Grossman-McKee, A. (1990). Affective expression in children's fantasy play, primary process thinking on the Rorschach, and divergent thinking. *Journal of Personality Assessment, 54,* 756–771.

Russ, S., Grossman-McKee, A., & Rutkin, Z. (1984). *Affect in Play Scale: Pilot project.* Unpublished raw data.

Russ, S., & Kaugers, A. (2000–2001). Emotion in children's play and creative problem solving. *Creativity Research Journal, 13,* 211–219.

Russ, S., & Niec, L. (1993, March). *Affective development and object relations: How much do we know?* Paper presented at the meeting of the Society for Personality Assessment, San Diego.

Russ, S., Niec, L., & Kaugars, A. (2000). Play assessment of affect—The Affect in Play Scale. In K. Gitlin-Weiner, A. Sangrund, & C. Schaefer (Eds.), *Play diagnosis and assessment* (pp. 722–749). New York: Wiley.

Russ, S., & Peterson, N. (1990). *The Affect in Play Scale: Predicting creativity and coping in children.* Unpublished manuscript.

Russ, S., Robins, D., & Christiano, B. (1999). Pretend play: Longitudinal prediction of creativity and affect in fantasy in children. *Creativity Research Journal, 12,* 129–139.

Russ, S., & Schafer, E. (2002). *Affect in Play emotional memories, and divergent thinking.* Manuscript in preparation.

Ryan, N. M. (1989). Stress-coping strategies identified from school-aged children's perspective. *Research in Nursing and Health, 12,* 111–122.

Saltz, E., Dixon, D., & Johnson, J. (1977). Training disadvantaged preschoolers on various fantasy activities: Effects on cognitive functioning and impulse control. *Child Development, 48,* 367–380.

Sandler, J., & Sandler, A. M. (1978). On the development of object relationships and affects. *International Journal of Psycho-Analysis, 59,* 285–296.

Sandler, J., Kennedy, H., & Tyson, R. L. (1980). *The technique of child psychoanalysis: Discussion with Anna Freud.* Cambridge, MA: Harvard University Press.

Santostefano, S. (1988). Process and change in child therapy and development: The concept of metaphor. In D. Morrison (Ed.), *Organizing early experience: Imagination and cognition in childhood* (pp. 139–172). Amityville, NY: Baywood.

Saracho, O. N. (1984). Construction and validation of the Play Rating Scale. *Early Child Development and Care, 17*(2–3), 199–230.

Saracho, O. (1992). Preschool children's cognitive style and play and implications for creativity. *Creativity Research Journal, 5,* 35–47.

Sawyer, P. K. (1997). *Pretend play as improvisation.* Mahwah, NJ: Lawrence Erlbaum Associates.

Schaefer, C., Gitlin, K., & Sandgrund, A. (1991). *Play diagnoses and assessment.* New York: Wiley.

Schaefer, C., & Millman, H. (1977). *Therapies for children.* San Francisco: Jossey-Bass.

Schneider, M. (1989). *Children's Apperceptive Story-Telling Test Manual.* Austin, TX: Pro-Ed.

Schneigher, M. (1974). Turtle technique in the classroom. *Teaching Exceptional Children, 8,* 22–24.

Seja, A. L., & Russ, S. W. (1998, May). *Children's fantasy play, emotional understanding and parents' reports of children's daily behavior.* Poster session presented at the Great Lakes Regional Conference on Child Health Psychology, Louisville, KY.

Seja, A. L., & Russ, S. W. (1999a). Children's fantasy play and emotional understanding. *Journal of Clinical Child Psychology, 28,* 269–277.

Seja, A. L., & Russ, S. W. (1999b). *Development of the preschool Affect in Play Scale.* Paper presented at meeting of Society for Research in Child Development, Albuquerque, NM.

Shaw, M., & Runco, M. (1994). *Creativity and affect.* Norwood, NJ: Ablex.

Shelby, J. (2000). Brief therapy with traumatized children: A developmental perspective. In A. Kaderson & C. Schaefer (Eds.), *Short-term play therapy for children* (pp. 69–104). New York: Guilford Press.

Sherrod, L., & Singer, J. (1979). The development of make-believe play. In J. Goldstein (Ed.), *Sports, games, and play* (pp. 1–28). Hillsdale, NJ: Lawrence Erlbaum Associates.

Shields, A., & Cicchetti, D. (1998). Reactive aggression among maltreated children: The contributions of attention and emotion dysregulation. *Journal of Clinical Child Psychology, 27,* 381–395.

Shirk, S. (1998). Interpersonal schematic in child psychotherapy: A cognitive-interpersonal perspective. *Journal of Clinical Child Psychology, 27,* 4–16.

Shirk, S. (1999). Integrated child psychotherapy: Treatment ingredients in search of a recipe. In S. Russ & T. Ollendick (Eds.), *Handbook of psychotherapies with children and families* (pp. 369–384). New York: Kluwer Academic/Plenum Press.

Shirk, S. R., & Russell, R. (1996). *Change processes in child psychotherapy: Revitalizing treatment and research.* New York: Guilford.

Shmukler, D. (1982-1983). Early home background features in relation to imaginative and creative expression in third grade. *Imagination, Cognition, and Personality, 2,* 311–321.

Shmukler, D. (1984-1985). Structured vs. unstructured play training with economically disadvantaged preschoolers. *Imagination, Cognition, & Personality, 4,* 293–304.

Sigman, M., & Sena, R. (1993). Pretend play in high-risk and developmentally delayed children. In M. H. Borstein & A. W. O'Reilly (Eds.), *The role of play in the development of thought: New directions for children development* (pp. 29–42). San Francisco: Jossey-Bass Publishers.

Singer, D. (1993). *Playing for their lives.* New York: The Free Press.

Singer, D. G., & Singer, J. L. (1990). *The house of make-believe: Children's play and the developing imagination.* Cambridge, MA: Harvard University Press.

Singer, D. G., & Singer, J. L. (2002). *Make-believe games and activities for imaginative play.* Washington, DC: APA Books.

Singer, D. L., & Rummo, J. (1973). Ideational creativity and behavioral style in kindergarten age children. *Developmental Psychology, 8,* 154–161.

Singer, J. L. (1973). *The child's world of make-believe.* New York: Academic Press.

Singer, J. L. (1981). *Daydreaming and fantasy.* New York: Oxford University Press.

Singer, J. L. (1994). The scientific foundations of play therapy. In J. Hellendoorn, R. van der Kooij, & B. Sutton-Smith (Eds.), *Play and intervention* (pp. 27–38). Albany: State University of New York Press.

Singer, J. L. (1995). Imaginative play in childhood: Precursor of subjunctive thoughts, daydreaming, and adult pretending games. In A. Pellegrini (Ed.), *The future of play theory* (pp. 187–219). Albany: State University of New York Press.

Singer, J. L., & Singer, D. L. (1976). Imaginative play and pretending in early childhood: Some experimental approaches. In A. Davids (Ed.), *Child personality and psychopathology* (Vol. 3, pp. 69–112). New York: Wiley.

Singer, J. L., & Singer, D. L. (1981). *Television, imagination, and aggression.* Hillsdale, NJ: Lawrence Erlbaum Associates.

Singer, J. L., & Singer, D. G. (1999). *Learning through play* (Videotape.) Instructional Media Institute.

Slade, A., & Wolf, D. (1994). *Children at play.* New York: Oxford University Press.

Smilansky, S. (1968). *The effects of sociodramatic play on disadvantaged preschool children.* New York: Wiley.

Smith, P. (1988). Children's play and its role in early development; a re-evaluation of the "play ethos." In A. Pellegrini (Ed.), *Psychological bases for early education* (pp. 207–226). Chichester: John Wiley & Sons.

Smith, P. (1994). Play training: An overview. In J. Hellendoorn, R. van der Kooij, & B. Sutton-Smith (Eds.), *Play and intervention* (pp. 185–194). Albany: State University New York Press.

Smith, P., & Dutton, S. (1979). Play and training on direct and innovative problem solving. *Child Development, 50,* 830–836.

Smith, P. K., & Whitney, S. (1987). Play and associative fluency: Experimenter effects may be responsible for positive results. *Developmental Psychology, 23,* 49–53.

Smolucha, F. (1992). A reconstruction of Vygotsky's theory of creativity. *Creativity Research Journal, 5,* 49–67.

Smolucha, L., & Smolucha, F. (1992). Vygotskian theory: An emerging paradigm with implications for a synergistic psychology. *Creativity Research Journal, 5,* 87–96.

Smyrnios, K., Kirby, R. I. (1993). Long-term comparison of brief versus unlimited psychodynamic treatments with children and their families. *Journal of Counseling and Clinical Psychology, 61,* 1020–1027.

Spielberger, C. D. (1973). *State-trait anxiety inventory for children.* Palo Alto, CA: Consulting Psychological Press.

Sroufe, L. (1989). Relationships, self, and individual adaption. In A. Sameroff & R. Emde (Eds.), *Relationship disturbances in early childhood* (pp. 70–96). New York: Basic Books.

Sroufe, L. A., & Rutter, M. (1984). The domain of developmental psychopathology. *Child Development, 55,* 17–29.

Stern, D. N., MacKain, K., Radnus, K., Hopper P., Kaminsky, C., Evans, S., Shilling, N., Mrahlo, I., Kaplett, M., Nachman, P., Trad, P., Polau, J., Barnard, L., & Spieker, S. (1992). The Kiddie-Infant Descriptive Instrument for Emotional States (KIDIES): An instrument for the measurement of affective state in infancy and early childhood. *Infant Mental Health Journal, 13*(2), 107–118.

Sternberg, R. (1988). A three-facet model of creativity. In R. Sternberg (Ed.), *The nature of creativity* (pp. 125–147). Cambridge: Cambridge University Press.

Strayer, J. (1987). Affective and cognitive perspectives on empathy. In N. Eisenberg & J. Strayer (Eds.), *Empathy and its development* (pp. 218–244). New York: Cambridge University Press.

Strayhorn, J. (2002). Self-control: Toward systematic training programs. *Journal of American Academy of Child and Adolescent Psychiatry, 41,* 17–27.

Suler, J. (1980). Primary process thinking and creativity. *Psychological Bulletin, 88,* 144–165.

Sutton-Smith, B. (1966). Piaget on play—A critique. *Psychological Review, 73,* 104–110.

Sutton-Smith, B. (1992). The role of toys in the investigation of playful creativity. *Creativity Research Journal, 5,* 3–11.

Sutton-Smith, B. (1994). Does play prepare for the future? In J. Goldstein (Ed.), *Toys, play, and child development* (pp. 130–146). New York: Cambridge University Press.

Sylva, K., Bruner, J., & Genova, P. (1976). The role of play in the problem solving of children 3–5 years old. In J. Bruner, A. Jolly, & K. Sylva (Eds.), *Play.* New York: Basic Books.

Terr, L. (1990). *Too scared to cry: Psychic trauma in childhood.* New York: Harper & Row.

Thompson, R. A. (1989). Causal attributions and children's emotional understanding. In C. Saarni & P. I. Harris (Eds.), *Children's understanding of emotion* (pp. 117–150). New York: Cambridge University Press.

Tomkins, S. S. (1962). *Affect, imagery, consciousness: Vol. 1. The positive affects.* New York: Springer.

Tomkins, S. S. (1963). *Affect, imagery, consciousness: Vol. 2. The negative affects.* New York: Springer.

Tomkins, S. S. (1970). A theory of memory. In J. S. Antrobus (Ed.), *Cognition and affect* (pp. 59–130). Boston: Little, Brown.

Toth, S., & Cicchetti, D. (1999). Developmental psychopathology and child psychotherapy. In S. Russ & T. Ollendick (Eds.), *Handbook of psychotherapy with children and families* (pp. 15–44). New York: Kluwer Academic/Plenum.

Tuma, J., & Russ, S. W. (1993). Psychoanalytic psychotherapy with children. In T. Kratochwill & R. Morris (Eds.), *Handbook of psychotherapy with children and adolescents* (pp. 131–161). Boston: Allyn & Bacon.

Udwin, O. (1983). Imaginative play training as an intervention method with institutionalized preschool children. *British Journal of Educational Psychology, 53,* 32–39.

Vandenberg, B. (1978, August). *The role of play in the development of insightful tool-using abilities.* Paper presented at the American Psychological Association Meeting, Toronto.

Vandenberg, B. (1980). Play, problem-solving, and creativity. *New Directions for Child Development, 9,* 49–68.

Vandenberg, B. (1988). The realities of play. In D. Morrison (Ed.), *Organizing early experience: Imagination and cognition in childhood* (pp. 198–209). Amityville, NY: Baywood.

Van Fleet, R. (1994). *Filial therapy: Strengthening parent–child relationships through play.* Sarasota, FL: Professional Resource Press.

Van Fleet, R. (2000). Short-term play therapy for families with chronic illness. In H. Kaduson & C. Schaefer (Eds.), *Short-term play therapy for children* (pp. 175–193). New York: Guilford Press.

Vernberg, E. (1998). Developmentally based psychotherapies: Comments and observations. *Journal of Clinical Child Psychology, 27,* 46–48.

Vernberg, E., Routh, D., & Koocher, G. (1992). The future of psychotherapy with children. *Psychotherapy, 29,* 72–80.

Von Klitzing, K., Kelsey, K., Emde, R., Robinson, J., & Schmitz, S. (2000). Gender-specific characteristics of 5–year-olds' play narratives and associations with behavior ratings. *Journal of American Academy of Child and Adolescent Psychiatry, 39,* 1017–1023.

Vosburg, S. D., & Kaufmann, G. (1999). Mood and creativity research: The view from a conceptual organizing perspective. In S. Russ (Ed.), *Affect, creative experience, and psychological adjustment.* Washington, DC: Taylor and Francis.

Vraniak, D., & Pickett, S. (1993). Improving interventions with American ethnic minority children: Recurrent and recalcitrant challenges. In T. Kratochwill & R. Morris (Eds.), *Handbook of psychotherapy with children and adolescents* (pp. 502–540). Boston: Allyn & Bacon.

Vygotsky, L. S. (1967). *Vaobraszeniye i tvorchestvo v deskom voraste* [Imagination and creativity in childhood]. Moscow: Prosvescheniye. (Original work published 1930)

Wachtel, P. (1977). *Psychoanalysis and behavior therapy: Toward an integration.* New York: Basic Books.

Waelder, R. (1933). Psychoanalytic theory of play. *Psychoanalytic Quarterly, 2,* 208–224.

Wallach, M. (1970). Creativity. In P. Mussen (Ed.), *Carmichael's manual of child psychology* (Vol. 1, pp. 1211–1272). New York: Wiley.

Wallas, C. (1926). *The art of thought.* New York: Wiley.

Warren, S. L., Oppenheim, D., & Emde, R. N. (1996). Can emotions and themes in children's play predict behavior problems? *Journal of the American Academy of Child and Adolescent Psychiatry, 34*(10), 1331–1337.

Waters, E., Wippman, J., & Sroufe, L. (1979). Attachment, positive affect and competence in the peer group: Two studies in construct validation. *Child Development, 50,* 821–829.

Webber, C. (1988). Diagnostic intervention with children at risk. In S. Altschul (Ed.), *Childhood bereavement and its aftermath* (pp. 77–105). Madison, WI: International Universities Press.

Weiner, I. (1977). Approaches to Rorschach validation. In M. Rickers-Ovsian Kina (Ed.), *Rorschach psychology* (pp. 575–608). New York: Kreiger.

Weisberg, R. (1988). Problem solving and creativity. In R. Sternberg (Ed.), *The nature of creativity* (pp. 148–176). Cambridge: Cambridge University Press.

Weisz, J. R., & Weiss, B. (1989). Assessing the effects of clinical-based psychotherapy with children and adolescents. *Journal of Consulting and Clinical Psychology, 57,* 741–746.

Weisz, J., & Weiss, B. (1993). *Effects of psychotherapy with children and adolescents.* Newbury Park, CA: Sage.

Weisz, J. R., Weiss, B., Alicke, M. D., & Klotz, M. L. (1987). Effectiveness of psychotherapy with children and adolescents: A meta-analysis for clinicians. *Journal of Consulting and Clinical Psychology, 55,* 542–549.

Weisz, J. R., Donenberg, G. R., Han, S. S., & Weiss, B. (1995). Bridging the gap between laboratory and clinic in child and adolescent psychotherapy. *Journal of Consulting and Clinical Psychology, 63,* 688–701.

Westby, C. (1980). Assessment of cognitive and language abilities through play. *Language, Speech, and Learning Serviced in Schools, 11,* 154–168.

Westby, C. E. (1991). A scale for assessing children's pretend play. In C. E. Schaeffer, K. Gitlin, & A. Sandgrund (Eds.), *Play, diagnosis and assessment* (pp. 131–161). New York: John Wiley and Sons.

Westen, D. (1995). *Social Cognition and Object Relations Scale: Q-Sort for Projective Stories (SCORS-Q).* Unpublished manual, Cambridge Hospital and Harvard Medical School, Cambridge, MA.

Winnicott, D. W. (1971). *Playing and reality.* London: Tavistol.

Withee, K. (1975). A descriptive analysis of the process of play therapy (doctoral dissertation, North Texas State University). *Dissertation Abstracts International, 35,* 6406B.

Youngblade, L., & Dunn, J. (1995). Individual differences in young children's pretend play with mother and sibling: Links to relationships and understanding of other people's feelings and beliefs. *Child Development, 66,* 1472–1492.

Author Index

Note: *t* indicates table

Subject Index

Note: t indicates table.